LITURGICAL DOGMATICS

DAVID W. FAGERBERG

Liturgical Dogmatics

How Catholic Beliefs Flow
from Liturgical Prayer

IGNATIUS PRESS   SAN FRANCISCO

Cover art:
The Trinity (detail)
Andrei Rublev
Tretyakov Gallery, Moscow, Russia
Wikimedia Commons Image
with
photograph by Fr. Lawerence Lew, O.P.
Chapel of the Priory of the Holy Spirit (Blackfriars), Oxford

Cover design by Carl E. Olson

© 2021 by Ignatius Press, San Francisco
All rights reserved
ISBN 978-1-62164-409-5 (PB)
ISBN 978-1-64229-146-9 (eBook)
Library of Congress Control Number 2020946391
Printed in the United States of America ∞

To the Bishops, Priests, and Deacons who have
been instruments of Christ for me

CONTENTS

Introduction   9

God and Revelation

    Chapter 1 – Liturgical Conditions for Revelation   19

    Chapter 2 – Knowing God through Awe and Fear   25

    Chapter 3 – Liturgy in the Trinity   29

    Chapter 4 – The Trinity in Liturgy   34

    Chapter 5 – Revelation, Liturgy, and Scripture   40

Created Being

    Chapter 6 – The Liturgical Potentiality of the Cosmos   53

    Chapter 7 – Liturgical Temporal Cosmology   59

    Chapter 8 – Angels and Men Doing Liturgy   65

    Chapter 9 – What the Angels Learn from Liturgy   69

    Chapter 10 – A Wrinkle in Cosmology   74

Man

    Chapter 11 – *Imago Dei* as Liturgical Description   81

    Chapter 12 – Liturgical Pilgrims   87

    Chapter 13 – Adam and Eve Confess   91

    Chapter 14 – Because We Are Sinners   95

Sin

    Chapter 15 – Satan's Hatred for Liturgists   103

    Chapter 16 – The Work of the Demons   108

    Chapter 17 – Sin as Idolatry   113

Chapter 18 – Evil   117

Chapter 19 – Liturgical Theodicy   123

Redemption

Chapter 20 – Grace, Liturgy, and Asceticism   129

Chapter 21 – The Liturgical *Soter*   135

Chapter 22 – The Beginning of Death's Death   141

Chapter 23 – Providence   146

Christ and Holy Spirit

Chapter 24 – The Liturgy in Christ   153

Chapter 25 – Christ in the Liturgy   158

Chapter 26 – The Perfect Liturgist   167

Chapter 27 – Liturgical Spiration   172

Chapter 28 – The Holy Spirit's Seven Gifts for Liturgy   177

Ecclesiology

Chapter 29 – The Church's Abcedarium   185

Chapter 30 – The Mystical Liturgical Body   193

Chapter 31 – Sacraments   203

Chapter 32 – Home-Sighting   210

Eschatology

Chapter 33 – Our Guide Home   219

Chapter 34 – The Harrowing of Hell   226

Chapter 35 – Eschatology   230

Chapter 36 – Mary (Liturgical Theotokology)   237

Conclusion   243

Subject Index   249

Scripture Index   259

INTRODUCTION

First, a word about what I want to do.

By an astounding gesture of grace, human beings are invited to liturgize God. My definition of liturgy is *the perichoresis of the Holy Trinity kenotically extended to invite our synergistic ascent into deification.* That is, the Trinity's circulation of love turns itself outward, and in humility the Son and Spirit work the Father's good pleasure for all creation, which is to invite our ascent into participation in the very life of God, which consists of glory, love, beatitude. This cannot be forced; it must be done with our cooperation. The twin purposes of liturgy, traditionally named, are the glorification of God and the sanctification of man. The former happens when the latter is accomplished. From the Trinity comes an energy that creates, a ray of light that illuminates, a fragrance of Torah that lures mankind, a symphony that gladdens man and glorifies God, a scroll whose sweetness is honey in the mouth, a thunder whose reverberation cracks stony hearts, a fire that alights upon unburned bushes and apostolic heads, a cloud that leads through the wilderness to the promised land.

Liturgy is a work of God, though it is an activity of man. The Uncreated gives being and mercy to his created ones, and, in this case, the uncreated energy of the Trinity climaxes in a created liturgy that God places in the hands of his Church, as the anaphora of John Chrysostom acknowledges: "We thank You also for this Liturgy, which you have deigned to receive from our hands."

A variety of human sciences can approach the human activity, but dogma is required to approach the character and work of God. When the Magi came to Bethlehem, their physical eyes saw a baby, but their *nous* was in a spiritual state suitable for a different kind of seeing, and, because of their inner knowledge, they worshipped God. Liturgical dogmatics uses noetic eyes formed by liturgy to see dogmatic truths. Liturgical dogmatics inspects the work God does when he conscripts members into his Church militant,

purifies members of the Church penitent, and allows members of
the Church triumphant to contemplate this liturgy without veil.
Leitourgia meant a public office, a service, a ministry that a citizen
undertook for the larger community, and if we want to understand
the duty, it is only right to look to the one who gives the charge.
The Holy Spirit is the primary commentator on liturgy because he
knows the work of the Son who is doing the will of the Father.
There is a cosmic liturgy as a result of the perichoresis of the Holy
Trinity kenotically extending itself to create, but this liturgy is sur-
passed by the Son liturgizing the Father and through the agency
of the Holy Spirit placing this liturgy in the hands of his mystical
Bride. The Incarnation makes this possible through the perichoresis
of divine and human natures in Jesus. Before the word "perichoresis" was used of the relationship between the Persons of the Trinity,
it was used to describe the relationship of the two natures in Christ's
hypostatic union. By no weak analogy, the society structured with
hierarchical organs and the Mystical Body of Christ can be compared to the mystery of the incarnate Word (*Lumen gentium* 8).

How can we do dogmatics when there is an absolute difference
between the Creator and the creature, an ontological and epistemological gulf about which apophasis ever warns? The answer is the
movement we find occurring from one side to the other and back
again. What knowledge cannot fasten together, love can unite, and
the story of that union is told by Christian dogma. The subject matter
of dogmatics is this movement, this divine economy, this liturgical
circulation between God and man. The two kenoses of the Trinity—
in creation, and then in the new creation—are investigated by dogma
metaphysically, mystically, economically, scripturally, traditionally.
All the chapter headings in a book of dogmatics are subdivisions of
this same, single story stretching from alpha to omega: the existence
and nature of God, the creating and redeeming and sanctifying acts
of God, the nature of man and the problem of sin, the purpose of
the Church and her sacraments, contact in grace and consummation
in parousia are all dogmatic investigation. And it turns out these are
liturgical verities. The truths dogmas talk about are celebrated in liturgy; dogmatics bobs in a liturgical stream. Liturgy is the catabatic
descent of God's loving mercy and the anabatic ascent of man's glorifying latria, of which all reality is made. What we stammer to say

cataphatically has been apophatically encountered in the Mysteries of Christ done (celebrated) liturgically. Cataphatic dogma arises from apophatic liturgy, *credendi* arises from *orandi*.

Liturgical dogmatics will therefore assume that liturgy holds a hermeneutical key by which to penetrate the meaning and use of a dogma, a torch by which to illuminate a dogma's interior surfaces, a nexus by which to conjoin dogmas holistically. On the one hand, liturgical dogmatics will treat dogmas as consequential for lives, not only for libraries; on the other hand, liturgical dogmatics will treat liturgy as consequential for credo, not only for cult. The goal of dogma is achieved preliminarily when the mystery has been protected from heretical corruption, but the final goal of dogma is achieved when the believer is united to the mystery that dogma propounds. Liturgical dogmatics will speak of a relationship between the liturgy and God's economy of salvation in such a way that what God does in his macrocosmic actions in the world, history, and eschaton can be detected in his microcosmic activity in our heart, asceticism, and deification. Liturgical dogmatics will examine dogma in light of liturgy. One can look *at* liturgy, or one can look *through* it to see—what? Everything. One can look through liturgy at the dogmas of theology: revelation, the nature of God, triadology, cosmology, anthropology, hamartiology, Christology, pneumatology, ecclesiology, and eschatology.

Second, a word about how I would like to do it.

An academic rarely writes without footnotes. Footnotes are a trail of breadcrumbs back to a book on the shelf somewhere; they are a way of establishing reputation by showing off whom else the writer knows; they are a net over which a tightrope walker walks. Sometimes they save one the trouble of thinking for oneself. The process of writing usually begins with a feeling (a feeling always precedes a proposition), which leads to a search for the quotation that initially gave that feeling. The writer returns to the book or the article containing the words of another author that once created a sensation he is now trying to re-create, and he stitches these other words together with the hope that they will have the same effect on his reader that they originally had on him. But there is no guarantee that they will do so. The quotation crystallizes an idea as a symbolic trophy of the struggle that occurred in the mind of the writer when he encountered it for the first time, but there is no assurance that the quotation will so function for his reader when this symbolic short-cut is employed. What was original and stimulating in the quotation depended upon the context of the whole page, the whole chapter, the whole book, and the point in life where the writer stood when he originally thought the thought. It might not be reproducible between the marks of quotation on a newly written page. Therefore, it behooves the tightrope walker eventually to attempt stating the concept himself, without a net, *sans* breadcrumbs. Can he convey the insight in his own words?

That is what I am going to attempt here, as intimidating as it seems. Instead of charting where I have gotten the thoughts, I am trying to have the thoughts again, for myself, to share with you. Instead of taking the easier path of collecting others' words, I am going to try to use my own words, with a minimum of footnotes. This should be an eventual goal for any theologian when reading in the great tradition. Sometimes it is their words and my thoughts, sometimes their thoughts and my words. As I look across the spines of my books, smiling down at me from the shelves above, I realize that *all* of them should be quoted; I could find material from *any* of them; *each* of them contains an element of the insight I want to communicate. It is shocking how much one forgets, so I turn for refuge to this word of hope from George MacDonald.

> Or have I forgotten a thought that came to me, which seemed of the truth, and a revealment to my heart? I wanted to keep it, to have it, to use it by and by, and it is gone! I keep trying and trying to call it back, feeling a poor man till that thought be recovered—to be far more lost, perhaps, in a note-book, into which I shall never look again to find it! I forget that it is live things God cares about—live truths, not things set down in a book, or in a memory, or embalmed in the joy of knowledge, but things lifting up the heart, things active in an active will. True, my lost thought might have so worked; but had I faith in God, the maker of thought and memory, I should know that, if the thought was a truth, and so alone worth anything, it must come again; for it is in God—so, like the dead, not beyond my reach: kept for me, I shall have it again.[1]

[1] George MacDonald, *Unspoken Sermons*, series I, II, III (Whitehorn, Calif.: Johannesen, 1999), 218.

I could have pulled down one book from this shelf, another from that shelf, thumbed through it to stop on a page with copious underlining, side margin notes, further extrapolation in the bottom margin, and exclaim, "Oh! There it is. That's what I want to say. It must be included." But since there would be no end to that process, I will instead try to build up what I mean from my own grasp of it.

Except in this introduction. Here are three sources to start us off on our journey. First, after I thought of the phrase "Liturgical Dogmatics", I wondered if it had been used by anyone else and found only a 1999 address by Metropolitan John Zizioulas titled "The Orthodox Church and the Third Millennium". Although he is not speaking in exactly my same sense, it was helpful to find confirmation of the phrase by so distinguished a theologian. The Metropolitan begins by asserting the need for an existential interpretation of dogma.

> Orthodox theology must review its language. We have inherited a rich dogmatic tradition and we must keep it faithfully and not change anything in it. We probably need no new dogmas. But this does not mean that we must conserve dogmas as archeological treasures. We certainly need an interpretation of our dogmas in existential terms. What for example does it mean for today's man that God is Trinity? Does it throw any light on problems such as those created by individualism, universalism etc., which mark our present culture.[2]

He refers to the failure to interpret the Gospel in existential terms. "Fundamentalism, confessionalism, and conservatism have killed the Bible and the dogmas of the Church, turning them into formulae to be preserved rather than lived and experienced. Dogma and ethics have been separated. And the same has happened with the *lex credendi* and *lex orandi*."[3] And so he concludes that the Orthodox Church must draw more and more from its liturgical life, particularly the Eucharist.

> In order to do that we must first pay attention to the way we celebrate the Eucharist and worship. Liturgical rite is not mere ritual. It is theology and it has profound existential significance. We must celebrate the

---

[2] John Zizioulas, http://theology.balamand.edu.lb/index.php/local-events/738-zizioulas lecture.
[3] Ibid.

liturgy properly if we are to offer anything to the world of existential significance. Secondly we must interpret our liturgy in existential terms. We need in other words a liturgical Dogmatics or a Dogmatics understood and expressed liturgically. This will be our specific gift to the world in the 21st century.[4]

In what follows, I do not mean to equate "liturgical" exactly with "existential", but it is the right starting place, and whatever I additionally mean will have to become clear on a case-by-case basis.

Second, a voice from the West. I found further confirmation of my hypothesis about the significance of liturgical dogmatics in a passage from Joseph Ratzinger where he is reviewing Western approaches to liturgy and sacraments. He identifies what appears to be a pendulum swing that has repeatedly missed the center balance point. Medieval theology swung to the one side when it "detached the theological study of the sacraments to a large extent from their administration in divine worship and treated it separately under the headings of *institution, sign, effect, minister, and recipient*".[5] Scholastic theologians analyzed the sacramental sign, not so much in terms of the living configuration of divine worship, but in terms of philosophical categories. "Thus divine worship and theology diverged more and more; dogmatic theology expounded, not on divine worship itself, but rather on its abstract theological contents, so that the liturgy necessarily seemed almost like a collection of ceremonies that clothed the essentials ... and hence might also be replaceable."[6] On the backswing, improvement was made by the liturgical movement. It came on the scene when "liturgics" was a kind of juridical positivism, Ratzinger says, and the movement sought instead to think of liturgy "not just as a more or less accidental collection of ceremonies, but rather as the organically developed and suitable expression of the sacraments in the worship celebration".[7] Ratzinger thinks the Constitution on the Sacred Liturgy of Vatican II was a much better synthesis than what had gone before and wishes that both theology and catechesis would understand the Church's divine worship in a more profound way.

[4] Ibid.
[5] Joseph Ratzinger, "Is the Catechism Up-to-Date?", in *On the Way to Jesus Christ*, trans. Michael J. Miller (San Francisco: Ignatius Press, 2005), 153.
[6] Ibid., 153–54.
[7] Ibid., 154.

But now, a third swing of the pendulum has passed the center point again, and "liturgical studies once again have tended to detach themselves from dogmatic theology and to set themselves up as a sort of technique for worship celebrations. Conversely, dogmatic theology has not yet convincingly taken up the subject of its liturgical dimension, either."[8] Does the duty lie on liturgical theology to take up dogmatic dimensions, or does it lie on dogmatics to take up liturgical dimensions? We could wish for both to take up their responsibility.

Third, two voices from the East. Although liturgy and dogmatics should both open up to each other, ultimately I think dogmatics leads to liturgy, which is why, although I use a structural outline from dogmatics, I am ultimately looking at the liturgical character of dogmas. This is described by Pavel Florensky in the first sentence of his great work, *The Pillar and Ground of the Truth*, where he expresses what he intends to do in that book. "Living religious experience as the sole legitimate way to gain knowledge of the dogmas—that is how I would like to express the general theme of my book or, rather, my jottings."[9] Living religious experience rests upon an ascetical capacitation for the liturgical mysteries that dogma describes and protects, but does not replace. This is explained by John Romanides when he writes,

> From an Orthodox viewpoint, someone probes more deeply into dogmas only when he uses them in his attempt to reach the stage of illumination. This is the Orthodox way to probe more deeply into the mysteries and dogmas. It is not an intellectual probing that aims at attempting to comprehend the mysteries or the dogmas or to enter their depths. Dogmas cannot be comprehended. In fact, dogmas are annulled in an experience of *theosis*, because they are replaced by the very living truth that they express. Dogmas are simply guides to God. When you behold God, then dogma is set aside.[10]

Finally, a concluding word about format.

I began by imagining an approach to various liturgical dogmas as if through a jeweler's lens, seeing first this facet, then that one. For that

[8] Ibid.

[9] Pavel Florensky, *The Pillar and Ground of the Truth* (Princeton University Press, 1997), 5, the first sentence of the book.

[10] John Romanides, *Patristic Theology* (Uncut Mountain Press, 2008), 252.

reason, I was inspired by the format of Francis de Sales' work, *Treatise on the Love of God*: short chapters that each consider an aspect of the same subject. I am not troubled by a certain amount of redundancy, therefore, and hope the reader is not, either. I hope this accomplishes a similar result that the Century genre in ascetical liturgy accomplishes, done there on a smaller, paragraph scale. A Century of paragraphs places two truths side by side and ignores the conjunctive adverbs between them. They are collections of what Florensky calls antinomies. For example, two truths are simply presented, like "we are saved by grace" and "work out your salvation with fear and trembling." What connecting word would you propose between these truths? Saved by grace *and* work out your salvation? *but, however, nevertheless, yet, meanwhile*? The truths are connected; they are meant to be connected; but the connection is as complicated as each part of the truth, and the reader is invited to do some labor himself. It is my hope to present liturgical facets of the same dogmatic truth and invite the reader to join me in the labor of connectivity.

GOD AND REVELATION

Chapter 1

Liturgical Conditions for Revelation

Knowing something requires an alignment between the knower and the object known. This is true on the level of sense faculties: I do not use my eye to apprehend music, my finger for sweetness, my nose for sunsets. This is also true on the level of the rational soul's faculties: I do not use my memory to apprehend the future, my instinct for concepts, my appetitive faculty for rationalizing. Reality imposes itself upon the various faculties of a human being and causes them to exercise. The object to be known determines the faculties we must use. We must align the *way we know* with *what we know*. Epistemology is conditioned by ontology.

Now, God is not an object and is therefore a special case. The ontological distance between the Uncreated and the created poses an equivalent epistemological distance between the Known and the knower. This is true for all creatures, visible and invisible. This is as true for the angels, who do not have bodies like ours, as it is for us. The gap between God and the seraphim is even greater than the gap between those seraphim and ourselves, although the spatial metaphor of "distance" is misleading because it fails to express the qualitative difference. Any two creatures compared are on the same line of being, but the Uncreated and the created are not. The starting and concluding point of apophatic theology is the recognition that God is beyond our conception, which is why he is beyond expression in words. Indescribable: "not-able-to-be-written-down". We dare not say anything about God without his permission. He must kenotically descend and reveal himself from apophatic heights to authorize our cataphatic expression in the valley below, which he has done in inspired Scripture and in warranted tradition. The Church Fathers sometimes spoke of the words of Scripture as a first incarnation: before

God clothed himself in human flesh, he clothed himself in human metaphors, names, and figures of speech.

Philosophy has deduced a set of attributes of God and composed lists of qualities such as infinite, perfect, simple, universal, true, good, immutable, eternal, omnipotent, omniscient, and omnipresent, but liturgical dogmatics begins by taking apophasis with even greater seriousness. If God eludes our rational grasp, we should employ our reason with a humility in the extreme, and these attributes should not be mistaken for descriptions. The transcendent one will always slip through our rational net. Theology is "firing where the enemy was last sighted": by the time we toss our rational snare in his direction, the Lion of Judah will already have moved on. The attributes are not meant to fence God in; they are meant to show us that he is invisible, make us perceive he is imperceptible, give reasons why he is trans-rational, and bring us to realize we cannot describe the indescribable. Theology is the writing down of what cannot be written down.

God is incomprehensible ..., but he is not unapproachable. And this antinomy undergirds the doctrine of God in liturgical dogmatics. We cannot comprehend the apophatic God, but we can take up the right posture to receive the signals he sends to us. It is a liturgical posture. And it is the posture necessary for receiving revelation.

Even after all these warnings about the illimitability of God, he is not off-limits to us. Even after all these warnings about the inaccessibility of God, he has given us access to himself. He welcomes us, encourages our advance, invites us to draw near, attracts our deepest selves, elevates even our natural desire, arouses our spiritual appetite, amplifies our longing, and magnifies our soul's eagerness. He is approachable, but must be approached correctly, which is what we meant by saying there must be an alignment between the knower and the known. In this case, we must align *the way* we know with *Whom* we know. And this is not a choice for us to make. God must determine the way we approach him. If I approach him as other than God, it is not God whom I am approaching. We can understand this with an example from the created realm as well. I do not approach a person truly if I do not approach him as a person, i.e., personally. Martin Buber made the point by saying we fail when we apply an I-It relationship to what should be an I-Thou relationship. If we approach a Thou as an It, we have violated the conditions required for knowing a person and miss him altogether. This applies to God as Supreme Person: he must be known personally, i.e., as a person.

Does Scripture give some advice for how we should approach the unapproachable, to know the unknowable? Yes. The seraphim cover their faces and feet (Is 6:2), they call out that the Lord of hosts is holy (Is 6:3; Rev 4:8), they carry live coals for purifying lips (Is 6:6–7). The cherubim stand attentively beside the mercy seat (*kapporeth*) (Ex 25:20), God is enthroned on them (1 Sam 4:4), and in glory they overshadow the mercy seat (Heb 9:5). It is the same for the other seven ranks of angels, whose entire existence is fearful worship of the Lord Almighty. It is the same for us human beings, whose entire existence is also fearful worship of the Lord Almighty. If we want to know God, then we must approach him in fear and worship and prayer. Insofar as we can speak of knowing God—that is, insofar as it is God whom we are trying to know—we must experience his glory and majesty in awe. If what we think does not produce awe in us, it is not God we are thinking. If the theologian does not feel awe, then he is thinking concepts with the philosopher, he is not thinking God. The subject matter of dogmatics is not the topic of God, it is the Subject himself. God himself. Liturgical dogmatics reminds us of this. If we want to know propositions—that God is universal, immutable, eternal, et cetera—we can know them by analysis. If we want to know God, we must fall down in adoration.

The philosophers say God is infinite, perfect, simple, universal, true, good, immutable, eternal, omnipotent, omniscient, omnipresent. What does he do with these talents? Why does he have this divine skill set? Of course, we do not mean that he was given them by anyone else; they are his nature. But what does he do with his natural attributes and characteristics? Toward what end does he use his qualities of omniscience and omnipotence? How do his infinity and simplicity serve him? What purpose do his goodness and beauty and truth have? What does the Being who can do anything do? Answer: he builds a bridge between himself and us, a liturgical bridge for us to cross and come closer. That is the liturgical use to which he puts the attributes the philosophers have concluded. He gives subsistence to non-divine beings that they might please him, glorify him, be ingredient to the divine happiness, extend the perichoresis, intensify the celebration, be loved and love in turn. The might of God enables our ministry, the strength of God makes possible our service, the energy of God calls forth our *leitourgia*.

Dogmatics expounds on knowledge of God, but on what does knowledge of God depend? Liturgical dogmatics will add the further point that the Subject sets conditions for the knower. How must we be in order to taste and see that the Lord is good? What must be our posture and attitude in order to know God?

Fear has already been mentioned. There is a fear that only the Lord should receive. The Greeks understood this so well that they employed two different words. Created things can receive *dulia* appropriate to the place held in the hierarchy of being. A teacher, civic official, a parent deserves a type of esteem, but we should not mix this up with the esteem that God deserves, which the Greeks named *latria*. God, only God, and because he is God, receives *latria*. To fear something other than God is idolatry. Besides this latreutic fear, with what else must a liturgical dogmatician approach the Subject God? With adoration, because he is worthy of our affection; with worship, because the whole earth is full of his glory; with meekness, because his commandments give life; with veneration, because hallowed is his name; with homage, because he is our master; with reverence, because he is holy; with sacrifice, because he is our joy; with laud, because he is worthy of eternal praise; with submission, because he is excellent; with righteousness, because he loves the upright in heart; with humility, because we know our sin and experience his grace; with love, because he is full of love. These are liturgical traits, liturgical characteristics, liturgical postures, and if we do not have them when we know this Subject, then it is not God whom we are knowing.

The General Instruction of the Roman Missal describes the chief elements that make up the Eucharistic Prayer, and instead of seeing them as a description of a prayer on a page in the sacramentary, we might now be able to see these elements as a description of the actions required of the liturgist in order to approach and know God. According to this prayer, what should people have in their hearts? (i) Thanksgiving, since liturgy is response to God's antecedent acts of salvation; (ii) acclamation, since this human congregation joins its voice to the song of the heavenly powers in the Sanctus when the Church militant gives praise in tandem with the Church triumphant; (iii) epiclesis, since the Holy Spirit is the principal liturgist and now consecrates the gifts offered by human hands, as well as consecrating the human heart that offers them; (iv) the Institution Narrative, since our liturgy has historical foundation in the *mirabilia Dei*; (v) anamnesis, since the Church glorifies God by keeping memorial of Christ's Passion, Resurrection, and Ascension; (vi) offering, since the Church offers the spotless Victim to the Father and offers herself with Christ day after day until the final consummation; (vii) intercessions, since offering is made for all the members of the Church, living and dead; (viii) doxology, since we come to liturgy in order to express and confirm the glorification of God. Knowledge of God—the unknowable one—comes when we stand before him and give thanks, praise, petition for the Holy Spirit, recite the holy history, and make memorial, offering, intercession, and doxology.

The definition of theology can be seen under an etymological lens: it is words about God; it is the search for words adequate to God; it is the struggle for words about God that are true. Ultimately, we only know God the Father through God the Son, in God the Holy Spirit. The second and third Persons of the Trinity lead us to the first Person, so Christian theology strives to repeat by the strength of the Holy Spirit what the *Logos* can say about *Theos*. This is *theology*. Liturgical dogmatics approaches the task of theology by insisting upon the antinomical fact that God is unknowable, yet approachable. Because unknowable, theology is not philosophy of religion; because approachable, theology has a price that simple philosophy is not expected to pay. Liturgical dogmatics seeks its language about God from a table for three set by Abraham at Mamre, from the foot of a ladder where Jacob wrestled wounded, from a bush that burns but was not consumed, from a tabernacle with a fiery column indicating that God is at home, from the *kapporeth* mercy seat of the ark, from the whirlwind of Job, from the still small voice that followed wind and earthquake, from a manger and a cross—all places that were consummated in the incarnate Christ and are now present in his body upon the altar. Liturgical dogmatics is louder than human theological efforts because of the echo chamber created by an emptied tomb.

God cannot be comprehended, but he can be loved. Therefore, in order for the dogmatician to practice his craft, he must become a theologian soul. Liturgical dogmatic theology rests upon liturgical asceticism because what we know depends upon the kind of person we have become. This is a fact true in natural knowledge: an avaricious person cannot understand generosity; an angry person cannot understand serenity; a lustful person cannot understand innocence. This is also a fact in the case of supernatural knowledge: a selfish person cannot understand God's motivations; an angry person cannot understand divine forgiveness; an idolater cannot understand beatific glory. There are things we cannot know unless we are charitable, meek, and chaste, and there is a Subject whom we cannot know unless we are reverent, obedient, worshipful, graceful, praiseful, pious, adoring, reverential, fearful, faithful, devoted. This requirement is placed upon the knower by the reality Himself.

Chapter 2

Knowing God through Awe and Fear

We human beings may feel a conflict or struggle within ourselves when facing God. On the one hand, there is dread that tempts us to escape the holy, and, on the other, there is desire that lures us toward the holy. We sense anxiety and attraction, fear and fascination, dread and calm, uneasiness and enticement, all at the same time. Religion is complicated, in the sense of being complex: more than one reaction happens inside. God is holy, almighty, numinous, so we react to a *mysterium tremendum*, and God is merciful, loving, delightful, so we react to a *mysterium fascinans*.

But we are thus far only describing the reaction of finite to infinite. There is now the added complication of sin. If we are honest with ourselves, we are overcome not only by the power of God, but also by the purity of God. His majesty overwhelms our mortality, and his immaculateness our immorality. Even though we cannot take our eyes off him, we are filled with an apprehension arising from a state that is both finite and fallen. The frequent result of this is a dishonest religion that replaces the true God with one more to our liking. If we lack fear of God, it is a sure sign of idolatry. But it is an equally sure sign of idolatry if we are not enraptured by God. For whatever reason we avoid him, we have joined Adam and Eve in the bushes from which will never arise true cult, genuine piety, acceptable sacrifice.

Liturgical dogmatics respects this complexity and will neither moderate God's power nor mitigate his purity. Leave God at full strength! Admit that the Holy One is beyond our control, and instead, adapt to God, liturgically. The liturgy functions on an antinomy wherein both poles we have described remain unabated, but wherein the two poles can be reconciled. Liturgy bridges fear and love, uniting them. Liturgy combines love and awe; it is an act of awe wrapped in love; it is an act of love imbued with awe. And the first degree of love is to fear God lest we grieve him. This is love mingled with fear. We do not fear God lest he find us out and punish us; rather, we fear God lest we cause him sorrow for having disappointed him. This is a totally different basis for fear. It does not belong to the category of fright and threat; it belongs to the category of liturgical lament. Therefore, this fear causes us, not to retreat, but rather to advance. Contra ordinary definitions and experiences of fear that make us run away, liturgical fear draws us toward the one we have no right to approach, toward the one we know we have frustrated, toward the one against whom we have sinned. Liturgical fear is a step of love that worries over having grieved God.

The liturgical soul stands before God with awe and love mingled, mixed together. Liturgy is an act of awe because God is the Lord; liturgy is an act of love because God is our Father. We began by observing an interior, psychological couplet of dread and attraction. Now we discover that this interior, human antinomy corresponds to an exterior, divine antinomy. That we have these twin reactions is due to the twin character of God. Liturgy reconciles fear and desire by keeping both reactions operative, by confessing God to be both Lord and Father. Letting them bifurcate wrongs God and produces faulty liturgy. The faulty liturgy insults God. If I describe the power and purity of God without any sensation at all, then I am merely doing metaphysics; if I describe the power and purity of God with nothing but fear, then I am having a religious reaction; but if I sense the power and purity of God with a fear of grieving him, then I am crossing a liturgical bridge between awe and love that is on loan from the Cross.

Liturgy is praise, yes, but praise infected with love. If one gives praise for no reason other than fear, then the praise becomes flattery, sycophantic, unctuous, a fawning. There is much bowing and scraping in some people's religious reaction, but this is not the mark of perfect worship. Often such homage is an act of self-defense, not self-gift. It is a mark of natural religion; I mean the kind of religion sinners find natural because it is inherent to a sinful nature. Natural religion had counseled "You who fear the Lord, run from him; you who fear the Lord, placate him; you who fear the Lord, bring the blood of bulls to conciliate him; you who fear the Lord, appease him with your morality." But the human race took a significant step forward when God taught Israel to link fear with love. The Psalmist makes a beeline from a cause to an unexpected effect: "You who *fear* the LORD, *praise* him!" (Ps 22:23; emphasis added). Fear is the cause of praise. This was a surprise. The religion of sinners had gone in a different direction, but Israel's religion moved from fear of the Lord to dearer terms, sweeter relations. If you fear the Lord, trust in the Lord (Ps 115:11). If you fear the Lord, turn away from evil (Prov 3:7). If you fear the Lord, then believe in the Lord (Ex 14:31). If you fear the Lord, then keep his statutes and commandments (Deut 6:2). If you fear the Lord, then walk in his ways, love him, serve him, cling to him, for he is your praise (Deut 10:12, 20–21). If you fear the Lord, then serve him in sincerity and in faithfulness (Josh 24:14). If you fear the Lord, then say out loud "His steadfast love endures forever" (Ps 118:4 [ESV]). If you fear the Lord, then give alms and praise him (Tob 14:2). The Psalmist urges, "Let all the earth fear the LORD, let all the inhabitants of the world stand in awe of him!" and then reveals the reason why a few verses later: "Behold, the eye of the LORD is on those who fear him, on those who hope in his steadfast love" (Ps 33:8, 18). God has his eye on those who have their eye on his stead-fast love. Fear is what comes out of awful love.

When a person loves, his desire is to talk of the object he loves. This is also the reason why liturgical dogmatics talks of God. Liturgy is praise; praise is the daughter of joy; joy results when the lover receives his beloved; the liturgist makes a joyful noise and breaks into joyous songs of praise when he sees the Trinity approach because God is dearly loved. When a person is in love, he will speak incessantly about what fills his attention. If all the waters of the oceans were ink, it would not be enough to record what he feels. The happiness of heaven will be, in part, not finding our joy restricted anymore. The acclamations will be uninterrupted; the lauding, unremitted; the homage, interminable.

At present, we tend to fear God because of his might and love God because of his mercy, but in the fullness that heaven will be, the terminals on the battery will be reversed: we will develop love for his power and fear before his mercy. The power of God will give us pleasure, and the mercy of God will make us reverent. Fear of God will be our delight, and love of God a cause for awe. Then

the characteristics of God that now make him seem distant (transcendence, omnipotence, majesty, perfection) will make him seem
dear and lovable. And the characteristics of God that now make him
seem near (charity, compassion, tenderness, clemency) will make
him seem majestic and regal, for we will be seeing him, not for only
our advantage, but for his own glory. Each person will behold the
glory according to the measure of his love: the more a person loves,
the more ardently he will set his face toward God in yearning. Even
on earth, this is true. Behold the glory of parenting according to
the measure of love for the child; otherwise, it is a chore and there
is no glory in it. There is a lesson here, too, for how justice and
mercy connect.

Chapter 3

Liturgy in the Trinity

Knowledge of the Trinity is not a conclusion; it is a confession. Knowledge of the Trinity is neither a deduction about the Uncreated God from created ontology nor an inference from other religious mythologies. Knowledge of the Trinity is an acknowledgment of the energies of God at work, and his energies are his activities; thus we make confession of the dogma of the Trinity when standing before the altar where all three Persons are acting. They are here mystically presenting the sum of their actions in the economy of salvation. What was accomplished by the providence of God as *mirabilia Dei* in history is united to the liturgical celebration: here the one who called Abraham summons our faith; here the Torah-giver's commandments are heard again; here the King of Israel's kings and the Spirit of Israel's prophets extend his sovereignty again; here the Incarnate One lays himself on the altar as once he was laid in the manger; here Cross and Resurrection still slay sin and raise life; here the full revelation of the Trinity on Pentecost is seen again in charisms alighting on the baptized. The gaze between the Persons of the Trinity, so beautifully depicted by Rublev, depicts the energies glancing from one Person to the next. It is a picture of liturgy: all things come from the Father, and the mission given to Son and Holy Spirit is to return all things to the Father for his glory. This liturgical *exitus* and *reditus* describes the energy of the Trinity, whose essence is beyond our comprehension. We cannot understand Trinity because it is mystery, but we can love the Persons of the Trinity because they have given themselves to be loved. The energy of the Triune God is theirs in common when it works for our sanctification. The consubstantial members of the eternal Triune community give and receive love, and liturgy is an activity of love. The perfect life with the Most Holy Trinity is called "heaven", and liturgy is a heavenly activity.

The uncreated glory even finds a way to hypostasize as created glory, then incarnate that glory in hypostatic form. The perichoresis of the Trinity was kenotically extended for the first time in creation and was kenotically extended for a second time in the Incarnation. In the former, being came from nothing, the cosmos was ordered, life was bestowed, and creation began. In the latter, the first Person of the Trinity sent the second Person of the Trinity to become incarnate by the third Person of the Trinity, and a new creation was begun. The Son who has eternally glorified the Father now does so as the God-man, does so in his flesh and by his human actions. The Spirit who has eternally glorified the Father now does so by directing all things to the Incarnate One and incorporating existence into the Kingdom that the God-man will hand over to his Father.

The Incarnation echoes the glory transacting across the Trinity. "Glorify your Son that the Son may glorify you" (Jn 17:1); "now, Father, glorify me in your own presence with the glory which I had with you before the world was made" (Jn 17:5). It is even shared with us unworthy sinners. "The glory which you have given me I have given to them, that they may be one even as we are one" (Jn 17:22). Jesus desires that "they also, whom you have given me, may be with me where I am, to behold my glory which you have given me in your love for me before the foundation of the world" (Jn 17:24). Any increase of the Father's glory is an expansion of liturgy. Any expansion of the love between Father and Son is an extension of liturgy. This is a pneumatological accomplishment, normally clandestine but here candid.

One cannot look at light, one looks by means of light; for that reason, we do not look at the Holy Spirit himself but, rather, at the one whom he reveals. In liturgy we see the Light of the world by the agency of the third Person of the Trinity, who illuminates him and enlightens us. One does not normally separate word and breath; one speaks a word by means of breath; for that reason, I hear the Word by means of the Spirit. And the Word and Spirit speak the revelation of the Father cooperatively, and we hear the whole Trinity in communication.

Knowledge of the Trinity's perichoretic unity does not come from philosophical deduction. Knowledge of this liturgical unity comes by our graced admission into the perichoresis among these

Persons—we know it from the inside—which is to say, it is an experiential knowledge of liturgical theology. Liturgical theology arises from our continued participation in the mystery-made-flesh (Son) and the spiritual-mystery (Spirit). Reason can marvel, but it cannot discover. The dogma of the Trinity does not come from religious studies because it concerns God. The dogma of the Trinity does not come from comparative religion because there is nothing to which the Trinity can be compared. Our knowledge of created things develops along the lines of comparison as we notice similarities and differences, but this is not a possible epistemology for the Uncreated One. When something is unique, it must be encountered on its own terms; and when the unique one (monotheism) is God, he must disclose himself on terms he chooses. These terms are his energies. His energies are his activities. The essence of God is unknowable because the Uncreated immeasurably transcends the created, which is why the first theological step must be taken with the apophatic foot. The energies of God are known by their effects upon us—we experience them—and then they invite cataphatic comment. The energies of God are creative and providential and redemptive and make up the subject matter of dogmatics, but even if dogma has tracks of where the Lion of Judah has passed, do not think that dogma can confine him with rational cages any more than liturgy can contain him with its ritual catnip.

The Trinity is the first mystery of God, although it is revealed late in the economy. Hints of the Trinity were given in creation, foreshadowings of the Trinity were given to Israel, but its perfect manifestation required one of the Persons to become a human being and one of the Persons to alight on the apostles as a tongue of fire. The Trinity is the only complete answer to the question "Who is Jesus?" Knowledge of the Trinity is participatory knowledge that comes from becoming one with the theandric Jesus, an offer made to us in the liturgy. The revelation of the mystery of the Trinity calls for a new love if we are to know it: a childlike love of God, a supernatural friendship, an adoptive state of unity with the Father of our brother. Knowledge of the Trinity is not a conclusion; it is a participation that happens when Christ gives us his Spirit so we can have a share in his filial relation to his Father in heaven. To have the Spirit within us is to have divine life within us.

On the one hand, we are intended to become what the Father said about Jesus: "this is my beloved Son with whom I am well pleased." On the other hand, we are intended to say to God what Jesus and the Holy Spirit say: "Our Father, who art in heaven". The dogma of the Trinity arises from liturgical prayer: God is whom we address, God is the pathway we walk, and God is the power by which we approach. Noetic prayer is the third Person of the Trinity speaking in our hearts, implanted there by the second Person of the Trinity, with permission to address the first Person of the Trinity as Abba. In spiritual-liturgical prayer, we discover ourselves surrounded by God, within and without, above and below, ahead and behind. In this womb of prayer, the dogma of the Trinity is begotten.

Grace is a gratuity; our praise is a debt. Participation in the divine nature is gratuitously communicated. The Trinity is a liturgical society in that it involves glory, praise, honor, joy, delight, self-giving. The Trinity is a liturgical society and our liturgical life consists of imitating, emulating, reproducing and mimicking—on our created level—the glory and praise and self-giving that occurs here. If the image of God in which we are made grows more perfectly into the likeness of God, it will be because we are becoming consummate liturgists. Every human being is created to be a temple of God, which means a temple wherein this liturgical life goes on. We become this temple when the Holy Spirit resides within us, and he brings with him the Father and Son, verifying the Trinity to our hearts. His testimony proves the dogma of the Trinity. The evidence of his testimony in our hearts proves the dogma of the Trinity. God continues his divine life in our souls when we are made into an image of the image of God by personally possessing the same Spirit that Jesus possesses. Jesus is Christ for being the Anointed One; we are Christian for being anointed ones. Baptism in Christ anoints us with the Holy Spirit, the same as he received when he came up from the waters of the Jordan. This is why liturgy commences with Baptism, why Baptism is the gateway to liturgy, why we are baptized in the name of Father, Son, and Holy Spirit. How could we liturgize the Triune God unless we had been baptized into their communion? How could we pray and praise and sacrifice to the Father unless we had been made baptized brothers of Jesus and sacramental servants of the Spirit in the Bride of Christ?

The Trinity is love; liturgy is based upon love. Love is liturgy's energy. The force of liturgy-in-motion does not come from us; it is God's energies stretching forth and picking us up on its waves. What occurs eternally within the Trinity somehow trespasses its celestial borders to reproduce in us, through sacramental channels, the internal relations of Father, Son, and Holy Spirit. Self-caused existence desires to appear in the lives of contingently caused existents.

Our symbolic liturgy is a reflection of mysteries that are occurring in heaven. Our symbolic liturgy is an external tracing of an internal delight. Liturgy is spiritual because the Spirit is its milieu; liturgy is theological because its words-about-God re-echo the Word's-communion-with-God.

Chapter 4

The Trinity in Liturgy

I defined liturgy in the thickest way I could by calling it the kenotic extension of the perichoresis of the Trinity, first in an act of creation and second in an act of salvation. I pictured our cosmos, and our life in it, bouncing off the walls of that Trinitarian life.

Now I am going to picture the Trinity bouncing off the walls of the Christian temple that houses the liturgy. Liturgy is a work of God and a human activity, and even as he invites us into his work, he joins us in our activity. Irenaeus described the second and third Persons of the Trinity as the right and left hands of the Father. The Father uses these two appendages to round up his favored people, the way a toddler will fill his arms to overflowing with his favorite toys. We might expect, then, both the Son and Spirit to be active even before the liturgy starts. Much preparatory work goes into developing an adept liturgist: we are brought into existence and must be brought to conversion, so the *Logos* and the *Pneuma* busy themselves with the rescue of another offspring of Adam and Eve, awakening the faculty for the supernatural that now lies dormant under a blanket of sin, reviving our appetite for a taste of the divine, raising our eyes above the temporal to the eternal horizon. Step-by-step the liturgist is cultivated and nurtured until he willingly passes through the font into the nave. There he is brought before the face of the Father, which is the purpose of this event. The Trinity is at work.

First, consider the work of the Father in our activity. His apophatic stillness puts our hearts in motion; his apophatic silence arouses our speech; his apophatic mystery attracts our souls. This is the mystery of predestination at work. "Those whom he predestined he also called; and those whom he called he also justified; and those whom he justified he also glorified" (Rom 8:30). Before the liturgical happening even occurs, and in order for it to occur, human beings are collected from their various locations throughout the city to make one hierarchical body; as the Didache says, grain is gathered from various hillsides to make one loaf. We are assembled. This does not mean "brought into proximity with one another", the way people are in the vicinity of each other in the shopping mall crowd. It means "being put together", put in place, put into hierarchical order. "To assemble" is a verb: the Father assembles his Church as I assemble the pieces of a dismantled pen by screwing them back together. The root of the word is *assimulare*, which means "to bring together into a whole". All the engine pieces may be lying about the floor of the garage, but a mechanic must assemble them properly if the engine is to run. All the pieces required for liturgy can be found in matter and souls, but God must put the Church together and put everyone and everything into their hierarchical place. We do not assemble to do liturgy, God assembles his Church so liturgy can be done.

The most significant moment happens in Baptism, where a laic is made, and out of the assemblage of laypersons God can order ministries by whatever charisms he wants to give. The liturgy is a collection of liturgies, done by many people in harmony, and the bishop, the priest, the deacon, the laic, the cantor, the choir, the lector, the servers (not to mention all the invisible angels) all have their part. This is why it is incorrect to say the laity cooperates with the priest in the liturgy and more correct to say the laity and priest *co-operate the liturgy*. This divine activity has many moving parts, all under the hand of God.

The liturgy is inaugurated by the Father, brought into being by the Father, caused to begin by the Father, as all things are. The phenomenon of liturgy is a spiritual instance of *creatio ex nihilo*. We, ourselves, could not bring liturgy into being. We could not bring about liturgy from the parts and pieces we possess. The supernatural event requires a divine dew to fall upon the natural elements we use in our performance (celebration) of liturgy. It is our duty and salvation always and everywhere to give thanks to the Father. Well, that works out nicely! By doing our duty, we receive salvation.

Second, consider the work of the Son in our activity. The liturgy is inscribed in our hearts by the same Word who inscribed the Father's words upon Sinai's stone tablets and who was made incarnate in the

womb of Mary so he could speak them in person. Christ is alone
when he comes from the Father, but he is not alone when he returns
to the Father. He comes from the Father as the eternal Son, but he
returns to the Father as the firstborn among many brethren (Rom
8:29). "In Christ Jesus you are all sons of God, through faith" (Gal
3:26). Normally a son receives more brothers when his father makes
more sons; in this case, the Father receives more sons when his Son
makes more brothers. Christ came down alone and returns as a crowd
(*totus Christus*); he came as the Only Begotten Son and returns with
a Mystical Body of siblings; he came down a bachelor and returns a
Bridegroom. And the Spirit of him who raised Jesus from the dead
now dwells in the members of that Mystical Body (Rom 8:11), so
maybe it is even more correct to say that two came down and one
remained. The Holy Spirit remains on earth now, not as an incarnate
one, but as the one who deifies others and equips them for their
ascent. The two hands of the Father work in accord. This was Jesus'
purpose upon incarnation; it remains his purpose as eternal Son and
high priest. The liturgy descends from the Father through Christ,
and it ascends through Christ back to the Father active in an *ecclesia*.

The *ecclesia* (*ek* + *kalein*) is called out by Christ, through Christ, in
Christ, for Christ, with Christ, under Christ, to Christ. *Adeste Fide-
les*. His people (the *Christifideles laici*) are not limp, however. He has
shared with them his power, his Spirit, which renders them capable
of giving homage and glory to God in a measure and of a kind they
could not otherwise have given. Liturgy does not operate off its own
energy; it is energized by the Paschal Mystery. Liturgy as a whole is
sacramental for having the mysteries of Christ operative in it, and
each sacrament, individually, is a liturgy for celebrating the Mystery of Christ in a particular application. Christ is mediator, which
is what it means to be a priest. He is mediator because of the hypostatic union of divine and human natures in his person, and now the
liturgy can reach through him from God to man and man to God.
Christ is a hypostatic bridge with two-way traffic on it. We find at
certain moments of the liturgy a divine descent, and we find at other
moments of the liturgy a human ascent. Christ is operating in both,
since he is both God and man. Both divine agape and human eros—
the former initiating, the latter responding—are to be found in the
God-man, and both agape and eros are to be found in his Mystical

Body, producing brotherly love as a result (*philia*). For liturgy to do so great a work as it does, Christ must always be present in his Church. A body cut off from its head is a dead body. A Church cut off from her head is a dead Church.

Liturgy is not one more cult of Adam to be added to the pile of religions that has littered history. Out of their natural thirst for God, the descendants of the first Adam developed innumerable religions (*re* + *ligare*, to reunite, to tie fast). Of course! They felt unmoored and loosed from their rock, the most high God their Redeemer (Ps 78:35). But Christ did not come to found another religion. He came to found the Church. Liturgy is the cult of the New Adam perpetuated in Christians. The Second Adam perfected the first Adam's human religious cults by replacing them with his liturgical cult; he perfected human religious sacrifice by substituting himself for the blood of bulls and goats that could not take away sins (Heb 10:4); he perfected human religions by bringing them to an end, bringing them to their *telos*, to himself. Mythology was a question, and religious cult was a quest, but both came to an end when the answer arrived and the treasure they were seeking bowed down from heaven to join us. The Church is the infection of new life being spread into human mortality.

There was no such liturgy as this before Bethlehem. This liturgy had a starting point, and the Church continues in spirit what Christ did in flesh before his Father. As there could not have been icons before Christ was circumscribed, so there could not be this mystical liturgy before Christ hypostatically unified divine and human (though it was foreshadowed in type by Israel, the womb that prepared the Church). The Christological mystery makes possible the mysteries of the liturgy. Liturgy can only be done through him, and with him, and in him, and in the unity of the Holy Spirit. This gives glory and honor to God, the Almighty Father, which is beyond our human capacity to give. Superior to religious cult is liturgical involvement in the perichoresis.

Third, consider the work of the Holy Spirit in our liturgy. The liturgy we do is the Breath of the Father exhaled to inspire prophets' speech and rest upon apostles' heads and, finally, work incarnation in the womb of Mary. Liturgy is the activity of Christ's Church, and Mary is the Mother of the Church. Jesus was incarnate by the Holy

Ghost and of the Virgin Mary, says the Nicene Creed; Christians are made kin, deified, by the Holy Ghost and of the Church. This liturgical platform exists so we can see the face of the Father and, this time, still live. "Man shall not see me and live", God warned Moses (Ex 33:20), and therefore showed him only his backside. But now we have become more audacious, indeed. The Holy Spirit frees us to liturgize with unveiled faces. "Since we have such a hope, we are very bold, not like Moses, who put a veil over his face so that the Israelites might not see the end of the fading splendor" (2 Cor 3:12–13). Such a veil drapes the natural and hardened mind, "but when a man turns to the Lord the veil is removed. Now the Lord is the Spirit, and where the Spirit of the Lord is, there is freedom" (2 Cor 3:16–17). The Holy Spirit frees us to liturgize while beholding the glory of the Lord, being changed ourselves into the Lord's likeness (2 Cor 3:18). To say that liturgy is a spiritual activity is to say that liturgy can only be done when the Holy Spirit is present. Without the Spirit's presence, this would just be a religious service designed by men.

The Holy Spirit unites the liturgy of heaven, the liturgy of the Church, and the liturgy of the heart. In a flash, the Holy Spirit moves between the ambo and our ear, making the reading of Scripture a spiritual proclamation. In a flash, he moves between the altar and our hearts to produce spiritual prayer, between the name of Jesus and our knee bending and tongue confessing, between the crystal river in Revelation and the living water in a font where neophytes are baptized, between the Liturgy of the Word and our conscience that strives to keep the commandments proclaimed there. Old Testament prophets and kings spoke by the Holy Spirit, and now, by his breath, the ink on the biblical page that he inspired becomes living word to inspire its hearers. He makes living stones out of those who are members of the living stone rejected by men. For Nicodemus, Jesus compares the Holy Spirit to a wind that blows where it wills, but this is not only geographic (blowing wherever it wants), it is also temporal (blowing whenever it wants). The Holy Spirit revisits every baptismal font, making saints, as once he descended as a dove at the Jordan. Every liturgy is a Pentecost: we are filled with a new wine unknown to the world. Whoever calls on the name of the Lord shall be saved, and souls are not abandoned to Hades anymore, but no one can say Jesus is Lord except by the Holy Spirit. At every Eucharist, the Spirit is sent down like dewfall to make the gifts holy so they may become for us the Body and Blood of Christ, and when we partake of them, that same Holy Spirit gathers us into one.

To conclude, the Father is the source and target of liturgy; it is the Son's liturgy that we do, not our own; and the Holy Spirit is the principal liturgist, with whose energy we synergize. Liturgy prepares us for beatitude—that is why it is so important—and our life of happiness, both now and in heaven, consists of koinonia in the Koinonia, fellowship in the Fellowship, union in the Communion. It is a good thing the Trinity is giving us the opportunity to practice.

Chapter 5

Revelation, Liturgy, and Scripture

Monastic ascetical texts frequently presented summaries of traditional wisdom in the form of paragraphs strung together. This was called a "century format" because they frequently strove for one hundred paragraphs to indicate perfection. This century format has two distinct advantages that make me use it here (albeit with only 76 items). First, it invites paradox. As mentioned in the introduction, truths are put side by side to be connected at a deeper level than might be indicated by conjunctions alone. Second, it invites the reader to do some work. He must become an active participant in perceiving the connections. I here propose truths about revelation, liturgy, and Scripture for the reader to connect.

1. Our topic here is Scripture, but we must set it within the bigger category of revelation, and revelation is activity. God is not an object to look at; he is a subject who approaches. He must give himself to be seen; he never just stands there to be looked at. We know him because he shows himself.
2. The reason God approaches is to call us home to himself. This same reason applied both before and after the Fall. God had the same intention in either case.
3. Revelation therefore initiates movement, pilgrimage, running forward. Revelation initiates liturgy. And because Scripture contains this revelation, we may say the existence of Scripture is for the sake of liturgy.
4. On this liturgical journey, the Church carries a *vade mecum*: "to go with". The Church carries a guidebook for ready reference, a constant companion, a manual, a reference book constantly carried. The Scriptures are this *vade mecum*.

40

5. This useful book serves the journey. The reason it is in our possession is to serve the journey. Although interesting in itself, although beneficial as a theoretical or didactic or historical text, although inspiring to the soul, Scripture is a travel handbook. It serves liturgical advance.

6. Scripture is to liturgy as Word is to sacrament.

7. Revelation, as an action of God, is a species in the genus of his mysteries.

8. The East made a distinction between the essence and energies of God. The essence of God is a truly hidden mystery, yet we can truly know God. He discloses himself in his action, his *energeia*, his deeds. It is similar, *mutatis mutandis*, with a human being: my essence is personal and unknowable in its depths, but I reveal myself in my activities.

9. God has his reasons. He has his reasons for what he shows and what he withholds, when he shows up and when he withdraws, to whom he appears and from whom he hides. Each revelation is crafted for a personal case. Revelation is never just once, and it is not the same for all. Yet we believe that God has revealed or will reveal himself to every person, and that gives us hope. The tradition speaks about every human being as an *actual or potential* member of the Church.

10. A first distinction: between natural revelation and the written word. Behind each type stands the same *Logos*. There are two books of revelation, nature and Scripture. Liturgical dogmatics should strive to read both books.

11. The spiritual essence of created beings is like alphabet letters still in need of a grammar. But in natural revelation, God has at least put mankind into motion by the pictures he sends, and human religious myths record them. But they are in the form of questions still in need of an answer.

12. God has scattered his revelations throughout the world (*logoi*), and liturgy pulls them all together.

13. A second distinction: between the written word and the incarnate Word. Both involve the same *Logos*. The Old Testament bears witness to the unincarnated Word; the New Testament testifies to the incarnated Word. That is why the Church can use Israel's written Scripture, the Hebrew Bible, in her liturgy.

Christians consider the Old Testament to be revealed Scripture by God. Old and New Testaments function together, like two lenses in binoculars.

14. Here we are especially concerned with the written and incarnate revelations, because both make their appearance in liturgy. There is a close link between Scripture and liturgy.

15. In her worship, the Church uses texts written by some of her members under the inspiration of the Holy Spirit.

16. There is an analogy between interpreting liturgy and interpreting Scripture. The literal-spiritual distinction formulated for the latter should also apply to the former. Philology alone cannot do justice to Scripture, and ritology alone cannot do justice to liturgy.

17. Without the Old Testament, Christians would not understand the grammar of temple, sacrifice, lamb of God, priesthood, mystery, glory, tabernacle-temple, prophecy, propitiation, Passover-Paschal, bread and wine, anointing, blessing, hand-laying, lamentation, memorial, *berakah*, *todah*, bath, martyrs, preaching, Psalm singing, the week, the Sabbath, or annual feasts. We could go on.

18. The typological reading of Scripture has always understood this. Insofar as biblical scholars today do *not* do typology, they do not understand this. Tradition said (voiced by Augustine) that in the Old Testament the New lies hidden, and in the New Testament the meaning of the Old becomes clear. Typology discovers the similitude between the two Testaments.

19. One symbol proposed for understanding the two Testaments (Gregory the Great) comes from the ark of the covenant. Two cherubim face each other over the *kapporeth:* that mercy seat is a throne, and they behold the Lord between them. Christ is seated between the two Testaments like that. And now his mercy seat is the liturgical altar between the two Testaments. That is why the liturgy has readings from both the Old and New Testaments.

20. What typology is to Scripture, mystagogy is to liturgy.

21. God said to Moses, "For this commandment which I command you this day is not too hard for you, neither is it far off. It is not in heaven, that you should say, 'Who will go up for us to heaven, and bring it to us, that we may hear it and do it?' Neither is it beyond the sea, that you should say, 'Who will go over the sea

for us, and bring it to us, that we may hear it and do it?' But the word is very near you; it is in your mouth and in your heart, so that you can do it" (Deut 30:11–14). The revelation that I give to you today is not far off; it is not in heaven, not beyond the sea, not in a book, not for biblical critics, not in manuals. It is very near you. At the ambo. Proclaimed for ear to hear and mind to embrace. It is God's first incarnation, said Ephrem of Syria: God clothed himself in words before he clothed himself in flesh.

22. Theology means teaching about God and divine things; theology depends upon revelation (otherwise it is humanly constructed religious philosophy); it is called revelation when the word of God is the principle of our theological knowledge; liturgical dogmatics supposes that if the liturgy's *lex orandi* establishes *lex credendi*, then the liturgy must be an instance of revelation; because both *lex orandi* and Scripture are revelation, therefore liturgical dogmatics must ask about the relationship between liturgy and the Bible.

23. Questions run through our minds: Are there two revelations? Does God stammer? Does the second extend the first, run parallel with it, or contradict it? Does the later revelation possess its own novelty? Has revelation fractionated? Into how many pieces? Is there one revelation, but two places to receive it? Why the redundancy? How is it apportioned? Is revelation conditioned for the consumer, with the Bible being for literates and liturgy for illiterates? These questions indicate fruitless courses. The Bible is revelation, and the liturgy is revelation, and we are asking about their relationship.

24. If revelation were nothing more than a pile of propositions, then we could reduce our question to asking where the biggest pile is to be found, or the first pile, or the most authoritative pile, or the best pile, or the most useful pile, or the definitive pile. But suppose revelation is something other than a pile of propositions.

25. We do not confront the content of Scripture chiefly as history; we chiefly confront the content of Scripture in its sacramental and spiritual aspects sparkling in the liturgy. That transition from historical meaning to spiritual meaning has already begun in the Scriptures. That is why the Bible reads the way it does; that is why the letter is read spiritually (one literal meaning, and three

spiritual meanings: typological, tropological, and anagogical). The trajectory has already begun in Scripture itself, and liturgy just continues it.

26. Revelation has a *telos*. It is a mind communicating to a mind, with a purpose. The purpose is not to make me smarter. The reason for the revealed law, natural or written, is to accomplish the preservation of worship of the true God.

27. *Scripture serves liturgy.*

28. Suppose revelation is not only what we see, but the gift of an ability to see it.

29. Christ is the revelation of the Father. He sees what the Father sees. He sees the way the Father sees. And to us, he not only shows us what he and the Father see, he also sends the Holy Spirit to give us the same sight: Christ's gift of revelation is to give us the eyes of the Dove.

30. Where is God's sight *revealed*? In Scripture. Where is God's sight *imparted*, communicated, transmitted, bestowed? In liturgy. That is why liturgy is primary theology: it is where we absorb Scripture as Scripture.

31. Revelation is not just a pile of facts from which we can select the ones we like. Revelation involves authority. In revelation, God speaks with authority. Therefore, there is a proper and appropriate attitude to adopt before revelation: it is the posture we should adopt before authority. That posture is obedience. The appropriate attitude toward revelation is obedience, submission, docility, conformity, observance, fealty, devotion, piety.

32. We have just crossed the line into liturgical matters.

33. Revelation of God demands from creatures due homage and the glorification of his Majesty. There is an appropriate liturgical attitude toward revelation. In order to live willingly under God's authority, we must turn ourselves over to Christ and be formed and conditioned to him by the Holy Spirit.

34. The highest revelation is in glory because it is the communication of the divine light necessary for the contemplation of God.

35. The Bible is content; the liturgy is light by which to see the content. Liturgy is revelatory in the sense of epiphany.

36. Liturgy is where art can function as icon; outside this liturgical viewing, art is a museum piece or artifact. Liturgy is where ritual

can function as *leitourgia*; outside liturgical usage, ritual is socially established. Liturgy is where a book can function as Scripture; outside this liturgical reading, the Bible is history or poetry or mythology.

37. The Bible can be read on multiple levels: a historian looks for chronology, an anthropologist looks for primitive behaviors, a psychologist looks for penitential motives, a scientist looks for cosmological descriptions, a sociologist looks for ancient kinship structures, a poet looks for samples of verse meter, a Hellenist looks for parallels between Jesus and a wandering cynic, a comparative religionist looks for similarities between Israel's temple and Hindu sacrifice, and we are not to the end yet. But in what would one have to be interested if one wished to attend to the Bible as Scripture?

38. A liturgical dogmatics of Scripture is the search for the name of that desire. And it turns out to be relevant to both the Bible and liturgy. Liturgical dogmatics concludes that for the book to be used as Scripture, and the ritual be used as liturgy, one must desire holiness.

39. The Bible records a history, a history of God's activity, and history is a line. Geometers tell us a line is made up of points, so we may imagine points of history making up the biblical line. We may further understand the line as a vector: "a line drawn from its original to its final position". History is a line tracing mankind's original place to its final place.

40. Points on that line cannot be erased, shuffled, reversed, returned, or repeated. But they can be climaxed ("brought to the point of greatest intensity or force in an ascending series"). The thaumaturgy of liturgy (working of miracles) is to climax those historical points on the line of revelation into a *hodie*: "on this day, as distinct from yesterday".

41. For example, we do not sing "Christ was born back then"; we sing *hodie Christus natus est*. In liturgy, it is always today. Ask "What time is it?" and you will always receive the same answer: "Today".

42. From the Gospel we know about the raising of Lazarus, but in the Church's *hodie*, that historical fact becomes an event for us. The story is climaxed, brought to a particular point, happens today, meets us face to face. Even though this is the sacred

history itself, found in the sacred text itself, this history must rise up (even as did Lazarus himself), be unbound (even as was Lazarus himself), and become an event today, on Lazarus Sunday in the Orthodox calendar and the fifth Sunday of Lent in the Catholic calendar.

43. We know that Lazarus would have risen again at the *last day*, at the resurrection of the dead. We know it as surely as did his sister Martha. But we are asked to believe that Jesus is the resurrection and the life *today*. In the liturgical day. If so, come forth and worship. If so, come forth and receive the Body and Blood of the one who raised him.

44. It is true that any person of faith could read Scripture existentially, as concerning him, too. He could consider the historical vector to be pointing directly at him and so be moved personally by Scripture. That is not untrue. It is only too circumscribed. The arrows coming existentially from Scripture do not merely hit targets in one individual person. They are not targeted at one individual person's belief, imagination, emotion, will, choice, prayer life, et cetera. That is too idiosyncratic.

45. Liturgical dogmatics does not overlook this personal use of Scripture, but right now liturgical dogmatics is thinking about the experience of the ecclesial subject, not the private subject.

46. Scripture must be read in the context of ecclesiality (Florensky's word).

47. It is an awful tragedy to read Scripture only historically instead of also liturgically. It becomes dry as a bone.

48. The Bible and liturgical theology make up revelation in this way: the dry bones (Bible) are moistened (liturgy) so the ecclesial subject can live.

49. Here is Ezekiel's account with some words changed, as indicated by the brackets. "The Spirit of the LORD ... set me down in the midst of the valley; it was full of bones.... They were very dry. And he said to me, 'Son of man, can these [writings] live?' And I answered, 'O Lord GOD, you know.' Again he said to me, 'Prophesy to these bones, and say to them, O dry [scriptures], hear the word of the LORD. Thus says the Lord GOD to these [scriptures]: Behold, I will cause breath to enter you, and you shall live'" (Ezek 37:1–5).

50. What is the result? The anatomy of Scripture is revealed. "The bones came together, bone to its bone." Passages from Scripture are no longer treated in isolation from each other, like treating the trapezoid bone of the hand in isolation from the whole skeleton. When the body breathes again, we will know how to organize Bible verses. The taxonomy of Scripture is revealed in its liturgical usage.

51. Irenaeus thought the Gnostics did not know how to organize Bible verses. Although the Gnostics had scriptural verses, they disregarded their order (*taxis*) and connection (*eirmos*). They had the same pile of Scripture verses as the Catholics had, like one artist might have the same pile of tesserae as another, but with those mosaic tiles they made the image of a fox instead of the image of a king because they did not know the order and connection the tiles should have.

52. The heretics did not know what Aristotle called the hypothesis, the first principle, the hypo-thesis, the "proposition underneath" the tiles.

53. *Lex orandi* is the theological hypothesis operating underneath the *lex credendi*. The *lex orandi* is operating there as an "understanding": it is the sub-stance of dogma.

54. Scripture's taxonomy must be revealed in the liturgical hypothesis.

55. The goal of health is the hypothesis for a doctor: it is his first principle from which all succeeding understandings and actions flow. If a doctor had a different hypothesis (principle), he would write a different prescription. With a different hypothesis, he would prescribe a different diet or different medicine.

56. Holiness is the hypothesis of the Divine Physician. Our deification. This hypothesis is the under-standing (substance) of liturgy's twin purposes: the glorification of God and the sanctification of man. Our deification glorifies God. God shows his glory by sanctifying mankind.

57. This first principle is assigned to all three of the *munera* (offices) Christ has left his Church: teaching, sanctifying, and governing (prophet, priest, and king).

58. Some will say they believe that the Lord suffered death for us, but if they do not attain to this love in their own souls, it will seem like an old story coming out of bygone days.

59. The events in the life of our Lord happen both in Judea and in the soul. What the Father accomplished by the Incarnation with his right hand in Judea, he does again by sacrament with his left hand in his Church.

60. The Fathers spoke of five ages depicted by the Old Testament (Adam to Noah, Noah to Abraham, Abraham to David, David to Babylon, and Babylon to the birth of Jesus), and the sixth age is the one we are in now, the age of the Church. It will be followed by a seventh age, the seventh day, the day of the Sabbath, the end of all ages. But there is one more. The eighth day.

61. We already taste the eighth day. We celebrate liturgy on the eighth day. We celebrate eighth-day existence in the liturgy.

62. The seven ages belong to the Bible; the eighth day belongs to liturgy.

63. Scripture thinks with words, because we have a mind. Liturgy thinks with symbols, because we have a body.

64. In class, Godfrey Diekmann described the overlapping and repetitive quality of the Psalms: they are God speaking to Christ, Christ speaking to God, Christ speaking to us, us speaking to Christ, God speaking to us, us speaking to God, us speaking to God through Christ, God speaking to us through Christ, us speaking to God about Christ, God speaking to us about Christ, Christ speaking to us about God—all conversations made possible by the Holy Spirit. Scripture is lifted up into liturgical conversation.

65. Liturgy has both an exterior and interior side. Scripture also has both an exterior and interior side. Man has an exterior and interior, too. It is almost like the three were made for each other.

66. Prayer is a continual intercourse of the spirit with God (Evagrius). Liturgy is prayer, and prayer gives wing to Scripture, that it might carry us aloft. By prayer, Scripture is saturated with praise and thanksgiving; Scripture gives words to our intercessions and petitions.

67. We do not just pray over Scripture; Scripture becomes prayer, which is always the prayer of the Church, which is liturgy.

68. Revelation invites us to behold; beholding is a kind of gazing at; gazing at is a form of contemplation; contemplation belongs more to *intellectus* than to *ratio*. We behold the Lord, whom we have met in Scripture, passing in liturgy.

69. Grace does not abolish freedom. In the case of Scripture, inspiration does not abolish the human character of the scribe. The Holy Spirit is the author of Scripture, but moves the writers according to their own character.

70. In the case of liturgy, the work of God does not abolish the development of structures across human history. There is a human quality to liturgy, but the Holy Spirit is analogously inspiring those liturgies. He can be called the author of the liturgy as he can be called the author of Scripture. This is the way grace works.

71. The Desert Fathers urged saintly ascetics to progress from mental communion to actual communion. In Scripture, we find communion with Christ through our mind and memory and imagination, but in the Eucharist he is present in a true, real, and substantial manner.

72. It sounds mystifying and obscure to move from mental to actual communion, but maybe it is simpler than we think. Do you have a friend, a spouse, a lover whom you got to know slowly? You gained first impressions of this person; such impressions dwelled in the imagination, in memory, in thought—they dwelled in a mental world. You were in mental communion with that beloved one, but are you still? Now she is there, and you are in her presence, in actual communion. *You are not thinking about her; you are with her.*

73. Being with her drives out mental images; there is no need for them. How foolish it would be to say to your beloved standing in front of you, "Wait, let me close my eyes and think about you. Give me that book, I want to read more about you."

74. If God in three Persons cannot be this actual to us, it is because we have restricted him and think of him as far away, sending us messages in a bottle.

75. We can read Scripture in actual communion with God. It is like a private exercise of public liturgical reading.

76. But love for another—whether God, spouse, or children—is different when it is in person, face to face, done with body and not only mind, with act and not only thoughtful memory. That is why I would rather make love than receive texts; why I would rather make liturgy than read texts.

CREATED BEING

Chapter 6

The Liturgical Potentiality of the Cosmos

Creation does not occur because of a deficiency in God. God is perfectly happy, and his perfection is happy. This is difficult for us to imagine since we are made for communion outside ourselves, but easier to imagine if we realize God has communion within himself. There is nothing God needs, nothing for which he goes in search, no shortage he suffers, since he is the abundance of existence and truth, being and beauty, love and goodness. We have never experienced such completeness and so cannot imagine the gratuity of God's creative act. Creation does not occur because of any insufficiency or inadequacy found in the Communion of Love; creation, rather, occurs because charity cannot be bounded. It is the nature of charity ever to increase. Even our contingent nature can sense the enlarging and expanding effects of charity, but in God's case those effects are ontological. The God who is Being is also Love and Goodness, and when these three attributes compound, then other creatures get willed into existence. He benevolently gives created beings a share in the circulation of love that flows between the Uncreated Persons.

Creation is not a past act of God; it is a present activity of God. Therefore, when we search for the reason for creation, we do not need to speculate about some past and distant origin point; we need only look around us. If we do, and do so in sufficient depth, we go past gratitude for good fortune, past amazement at being alive, and reach astonishment at being at all. I have been today; I might also be tomorrow, though there is no necessity to that; I am today. That is reminiscent of the name God revealed to Moses from the burning bush. "Tell them I Am sent you." God is Being, and even though this characteristic in God is apophatically different from this characteristic in us, we have a creaturely version of it. When I am, it is in the

image of I Aм. To have being is to be in the image of God, who is I
Aм. Though human language has only created the present participle
"be-ing" out of the verb "to be", it could as easily go on and create
"am-ing" out of "am". My is-ing is the very first case of being an
image of he who Is. This is true for every creature, without any risk
of pantheism.

Why does I Aм share be-ing? We have said it is not out of a meta-
physical crisis on his part; it is, rather, out of liturgical largess toward
us. The cosmos' *raison d'être* is to glorify God. God creates (present
tense), first, in order to have creatures whom he can love and, second, to have creatures who can love. He can accomplish the former
by calling irrational creatures into existence, but the latter can be
accomplished only by the appearance of rational spirits. And liturgy
functions in both cases, the former being cosmic liturgy and the latter
being *logike latria*.

In the first place, irrational creation is for liturgy. Visible and
material creatures glorify their Creator by their existence and operation. Their existence exclaims, without words, "Bless the Lord",
and they magnify God by their subsistent obedience to the orders
of nature established by him. To purify gold, refiners heat it to an
extreme temperature. When Nebuchadnezzar heated the furnace
seven times more than accustomed, then the three youths who were
cast into it discerned the praise that all of purified cosmos offers up:
the heavens, the waters above the heavens, the powers, sun and
moon, stars of heaven, shower, dew, winds, fire, cold, rain, frost,
snow, night and day, lightnings, clouds, earth, mountains, hills,
every growing thing, springs, seas, rivers, sea monsters, water creatures, birds of the air, wild and tame beasts, and all mortal human
beings—let every created cosmic thing bless the Lord (Dan 3).
God made the furnace a temple of prayer, and he can make the
cosmos a temple of prayer, too. If irrational creatures like stars and
waters could reason, then they would put their liturgy into intelligent form, but as they cannot, they glorify God by being, being
obedient to the laws of their nature, being instruments of theophany, and directing man to their Creator. Ephrem said it was a suffering for the creatures when men began worshipping them instead
of the One to whom they were trying to lead men. In their *logoi*,
they bear witness to the *Logos*.

In the second place, rational spirits are for liturgy. First among the rational spirits are the invisible angels, created for liturgy. They surround the throne as an echo chamber of glorification. All the angels live a life of adoration (which is why monks are said to lead an angelic life), with seraphim chief among them. The icon of the synaxis of the angels shows the bodiless powers adoring Christ, the embodied one. They assemble for the glory of the Incarnate Son, who gives glory to the Father. The angels of heaven, the angels of earth, the angels of the nations, the guardian angels of each person all cooperate in lifting acclamation upward and channeling grace downward. This is the liturgical business of the celestial hierarchy that Dionysius detected.

Second among the rational spirits are hybrid human beings, created for liturgy. Man and woman were created as mediators, standing at heaven's nadir and earth's zenith and weaving the praise of the visible cosmos with the praise of the invisible cosmos. They are the spiritual tongue of mute creation and the corporeal ear that can hear incorporeal laudation. The fact that man and woman can join their voices to the seraphim (the very ones on whom Isaiah eavesdropped in the year that King Uzziah died) lifts men and women from a merely mundane existence to exalt them to a heavenly vocation. The whole earth is full of God's glory, which is why the seraphim say the Lord of hosts is holy, holy, holy, but a priest is needed to translate this material glory into spiritual sacrifice. We shall see that Adam and Eve were created to be this cosmic priest and how they failed their vocation.

We are often reluctant to say that God created for the liturgical purpose of his glorification, but that is because our understanding of glory is now corrupted. We falter because we apply our categories to God. When we seek our own glorification (not a hypothetical example!), it is for selfish reasons. Vanity is the motive for drawing glorious attention to ourselves. But this is not the case with God, because it is just for him to receive glory. Aristotle said justice is giving what someone or something is due: giving the right thing, to the right person, in the right measure, in the right way, at the right time, for the right reason. When the Mass invites us to lift up our hearts and give thanks, we instantly and instinctively respond that it is right and just. (That is, we respond that way if we are standing aright, standing in awe, being attentive in order to present the Holy Offering in peace.) In that brief response, we have affirmed liturgical cosmology. Religion is giving God his due, which is why Thomas treats the topic within the context of the four cardinal virtues, specifically within the context of justice. Religion is giving God what he is due as God. God, and only God, is due *latria*, more than *dulia*. Religion professes God to be of ultimate value, ultimate worth, and deserving of *worthship* (the etymological root of our word). Someone is worshipped if he is in the condition of being worthy. It is only right and just to give God this kind of glorification (*latria*); if we took such glory for ourselves, it would be wrong and unjust. Even worse, it would be idolatrous. We hesitate to say that God creates liturgically, i.e., for his own glory, because we impose our own reasoning upon his case. But it is not idolatrous for God, as God, to do things for his own glory, i.e., liturgically, and we may affirm liturgical cosmology without wavering. Liturgy is an end in itself because glorifying God does not need to be justified. It is the end, the *telos*, of both man and the cosmos.

This liturgical cosmology will have a twofold effect. It will not only condition our understanding of the cosmic liturgy, as we have been describing, it will also condition our understanding of the cultic liturgy. The symbolic, sacramental liturgy offers us innumerable benefactions. At this throne of grace, we receive forgiveness, redemption, justification, and sanctification, but they do not make up the total activity of the cultic liturgy. These gifts are preparatory requirements only. They ready the liturgist for the primary task of liturgy, which is glorifying God. When we have been forgiven, redeemed, justified, and sanctified, then we can give proper glory to God. This kind of worship is only accomplishable by the sons and daughters of the old Adam after they have been incorporated by Baptism into the New Adam. Christ is the only human being who can give dignified and just worship (*dignum et iustum*) to the Father, but every human being initiated into Christ joins him in this kind of worship because through the Holy Spirit they are in him and he is in them. The *work* of the Incarnate One is done in the *activity* of the cultic liturgy of his baptized brothers and sisters. And so a proper liturgical cosmology would help restore the latreutic dimension of worship front and center in the Christian cult.

It would furthermore repair any faulty notion of sacrifice by recovering it as a natural human religious instinct. The motive in sacrifice is to glorify God, to thank, exalt, and adore God, to give oneself to God. Sacrifice as propitiation for sin is a necessary preliminary, but it is not the end of sacrifice. According to Augustine, the end of sacrifice is doing every action clinging to God in the communion of holiness.

Liturgical cosmology answers the question, "What is matter for?" And the answer comes in the form of a liturgical Jacob's ladder: matter is designed for both ascending and descending traffic. On this ladder, Jacob saw God's angels ascending and descending, and when he recognized the gateway to heaven, the house of God, he took the stone that he had put under his head and set it up as a sacred pillar, pouring oil on top of it. Every place where we stop, every stone that we take, has the potential of becoming a temple if God begins trafficking to it. The liturgical potentiality of the cosmos is astonishing. Matter is configured for sacramental outreach from heaven to earth, which makes possible a sacrificial reach from earth to heaven. Matter becomes theophanic when God self-discloses through it, and it furthermore becomes sacramental when God graces through it. In response, matter becomes sacrificial when man's thanksgiving and self-offering return upward through it. The cosmos is a locale for catabatic and anabatic movement.

The light of each liturgical Tabor gives eye beams with which to see the world differently. Sacramental theology concerns the importation of the material cosmos into liturgy, but liturgical cosmology concerns the importation of liturgy into our daily cosmos. Earth looks different after we have stood before the altar mandorla and glimpsed heaven. The flash of eschatology in liturgy does not blind our eyes; it opens them, heals them. The resultant transfigurative teleology understands all things according to their *telos*, their end: at liturgy we see the alpha and omega of the cosmos, and thus we see the cosmos' nature more truly than any science can depict it. The scientist investigates the "what" of the thing; the liturgist contemplates the "wherefore and whereto" of the thing, and the "why" of a thing is more evident in the latter than in the former. The liturgical eye beam is contemplative knowledge now exercised on our current space and time, and contemplative knowledge deals with substance and not surface. As a result, the whole world looks different, deeper. There is a will behind it, and not merely a force, and a will can love, whereas a force cannot. That, in itself, totally transfigures our world. We discover that the world is gift, not mere utility. This fact transfigures our otherwise selfish approach to the world. We are transferred from *philautia* to philanthropy, from egoist to altruist, from profiteer to protector. With God overhead, we tread differently upon the earth under our feet. The royal priest has a submissive dominion, not an arbitrary domination.

We will not understand man's place in the world, or the world's design for man, if we do not combine liturgical cosmology with liturgical anthropology. The cosmos is a quarry for mining stones out of which to build the temple of our lives. It is the most dignified and just use we can make of matter, even though there are a hundred other ways to approach the material world: the hedonist embraces it for sensual pleasure; the scientist probes it with curiosity; the capitalist organizes it for profit; the Marxist restricts himself to a materialism that is dialectical; the aesthetic admires it; the artist mimics it; the naturalist wants to return to it; the positivist strips it of spiritual content; and the spiritualist ignores its potential transfiguration. So many philosophies, so little insight into the real purpose of our cosmic existence.

Chapter 7

Liturgical Temporal Cosmology

Time is also an element of liturgical cosmology. Besides matter and space, the cosmos involves time, because space and time came into existence simultaneously. As soon as there was a point A and a point B, it took time to go from one to the other. And if matter glorifies God, then we will not be surprised to find that time does, too. There is a temporal component to the adoration of God in the cosmic liturgy. Even if creation had only existed for one brief flash, like a lightning strike in the darkness, sandwiched between a nothingness on both sides, that momentary blaze of being would have honored God. But to our astonishment, creation continues, from one moment to the next, and time unfolds in an undying glow of glory. And when it comes to human rational creatures with memory, we begin dealing with history in addition to brute time—both the sense of history grasped by persons and their own personal history. The loom on which we weave our lives has both a spatial warp and a temporal woof, and for us the created world involves both objects and histories.

The fact that the Church is sacramental means that God reaches out through material things like water, bread, wine, oil, and hand-laying when material things are spiritualized by the Holy Spirit. But man also lives in time, spiritualized by the Holy Spirit resulting in a Church of sanctified time. God reaches out through history as well as through matter. Liturgical cosmology deals not only with things, it also deals with moments. By daily experience we know that any material thing is only properly understood if taken in the context of the events in which it plays a part. Similarly, the real meaning of the material world is only understood properly when it is placed in the context of divine providence. When time makes contact with eternity, time is filled to overflowing.

Cultic liturgy is an expression of the cosmos' liturgy, a kind of symbolic microcosm of what is going on below our feet and above our heads, and insofar as that liturgy of the world includes a temporal reality, we may think of cultic liturgy as being a time-lapse image of the cosmic liturgy. In time-lapse photography, exposures are taken at intervals so that, on playback, a naturally slow process may be viewed at an accelerated pace. The natural liturgical rhythm of the spheres is given an accelerated view in the cultic liturgy so that we can see it unfolding. This was better understood by medieval man, who expected the music of the spheres to praise God with the harmonies that sounded from their revolution. After all, the heavens rejoice (Ps 96:11).

Cultic liturgy is also an expression of internal liturgy, a manifestation and symbol of what is going on within our hearts. A noetic liturgy occurs in symbiotic conjunction with the external liturgy. Thus does a personal *leitourgia* extend across the various units of time that we occupy. The eighth day, the Liturgy of the Hours, and the liturgical year are a manifest organization of the Paschal Mystery as it permeates our lives to its smallest moments. Time does not need "redemption", since it is a creation by God and is good. But time is consecrated when it is presented before the Kingdom of God to be blessed, as all creatures are. No part of our day or week or year is excluded from receiving this blessing. We liturgically confess that we are totally dependent upon God when our temporal rhythm of prayer acknowledges the dominion of God over us. There is no part of our work or play that he does not govern. The Divine Office makes a liturgy out of our hours—makes an actual Liturgy of the Hours—like an architect makes the Church out of stones. The Divine Office breaks the Paschal Mystery into bite-sized pieces that we can chew on over the year. The whole life of the faithful is a *leitourgia* in which we are identified with the action of Christ. The hymn that Christ introduced into his world is sung as one long, sustained note.

Liturgy gives us the only accurate perception of the world because liturgy keeps our eye trained on an eschatological horizon that admonishes us about this world's passing. To admonish means "to reprove gently but earnestly, and counsel against something to be avoided". Liturgy counsels us, gently but earnestly, not to place our hope in the wrong source, not to put our faith in the wrong wellspring, not to give our love to the wrong author. The world will never redeem us, no matter how far along its history we journey. It is not just that the world has not redeemed us yet, it is that it will *never* redeem us because it does not wield such power. Eternity must irrupt into temporality. The world will feel this irruption as forcible and uninvited because a consequence of sin is the world's resistance to the eternal Kingdom. It comes from an exaggerated and unhealthy valuation of earthly, material life. It comes from preferring to imagine, fancifully, that the world is the center of meaning, and its history will go on perpetually. The world would prefer to consider itself in autonomous control of the passage of time. It will resist being told that it is impermanent and was created to lay itself down for the glory of its Creator. As a result, the world will never come to a correct reckoning of time.

Therefore, the Christian liturgist must practice at dying in order to remember that we do not have our true homeland here. Taking time liturgically reveals the world as a pathway, and our liturgy begins by dying at Baptism, then continuing to practice at it daily until our sacramental death is consummated in our biological death. Liturgical time recognizes and proclaims the world's temporal character, by which we mean the world's temporary character. This does not mean time and matter are denigrated, as was done by most Gnostics, but neither does it mean being satisfied with less than fully consecrated time and matter, as most worldly people are. Liturgy habituates us to our true home, and that makes us tread gently in this halfway house, which, in turn, conditions the way we use all material things: they do not belong to us; they are not permanent; we do not find our meaning or satisfaction in them. Liturgy and eschatology impact time and matter. The world is a pathway, not a home, and a pathway is exactly what its name says: a route to walk. The liturgy reveals this fact about the world by providing a foretaste of our real home. Earthly wealth and property and honor change hands constantly, proving that they are only ours to watch over temporarily—i.e., while in our temporal state. Once we leave this state, temporal riches and properties and esteems fall limply from our hands. A cadaver cannot clasp anything. This we are taught by liturgical time when it takes death into account. When the moment arrives for our true identity to appear, we will drop everything and obey the summons—either voluntarily, as believers should have been practicing since Baptism, or involuntarily, as happens to people unprepared for the stripping that death does.

We have time to unite with God. We have time in order to unite with God. The reason there is time is so we can unite with God. At death time will run out—like a child might run out of the yard—and there will be no time left to unite with God. If we do not begin the process now, we cannot finish it later. If it is not initiated during this life, it will not occur at all.

This should give us a new and sober recognition of what happens in the Sacraments of Initiation. *Baptism* does not pickle us in holy water until Judgment Day; it inaugurates something that, if not started now, will be stillborn at our death. It is a Sacrament of "Initiation" precisely in the sense that it initiates a spiritual dimension that should occupy each moment. *Confirmation* bestows gifts of the Holy Spirit, not with the intention that they remain idle, but rather with the purpose of conforming us to Christ's apostolic ministry in mature participation in bringing the visible Church's mission ever closer to fruition. And the third Sacrament of Initiation, the *Eucharist*, is not a nibble of mercy; rather, its sustenance builds up a spiritual body that one day can digest the consummating messianic feast, the beatific banquet. These sacraments do what their name declares: they initiate. The Sacraments of Initiation place our feet upon a liturgical causeway: a road raised above swampland by stone and timber (altar and cross). On it, we tread across time with purpose and design. On it, we tread over history's temporal arc to everlasting life.

Even more astonishing than our traffic across the temporal to enter the *everlasting* Kingdom of God is God himself trafficking along the temporal to bring us *eternal* life. Eternal is different from everlasting. We have to wait for what is everlasting until time ends, but we are met by the eternal already, now, even before we leave time. The world does not last forever, so we cannot find the everlasting in it. But even in this passing world we can find the eternal, because the Eternal One has made history his manger.

This makes liturgical time the most surprising mix of all—more surprising even than the sacramental mix of spiritual with material. There is a certain connaturality between the human person and a sacrament: it befits our nature because we are a hybrid of spirit and matter ourselves. To find spiritualized matter in the sacrament is miraculous, but not astonishing. But it is both miraculous and astonishing to find the presence of the eternal already, in time, ahead of the parousia. The eighth day does not wait for the end of the sixth day (the age of the Church) or the end of the seventh day (the Sabbath rest, the end of ages) before it appears. It is one thing to rest in the Lord everlastingly, as signified by the seventh day; it is another thing to go beyond all time already and rest in the Artisan of time himself, while time is still extending its web. Sunday is the eighth day, and the eighth day is the *hodie* of liturgy. The Sunday on the calendar is bigger on its inside than it is on its outside, because the eighth day can be found in it. Sunday is a unit of time in each week of the year, but the one who holds the expansive history in which Sundays occur is the one who kenotically enters each week on every eighth day. Sunday is an antinomy because what time cannot contain is contained in liturgical time, just as what heaven and earth could not contain was once contained in the womb of the Theotokos.

We are temporal creatures. Temporally is the way we are. Things come to us in spasms, modulated flux, oscillation, and undulating rhythm. Sharing in such temporality belongs to our nature as microcosms. Not only does the microcosm, man, share citizenship in both the intelligible world and the sensible world, but the microcosm, man, shares citizenship in both the eternal world and the temporal world. Our priesthood extends not only over matter; it extends over time as well. Only by participating in materiality could we be lord of it, and only by participating in temporality could we be lord of it. Our lordship over time should have consisted of gathering in our intellect the whole as it came into being. In time, realities are not entire; they become, and the human intellect should have known the whole entity even as it came into being part by part. But the loss of our cosmic and temporal priesthood in the Fall has damaged this ability. In order to raise up man and woman and restore their cosmic priesthood, Christ was (to say it by temporal metaphor) and came (to say it by spatial metaphor). This God is beyond the measure of either time or space, and he can neither start nor arrive, yet the mission of the *Logos* was to come, take up residence in time, and begin life in the womb of the Theotokos. To participate in time, then, belonged to man's nature originally, and redemption involves returning man to a proper rule over time. This temporal view of creation supports liturgical time the way a material view of creation supports liturgical sacraments.

Do not be discouraged if God is not constantly present to you; in this life it is a sign of progress that God is frequently present to you. He comes with regularity on each Sunday. Adam and Eve saw God frequently in paradise, though not constantly. Heavenly beatitude is a condition of constant presence; for now, temporal creatures both before and after the Fall should be glad that God comes frequently.

But now that the new age has overlapped the old age—*felix culpa*—throwing time into havoc, the monks, those forward-living vanguards, want to dwell in this new age already, so they desire to remember Jesus constantly. To pray without ceasing is a quality of the new age. Paul gives this commandment, not Moses; it could not be done before the *Logos* entered time or if our destiny were not eternity. May we make a move from frequent to constant communion with God even before we reach the end of our lives. Liturgy falls upon the eighth day every week, and we step into the eternal and unending day that was the *telos* of Adam and Eve. The Incarnation is the miracle of bringing eternality into temporality, the new eon into the old, the infinite into the finite, the divine state into the created state, God's mode of life into ours, which equals deification. Liturgical time is not lived under the countdown of *chronos*. Liturgical time is lived under the power of *kairos*.

Liturgy: the Son's Christic energy possessing those baptized into his body, enabling them to do before the Father, by Divine Breath, the very work that the Son does. Liturgy, then, is to enter into the Trinity. Theology is knowledge of the Trinity: therefore liturgical theology. This divine knowledge can be had even now: therefore liturgical temporal cosmology.

Chapter 8

Angels and Men Doing Liturgy

In order to consider a liturgical angelology, we will have to consider what angels could possibly have to do with human beings. Men and women are corporeal and corruptible; they die; their habitat is earth; their knowledge is discursive; what they know in their mind must first be in the senses; they come in two sexes; they are given in marriage; their movement is local; each one proceeds from procreation; their number continues to increase. It is not the same with spiritual, celestial, non-corporeal creatures, so the human beings and the angelic beings seem to occupy two different planes. Nevertheless, Scripture suggests an engagement between them. Leaving aside the fallen angels for now, we discover Scripture suggesting that angels and men mix it up with each other. The nine ranks of angels compose an invisible hierarchy between God and the visible creation (Eph 1:21, Col 1:16); angels are given to those who dwell in the shelter of the Most High to guard them in all their ways (Ps 91:11); the angels are sent out to serve those who are to inherit salvation (Heb 1:14); they are joyful over one sinner who repents (Lk 15:10); we might entertain them unawares (Heb 13:2); the little ones have angels who behold the face of the Father in heaven (Mt 18:10); at the end, angels will be sent to gather the elect from the four winds (Mt 24:31) and gather out of the kingdom what offends to be burned (Mt 13:41–42). From the highest cherubim and seraphim to the lowest guardian angels, these heavenly servants and messengers praise God and will cross paths with men whenever God sends them on a mission. They come to people in dreams (to Joseph, Mt 2:13) and to people wide awake (to Mary, Lk 1:26–27). An angel of the Lord inflames a bush (Ex 3:2), serves as Israel's GPS in the desert (Ex 14:19), instructs Joseph (Mt 1:24), stirs up healing waters (Jn 5:4), and the angelic servants become particularly active in the Acts of the Apostles, unlocking jail doors (Acts 5:19), steering Philip (Act 8:26), lighting up jail cells (Acts 12:7), striking kings dead (Acts 12:23), and comforting an apostle at sea (Acts 27:23).

But here in liturgical angelology, we are not going to consider their exceptional and extraordinary work but, instead, consider a commission that men and angels share in common and with regularity: they liturgize God cooperatively. Without the angels, our view toward liturgy would be very much too local. After the Lamb opened the seventh seal, and there was silence in heaven for half an hour, an angel came "and stood at the altar with a golden censer; and he was given much incense to mingle with the prayers of all the saints upon the golden altar before the throne; and the smoke of the incense rose with the prayers of the saints from the hand of the angel before God" (Rev 8:3–4). David pleaded, "Let my prayer be counted as incense before you" (Ps 141:2), and God's prayer-attendants responded. The altar of the Lord in the Church is the hearth place for our prayer life, so we are not surprised to find angels surrounding it. The sanctuary is a place for human and angelic cohabitation. The invisible and visible liturgists reside in a common environs; liturgizing is the reason for the two parties to keep company with each other. We sinners ask them to pray for us, and with them we declare God's glory with one voice (Eucharistic Prayer II); we confess God's name and exaltation with the countless hosts of angels who serve God day and night, gazing upon the glory of his face (Eucharistic Prayer IV).

The angels surround the sacrifice (*thysia*) on the altar (*thysiasterion*). Like moths to a flame, the angels were drawn to the tabernacle in the wilderness by the Shekinah that resided there; now angels are drawn by a similar impulse to the altar of propitiation that holds the new mercy seat. This altar draws angels down and people over; it is like a landing pad for descending angels and a launching pad for ascending humans; it is the place upon which angels alight regularly and the bottom rung of a memorial ladder for humans. Moses was instructed to put two cherubim face to face atop the ark of the covenant to honor the Shekinah of God seated there. The cover of the ark was called the mercy seat, and it is the throne of the Merciful One who sits now upon every liturgical altar, his seat of resurrection. Faith can see two angels at the head and foot of the altar of resurrection, as Mary Magdalen had seen them sitting where the body of Jesus had lain in the tomb, one at the head and the other at the feet (Jn 20:12). Jesus continues to fulfill the job description given him by the prophet Isaiah to proclaim good news to the poor, proclaim liberty to the captives, recover sight for the blind, and set the oppressed at liberty. For such gifts as these we approach liturgy, and although the High Priest has now ascended to the right hand of his Father, the Spirit of the Lord that was upon him continues the year of the Lord's favor as the liturgy in heaven is united with the liturgy on earth by rising incense prayers administered by angels. "The smoke of the incense rose with the prayers of the saints" (Rev 8:4, again).

The angels are thurifers. An angel tells Cornelius of Caesarea that his prayers and alms have ascended as a memorial before God (Acts 10:1–4). In some sacrifices the gift is burned: literally, becomes incense (*thyein*). If God and man are to share the common meal that culminates the sacrifice, they will each have to do so in his own way. We have mouths and teeth; God does not. So for God to take in the sacrifice, it will have to be turned into smoke so he can smell the pleasing aroma, as he smelled Noah's burnt offerings (Gen 8:20–21). Now a still more pleasing aroma exists. "Therefore be imitators of God, as beloved children. And walk in love, as Christ loved us and gave himself up for us, a fragrant offering and sacrifice to God" (Eph 5:1–2). The altar sacrifice is a meeting place between God and true worshippers.

A deacon is compared to an angel because one of his ministries during the liturgy, as well as after the liturgy, is to proclaim the good news. A message needs a messenger, and indeed the word "angel" (*angellein* means to announce) is contained in the center of the Greek word for Gospel: *evangelion*. The Second Vatican Council recovered the permanent diaconate order, dedicated to liturgy, word, and charity. The deacon is not primarily a server of food, but is, rather, a minister of the mysteries of Jesus Christ, and although the deacon will conduct much of his triple ministry beyond the walls of the Church, he must never lose contact with the thread that connects him to the courts of the Lord. Therefore, as a second sign of ordination (after his vesture of stole and dalmatic), he is given the Book of the Gospels, whose herald he will become. He is mimicking angels. In a regular liturgy, he bears this book to the altar in the entrance possession; he proclaims the Gospel from it at the ambo and may preach on it; he is the keeper of the thurible and assists the priest incensing the altar, and he himself incenses the Gospel Book, the priest, and the people. Deacons serve with alacrity, as do the angels, and the similarity of the two led liturgical commentators to see a resemblance: when deacons fanned the gifts on the altar, they saw angel wings fluttering.

In every form under which we experience liturgy—Eucharist, sacraments, the Hours, the year—we are lifting our eyes from earth to heaven. This is a perfectly good creation, but it was never meant to be our permanent abode, only a pathway home. If we drop our sightline from the mansions Jesus has prepared for us, we wrong this world for expecting too much of it. The angels are ministers to our liturgical vision, mediators of hierarchical sights. We see them when we look up liturgically. And no wonder, for Holy God "is resting among the holy ones, praised by the Seraphim with the thrice-holy voice, glorified by the Cherubim, and worshipped by every celestial power" (Liturgy of Saint John Chrysostom). In the Divine Liturgy of the Eucharist, we see the vapor trail of one in particular. The Roman Canon asks almighty God, in humble prayer, to command the Eucharistic gifts be borne by the hands of his holy angel to his altar on high in the sight of his Divine Majesty. Why? So that all of us may receive the holy Body and Blood of his Son through our participation at this altar and be filled with every grace and heavenly blessing. No wonder we bump into angels as we approach God in our liturgy. We have to elbow our way through them. And there, at the vertex of the liturgical column, we see one of our race, Mary, who is more honorable than the cherubim and more glorious beyond compare than the seraphim. The angels hold her in special esteem because they rejoice in our redemption, delight in serving God, thrill from praising God, and mingle much incense with our prayers. That is why they like to join us in liturgy. Christ has made a Church of angels and men.

Chapter 9

What the Angels Learn from Liturgy

There are things the angels know that men want to know. Because it belongs to angels to see the face of God continuously (Mt 18:10), and because this is the face we also hunger to see, it can therefore be said that men are seeking a knowledge proper to the angels. If only it were possible for man to eat of the bread of angels (Ps 78:25). Wait. It was not Moses who gave the Israelites that bread from heaven, it was the Father who gave the true bread from heaven, and Jesus said "It's I" (see Jn 6:32–35). The Jews murmured, but Jesus persisted. "Not that any one has seen the Father except him who is from God; he has seen the Father" (Jn 6:46). "He who has seen me has seen the Father" (Jn 14:9). Our Eucharistic diet affects our vision. For now, our liturgy is periodic and the angelic liturgy is continuous, but one day we will join their schedule, and they already join ours. The earthly economy of salvation has been completed, and we await the resurrection. The angel exclaims it, with awed voice, through the deacon. Where is this resurrected Christ? At table with the disciples behind locked doors in Jerusalem? At table with the faithful behind the open-doored iconostasis? At the right hand of the Father? Yes. He is in all those places. He was, and is, and shall be.

But there are also things men know that the angels want to know. After the Fall of Adam and Eve, the angels felt the disruptive reverberation throughout the cosmos. An angel had been given care of each nation, but they found their ability to guide the peoples stymied by fallen mankind's darkened intellect. A guardian angel had been given to each soul, but he found his ability to protect his charge thwarted by a rebellious will. Unless human nature were repaired, the angels' ministry would be restricted. The help they

69

wanted to give had been crippled by our fault, and they were frustrated, so they watched closely to see whether the Lord Almighty would set things straight. He did. And he did so by an extension the angels had not foreseen.

They had eavesdropped on the prophets. The Old Testament prophets had prophesied about the grace that was to be ours and "searched and inquired about this salvation; they inquired what person or time was indicated by the Spirit of Christ within them when predicting the sufferings of Christ and the subsequent glory" (1 Pet 1:10–11), but things were not yet sufficiently clear. The prophets had types and foreshadowings of the maneuver God would pull off, but it was not until it actually happened, not until salvation history climaxed in the Paschal Mystery, that things were revealed "which have now been announced to you by those who preached the good news to you through the Holy Spirit sent from heaven, things into which angels long to look" (1 Pet 1:12). "To look into" means to bend over and look deeply into something, to see the bottom of something. Like the cherubim above the ark directing their gaze at the mercy seat, the angels now gaze intently at the Merciful One in the flesh.

The angels learn something new when they watch the activity of the Trinity descend from eternity to unfold in history. The apostle Paul describes this three-Person, three-part activity in his letter to the Ephesians. First, he says the Father has always had an eternal plan in his mind. "He chose us in him before the foundation of the world, that we should be holy and blameless" and "destined us in love to be his sons" (Eph 1:4–5). Second, the Son accomplished this plan when all things were summed up in him, in heaven and on earth (Eph 1:10). Preparatory work was done by Israel, whose *leitourgia* was to prepare for the coming of the Messiah. Third, we "were sealed with the promised Holy Spirit, who is the guarantee of our inheritance until we acquire possession of it" (Eph 1:13–14). This mystery is summed up by John Chrysostom as God desiring to have man seated up on high. The angels had hoped to see the peoples entrusted to them liberated from idolatry; they were glad when they saw God save his people Israel; but to see the Gentiles deified and numbered among the Church was astonishing! An eternal mystery became historically visible. The love within the perichoresis of the Trinity was being liturgically unpackaged to all of mankind, Jew and Gentile.

Thus the angels learn something new about the Bridegroom when they see him in the Bride. Paul writes, "Great indeed, we confess, is the mystery of our religion: He was manifested in the flesh, vindicated in the Spirit, *seen by angels*, proclaimed among the nations, believed on in the world, taken up in glory" (1 Tim 3:16, emphasis added). When angels see his Body on earth, they learn something hitherto unknown in heaven. The angels learn something about the Son in the brothers and sisters he brings to the Father for adoption; they learn something about his grace when it is extended sacramentally into the lapsarian world; they learn something about the extent of his love when he descends to add one sheep to their ninety-nine, namely, the human race among all their ranks; they learn something about his majesty by his *kenosis*, his glory by his humility, his royalty by his obedience, his strength by his weakness, his wisdom by his foolishness, his nobility by his lowliness, and his honor when he was scorned. The Cross reveals something about the sacrificial relationship the Son has had for all eternity to the Father but that was unclear to others until it was acted out manifestly in the flesh. Inquiring minds would want to know. As ministering spirits to the heirs of salvation (Heb 1:14), the angels would naturally want to penetrate this mystery and reflect upon the love and justice and wisdom and power of God. They know the mystery through its manifestation in the Church, which is why they like to hang around liturgy. They witness the power of conversion there. They witness the perichoretic relationship between Father and Son when the Spirit of love proceeds from them to invite our synergistic ascent into deification.

The liturgy celebrates the Incarnation, death, Resurrection, and Ascension of Jesus. The Church Fathers describe the angels' reaction as if they were simultaneously shocked over Christ's reckless itinerary and overjoyed by its consequences. The New Testament describes it unfolding in four stages. First, at the Incarnation, the heaven-angels called out to their counterpart earth-angels that the Savior was descending to Bethlehem and would tarry on earth. They came along down to earth in his wake, entering by the way he had opened, joining the angels in charge of the nations who were rising up to welcome him with great happiness. That is why the sky around Bethlehem was filled with angels: they surged from above and below. Second, at the crucifixion, Christ storms Hades' fortifications as a royal conqueror coming to annihilate the realm of the devil, and Church tradition has said he was accompanied by hosts of angels singing Hosanna. Why did the angels accompany him to the realm of the dead? To watch joyously the rescue of the righteous, to do what they could to assist citizens of liturgy being raised up, even as they watch catechumens carefully during their last days of asceticism before Baptism. Third, the angels prepare for breaking the good news of Resurrection by rolling away the stone and sitting upon it, by terrifying the guards at the tomb, by telling the women not to be alarmed, by telling them not to seek the living among the dead. And fourth, at the Ascension, the earth-angels call out to their counterparts to welcome the Savior returning home. "Lift up your heads, O gates! and be lifted up, O ancient doors! that the King of glory may come in" (Ps 24:7). But the angels above did not recognize him because of his wounds. "Who is this that comes from Edom, in crimsoned garments from Bozrah...." (Is 63:1). The earth-angels who had witnessed the Lord's sufferance of these wounds knew he was bearing them as trophies of his victory over sin, death, and Satan, and identified him as the Lord strong and mighty, mighty in battle. So, to the disciples still gazing into heaven, two men in white apparel whispered that they should not be sad, because he would come back, the same Jesus, in like manner: personally, visibly, gloriously.

The hope that animates the liturgy derives from faith's certainty about love. *Faith* in Christ's incarnational *kenosis* is coupled with *hope* in his eschatological return and *love* rejoicing in his sacramental presence. He has died, he is risen, he will come again, and in the meantime he has not left us without an Advocate. This Counselor will bear witness to him and form us into *sequela Christi*. We therefore celebrate two movements in every liturgy, identified in Greek as anabatic and catabatic. The suffix *basis* means to go; in these cases, to go up and to go down. The anabatic movement of liturgy is man's ascent into the heavenly realm ("Lift up your hearts"), and the catabatic movement of liturgy is the Spirit's epicletic descent. There is also a meteorological description. Anabasis is an uphill wind that has been produced by effects of local heating. Wait, I suppose that is actually a Pentecostal definition. And there is also a spatial definition of anabasis as a march from the coast to the interior, while catabasis is a march from the interior to the coast. Put them all together, and we find that every liturgy is a one, holy, catholic, and apostolic parade up to God because he has come down to our soul; a movement inward to the Holy Spirit and outward to a world in need. The prefix *acro* means "aloft". The Holy Spirit restores Adam's wings and makes us Eucharistic acrobats, tumbling, twirling, doing barrel rolls with the angels. The angels seem to like to be on the move. There is so much angelic traffic above the altar that we can imagine the deacons as air-traffic controllers.

Chapter 10

A Wrinkle in Cosmology

One of the challenges to clear thinking is the fact that, unlike stones rolling through moss, words do gather meanings when they roll through human use. Words are not frozen like a mammoth in the ice, and dictionaries must swell. The word "world" is a case in point and relevant to liturgical cosmology. The Oxford English Dictionary gives me nineteen definitions; I will settle for four. But I need all four because the last marks a turn in cosmology, a departure from the trajectory that creation had been following. It makes a wrinkle in the doctrine of creation, but a liturgical cosmology is prepared to deal with it.

(1) "World" can mean the cosmos, the universe, God's good gift, things as they are, the affairs and conditions of life, the world of Genesis 1. This includes human existence, but this first definition pushes us beyond merely an anthropocentric understanding to what I suppose could be called a cosmocentric one. It is a focus upon the objective world that human beings inhabit. And this first meaning of "world" also extends beyond individual material things to include the orderly arrangement of things, a sense of the harmonious whole, the blueprint imposed upon the pile of bricks. Cosmos is the opposite of chaos. Cosmos is not just things; it is things arranged. God is the Creator of the world in both senses: he is the Creator of being (*creatio ex nihilo*) and the Creator who orders (*Logos*). If God withdrew his hand from the world for a single moment, it would slide backward into chaos and be "uncreated". Only by his steadfastness does the world continue as a stage for man's work and growth. This first meaning of world designates the sphere of activity for man, which is why it also includes a temporal sense. Time goes by in the world. Into the spatial warp is woven a seasonal woof.

(2) "World" can mean a subjective state, a world we create, an interior realm, a domain of mind and soul. Unlike the objective state of affairs in the previous definition, the world in this definition is a human artifact, a product, one might even say a person's life accomplishment. Philosophers have quipped that the world of the happy man is completely different from the world of the unhappy man, and psychologists have observed that the child's world is different from an adult's world. Under this second meaning, the world is not given to us from outside; it is, instead, the world we construct inside out of stories and mythologies and imaginations, and it includes the attitudes we take. This subjective world involves resolutions of will. We have no choice as to whether we accept or decline the construction of this second world; the resolution of will concerns whether we construct this world intentionally or accidentally, deliberately or reactively. We should strive to be aware of the components we bring into this subjective world and of the vices or virtues that determine it. We should be on guard against the slight danger of solipsism here, lest we think that by living in our own world we share no objective reality or that our human nature is not shared with others. This is not correct, of course. However personal everyone's world is, there is a connection to reality.

(3) "World" can mean present, current, contemporary, what is still in progress as opposed to what is finished, future, final. This third definition understands the world as still partial and waiting to be filled full. The accent is upon its incompleteness and unfinished quality. The first world waits for heaven; the second world waits for fruition; this third world waits for the eschaton. This world is still becoming; it is potentiality awaiting actuality, a thicker ontology that has yet to be acquired. The teleological mystery moves the world toward its end, and this third definition comes out of that sensation. We should not, therefore, think of the apocalypse as escape from the world but, rather, as the consummation of the world. Eschatology is the world beautified, splendored, graced, verified, substantiated, fulfilled.

(4) "World" can mean the fallen world, a sinful state, corruption, rebellion, estrangement, Genesis 3. It is usually possible to distinguish the first from the fourth definition by its context. We can detect the meaning of the word from its language game. The same Gospel that says God so loved the world that he gave his only Son for it (Jn 3:16)

goes on to say that Jesus' disciples do not belong to the world (Jn
17:16), that the world hates them (Jn 15:19), that they must hate their
life in this world (Jn 12:25), that they should long for the judgment
of this world at which time the spirit that rules this world will be
driven out (Jn 12:31). The Gospel of John is speaking both of the
good "world" that the good God creates and the fallen "world" in its
corrupted, hostile, fallen state. One is carnal, and the other is spiritual.
Do not translate this as "corporeal and incorporeal", because corporeality is not the source of the problem. Our souls have fallen as well
as our bodies. Indeed, the rebellion of the spirit has affected the body.

One could approach the different types of "worlds" in a variety of
ways, each intellectual approach being suitable to the different definitions. The first world would be approached by phenomenology, the
second by psychology, the third by eschatology, and the fourth by
soteriology. Theology is relevant to all four definitions, and therefore
all four are engaged by liturgical cosmology.

(1) Liturgy assumes the whole of world one. Liturgy is performed
with every piece of creation. As our spirit is soul to our bodies, so
liturgy is soul to the cosmos. Cosmos without liturgy would be a
corpse, as would be a body without a soul. We only have an inkling
of what angelic, invisible, and incorporeal liturgy is like, but human,
visible, and corporeal liturgy requires the world according to its first
definition. By the matter of the world, liturgy moves, expresses,
speaks, manifests, actuates. We do not inhabit an accident, and the
world, while graced, is not inadvertent. God created the world out
of nothing and directs it by his uncreated energy, which means the
world has not been left to spin aimlessly. It has a liturgical aim. Both
the astronomic and the subatomic move in liturgical orbit; the *musica
universalis* and the *musica humana* harmonize with God's *Logos*. That
we live in a cosmos, not in a chaos, means that the world is dis-
posed, prepared, ordered, and arranged (*kosmein*) for liturgy. It has
the capacity to glorify God, and men have a place at the head of that
purpose. What happened to the cosmic priesthood of Adam and Eve
must be addressed later, but its result is anticipated in the fourth definition of world below.

(2) Liturgy assumes the whole of world two. If men have been
placed in this perpetual Eden to serve as priests of the cosmos (cosmic
priests), they have also been placed among the living creatures to

offer a *logike latreia* (rational worship). Our liturgy is intelligent. The liturgy of man should be patterned after the divine Reason, Wisdom, *Logos*, Sophia, and so should be offered up with full attentiveness, piety, mindfulness, and circumspection about our conceptual world. The praise on our lips must come from our minds. Since the bloody oblation of the Lamb of God was rational, spiritual, and obedient, so also should be the unbloody oblation. We rally all our soul's energies to seek the Lord and contemplate the fact that we have been created by God, that worship of God is justice, and that we should seek God as our highest good. Serving God is reasonable. The adoration that inspirits liturgy arises from the *nous* of the human person, which is filled with the light of liturgy. When the second world is irradiated with the light of Mount Tabor, the first world looks completely different. The world of the spiritual person is completely different from the world of the unspiritual person because when the Word unites himself to our words, then we can make our litany of prayer and supplication "with all our soul and with all our mind" (Liturgy of Saint John Chrysostom).

(3) Liturgy assumes the whole of world three. We cannot find in this world a perfect liturgy because this world is imperfect in the sense of incomplete. This fourth world is the eager anticipation of the promise of God being accomplished and carried into effect. The world's purpose and design is not yet achieved, though one day it will be, and in the meantime, while its completion is still underway, we liturgize like someone living in a house still under construction. Creation exists for the sake of becoming Church, and the work is as yet unfinished. Liturgy in this world reveals the vocation of all things: matter as sacramental, man as priestly, history as precursory, sepulcher as birth canal. The cosmos has a *telos*, and liturgy picks it up to carry it across its teleological finish line into the Kingdom of God. There is not a breach between this world and the heavenly Jerusalem, but they are not identical, either. Faith must become beatific vision, hope must become certainty, love must be consummated, and our temporal, symbolic, and ceremonial liturgy must become eternal, face-to-face, and intimate liturgy. The liturgy of this world waits for fulfillment.

(4) Liturgy combats the whole of world four, and yet, in a way most surprising of all, liturgy does so by assuming the whole of world four, too. What has not been assumed has not been healed,

Christology tells us, and healing this odd-world-out is a task accomplished in the same manner: the fallen world must be assumed and healed by liturgy. As I say, it is startling. What does darkness have to offer to light, what does death have to offer to life, what does iniquity have to offer to liturgy? And yet the miracle of the Divine Exchange is that Christ joined us in this, our perishing world, precisely so that it could be redeemed and returned to the hierarchical cycle of *agape* and *eucharistia* from which we had bolted. Locked to Christ, even sinners can liturgize. For our sake, God "made him to be sin who knew no sin, so that in him we might become the righteousness of God" (2 Cor 5:21). What good would liturgy be if it could only be done in Eden and on Mount Zion, the city of the living God (Heb 12:22)? What good if it cannot be done now, in this fallen world, betwixt paradise and heaven? What good if only saints and angels could glorify God? The liturgy of this fourth world is the liturgy of Zacchaeus, Matthew, Saul of Tarsus; of the woman taken in adultery, the man with seven demons, and the sinner whose darkness is overcome; of the younger brother whose forgiveness caused more joy than the elder brother knew. This is a liturgy of contrition and sorrow, repentance and remorse, guilt and shame, which, under the touch of God's hand, is transformed into joy. We cannot find in this world a pure liturgy because this world is sinful, but Christ is taming the world made unwieldy by Adam's sin.

When the holiness of Christ is put on loan to us, then there is no world, no dimension of reality, to which liturgy is irrelevant.

MAN

Chapter 11

Imago Dei as Liturgical Description

The dignity to which men and women are called according to liturgical anthropology can hardly be comprehended. Various other philosophies and myths and social campaigns have sought to place man on a high pedestal, but their efforts fall short compared to the dignity that derives from man's liturgical identity. The cosmos is temporal, and any honors we receive from it and in it are temporary. Any glory a man attains here is like grass (Is 40:6–8; 51:12; Ps 37:2; Jas 1:10; 1 Pet 1:24). The flowering is even briefer than the grass itself, "which is alive in the field today and tomorrow is thrown into the oven" (Lk 12:28). Yet, brief as the cosmos is, and short as is man's glory, both contribute to the splendor of God. *Splendere* means to shine, and glory shines back to God from these two mirrors. The human creature, however, splendors God in an even more profound way by means of his gift of reason. Plato said that beauty is the splendor of truth, and when man searches for truth, and finds it and shines it forth, there is a greater beauty in the universe. *Christologically*, the worship of the Church stands between Christ's Ascension and his return; *individually* it stands between a person's baptismal death and his physical death; and *cosmologically*, it stands between the worship of the heavenly creature and the earthly creature.

The splendor of the cosmos derives from giving glory to God, and the liturgy in which the cosmos plays its part is eternal, and thus the human priests of the cosmos can engage in an activity that is of greater consequence than any other human activity, whether social, political, artistic, scientific, or scholarly. The honor of a servant is determined by the magnificence of the one whom he serves, and there is more nobility in Mary being handmaid of the Lord than in Caesar creating the Roman Empire. The worldly honors one receives will soon

81

terminate; the talents of intelligence, wealth, or might that earned those honors will terminate even more quickly. Dust to dust awaits every person, and it is impossible to find true human dignity by digging in the dustbin. Chesterton said that man cannot love mortal things; he can only love immortal things for the brief instant during which they appear; *mutatis mutandis*, man does not receive dignity from serving a mortal cosmos that is subject to death; he receives it from serving the eternal liturgy of the eternal God during the brief instants it appears in cosmic history. It is a curious fact that human dignity entails the divine. Human dignity comes from being bound to God, not from breaking free of him. The grammar of the Incarnation is already hinted at in Genesis.

Philosophers have made noisy work of defining man ever since Plato suggested "featherless biped" and the smart aleck Diogenes brought a plucked chicken to class with the words "Here is Plato's man." Evidently, one can get off-topic rather quickly. The last few centuries have also offered up some definitions of man that are no less off-topic, although the bloody consequences of a purely materialistic definition have been less amusing. Define a person as mere body without mystical spark, and he can be abused without scruple; define a person according to the role he plays in the social machine of the state, and he can be battered into whatever shape the state machine requires; define a person as brain and not mind, and he can be behaviorally conditioned without regard to freedom. If a bird is made with wings, one cannot understand it adequately by observing its pedestrian patterns, and if man is made with a soul, one cannot understand him adequately by observing his carnal activities.

Liturgical anthropology is interested in discovering man's place in the cosmos, and it turns out to be a liturgical place. Man's home in the cosmos is a liturgical domicile, and residing anywhere else leaves him unfulfilled. His nature is revealed in his function, and his function is revealed by his nature. Instead of using a social or psychological or philosophical definition of man, let us hold ourselves to the biblical view. When Scripture thinks about man, it does not start with the idea of an autonomous biped who stands on his own two feet ("Here is the Rationalist's man"). Scripture, instead, starts anthropology with relationship, which is what the term *imago Dei* means. It refers to a relationship, a kinship, a way of being that

depends upon the gift of God. It does not refer to something tick-
ing inside us, like Plato's reason bottled in a body. It is an icono-
graphic term of relationship between type and ectype: the image
must have a prototype; the *imago* must have a *Dei*. A person can
neither bring himself into existence nor keep himself there, so we
are an image of *I Am* (the name revealed to Moses when he asked).
We are because he is. We are who we are as image of the one who
is as he is. Because God is a Trinitarian community of love, progress toward fuller humanity, fuller imagery of our prototype, means
that we must grow in love's communion. The Incarnation assumed
our human nature in order to restore this possibility after we had
abandoned this scheduled task. As *imago*, we are fitted for communion, and one cannot participate in the kenotic extension of our
prototype's perichoresis without increasing in love. Our capacity for
liturgy demands this.

Teleology explains a thing according to its *telos*, according to its
end and purpose. Why is this watch? To tell time. But teleology
goes farther to say something about a thing's design. Why does this
watch have hands, a mainspring, and a balance wheel? So it can perform the function of telling time. The teleological definition defines
both the purpose of the thing and the design of the thing. The thing
is designed as it is in order to accomplish the thing's purpose. Liturgical dogmatics operates with a teleological anthropology. Liturgy
explains man's end and design. The *telos* of a watch is to tell time, of
a knife is to cut, and of man is to be a liturgist. Human beings possess
the nature they do in order to accomplish this end.

Man and woman are the climax of God's creativity. For five days,
God busied himself night and day, creating, and at the end of it all,
to top it off, he made a special kind of creature. This creature would
be a being of clay alive with a soul; an embodied soul, an ensouled
body; and into that living clay-creature God would breathe his Spirit
as a grace to raise him to Godlike dignity and would take a partner of
identical nature from his side. Their *telos* explains their design: they
were made for liturgy. Their cosmic priesthood explains their nature.
They have the capacity to know sensibly the visible world (unlike the
angels) and the capacity to contemplate the invisible world (unlike
other animals). Adam and Eve are a new universe, a microcosm,
hybrid worshippers, according to the Church Fathers. God created

man in his own image, after his likeness, male and female, and then
told them to multiply and fill the earth and subdue it and rule over
it. Such beings have dominion over matter in order to gather it up
to serve the cosmic liturgy. They were designed as beings of earth
with a heavenly capacity. God designed a royal priest: royal because
Adam and Eve rule with dominion over what stands below them,
and priestly because they serve with devotion the One who stands
above them. This is man's middle place, his mediatorial place, his
royal-priestly place, his liturgical place. Any failings man has committed in his stewardship of creation are a result of letting these two
dimensions disconnect. Something goes wrong when a person exercises dominion without submission. One does not subdue the earth
and rule it justly if one does not do so as an ambassador. Our kingship
over the earth is exercised from a court under the high King, from a
caer paravail. Reason and free will are given as faculties for performing
service, and they can be used to ill effect for any other reason. The
restoration of justice will come from reunifying the royal-priesthood
link, even as it concerns small things, daily decisions, sovereignty
over our own bodies, authority over natural desire. This is the liturgical asceticism of the children of Adam and Eve.

No other creature is enrolled as simultaneous citizen of both realms.
An animal shares man's corporeal nature but has no intellect to know
the *kosmos noetos*, to perceive the invisible, to compose songs of praise,
to make rational worship, to pull sense perceptions into an abstract
notion under the power of an active intellect, to add the splendor of
the created world to the celestial praises. An angel's intellect exceeds
ours, but he has no corporeality by which to know the *kosmos aisthetos*,
to know the visible sensibly, to go beyond intuitively apprehended
intelligible essences to their material particularity, to weave into the
celestial praises the splendor of the created world known firsthand.
The liturgical role of man and woman depends upon the twin capac-
ities of sense and intellect, body and soul. They perform a liturgy that
neither angel nor animal can celebrate.

This participation in both the visible and invisible worlds is the
anthropological potential for the Incarnation. Any actuality must
come from a potency, and the actual Incarnation comes from a potentiality built into the human. The Incarnation is not simply a stopgap
measure, intruded by a *deus ex machina* thrust from beyond. Rather,

the Incarnation is fitting to God's providence from the first chapter of Genesis onward. Furthermore, our unity of soul and body means that spiritual life concerns the body, and bodily life concerns the spirit. The two do not collide in man, they do not run in parallel irrelevance to each other. Rather, the unity of soul and body is the anthropological foundation of asceticism (which can discipline the body to purify the soul) and of liturgy (which can use matter for symbol).

Imago Dei is a liturgical description. As the image of God, man stands at the apex of visible creation to mediate God's descending love and creation's ascending worship, both currents fluxing through the human. In addition, man is a *homo viator*, a "being-on-the-way", not yet complete and beckoned onward toward deification by growing from the image of God into the likeness of God. We are a verb (human *beings*) until we finally become a noun (saint). There is an unfinished quality to each person because God has chosen to enlist our own participation in our own development. The Church Fathers expressed this by saying that the image is like a charcoal sketch of a king, while the likeness is his countenance being filled in with painted color, and we are co-laborers with the Spirit by gathering colorous virtues for the final likeness that God is painting. As image, man has the gifts of creation that include rationality and volition, personhood and responsibility, but to "image God" (a verb) in a likeness that is more perfect, complete, and final requires us to become more pure, more holy, more sanctified. This was a command given to Adam and Eve. They were set to run the race to glory, but they ran into the bushes and hid themselves before the starter's pistol could go off. The icon should not be afraid of his prototype, and yet, when the Lord God called and asked "Where are you?" the man admitted he heard God's voice in the cosmos and was afraid, so he hid himself. The human race has been hiding in the bushes ever since. There it has falsified sacrificial cult to the point that what should have been a means of contact with God has been made into a way of keeping ourselves "safe" from God by keeping him at bay. Ever since our ancestors disobediently seized what they had not yet been given permission to have, our religion has been faulty, and salvation consists of the New Adam training us for refurbished liturgy in a restored cosmos.

We have a true humanity only insofar as we are fulfilling this function, and the function will be filled more fully than we can imagine it now. It was filled more fully after the Garden of Gethsemane than it had been in the Garden of Eden, because an anthropological reboot (called recapitulation) was required for the image to grow into the likeness. The head of the human race had sinned, and mankind needed a new head. The New Adam did what the old Adam failed to do, namely, liturgy. The New Adam must conquer the reign of the old Adam in every heart so that it can be restored to its proper activity, namely, liturgy. Then we will be brought home; then we will be brought to our proper place in the cosmos, where service and submission, prayer and praise, glory and gladness overflow.

Chapter 12

Liturgical Pilgrims

What shall we do with our time? Walk while there is daylight.

There is a post-communion prayer that is peculiar on account of its timing. At the Easter Vigil, the people pray: "with your help may this Easter mystery of our redemption *bring to perfection* the saving work you have begun in us." Even on the greatest night of the year, we recognize that something is incomplete and pray for perfection: *perficere* (to accomplish, finish, complete), from *per* (completely) *facere* (to do). It is an odd craving that God has planted in us: to feel like we are not finished. Should an animal be gifted with consciousness, I do not imagine a dog concluding he is insufficiently canine or a giraffe wondering if he would be better off with another three inches on the neck, and yet these beings called human do feel like something is wanting. All the odder, they still have that sensation on the very night when death has been trampled down, neophytes have been birthed, and the community of believers remembers its deliverance. In the face of the *mirabilia Dei*, we beg God not to end his work prematurely, before it has been finished, before it has been thoroughly perfected in us. We beg, "Do not quit until the regeneration has penetrated every corner of our lives, every faculty, every thought and emotion and act and memory. Be thorough, O Lord, in your redemption. Bring it to perfection. Overlook nothing."

We can understand this better if we perceive perfection as a process and not a state. The problem we are thinking of right now is not due to the fact that raw material is recalcitrant in the potter's hand, although that is also true of us sometimes. The problem under consideration now is due to the fact that redemption must affect all of me, and I am not all here yet. There is more of me to come. I am becoming. I am a pilgrim. I am more today than I was yesterday, and

I will be more tomorrow than I am today. I am under construction (unlike the angels or the animals), and as a historical being I not only want my yesterdays perfected but my tomorrows, too. Perfection is a process not only because I am a sinner, but also because I am finite. Even before the Fall, Adam and Eve could have looked at themselves and prayed, "Bring to perfection the work you have begun."

Perfection has sometimes been defined as when a thing works. Perfection is not just a matter of adding the last piece under the hood; perfection is when the engine runs because everything is in its place and working. Perfection is not simply the accumulation of parts; it is the arrangement of those parts in such a way that the entity or organism or system or institution can do what it was made to do. This gives a different understanding to the question about human perfection. What is a human being made to do? For what purpose was he made? The answer of liturgical anthropology is to say that our perfection is liturgical. For what reason do we exist? To do what? The end of man and woman is to be a *homo adorans*—to worship and pray. Ontology merges with teleology. Our nature, our ontological condition, is aimed at the end of liturgy, and it is insalubrious to frustrate this human purpose. It harms us to forget our true end. In such a case, our faculties fail to operate correctly because they are not being put to their proper use, which distorts them. We could read each of the eight passions mentioned by Evagrius as instances where our intellective, irascible, and concupiscible faculties stop us up short from celebrating liturgy.

Ordinary religion will not suffice. We were created not only to worship *before* the Father, as religion does, but to worship *in* the Son, as liturgy does, and we stop short if we do not put our religious sacrifice into his liturgical hands. The Church's evangelism is motivated by a completely new datum. Theosis is our calling, and the Church's reason for being is to iconograph this in dogma, painting, and cult. Every righteous person seeking God is on the way, even if he has no idea what he is on his way to until the new datum is revealed. Every righteous person is on his way to membership in the Church as an assembly of liturgists. There is no point at which the human race will have the sort of unity for which it yearns until the human race stands as a corporate liturgist. The Church-at-liturgy is not a group of individuals doing something together; it is a single corporate body doing something.

But the Easter Vigil prayer is asking for even more. It is begging for a kind of perfection that will only come finally in heaven. Now the seed below is being coordinated with a fruit above. What has begun on earth cannot find its fulfillment anywhere on earth; what has begun in time cannot find its fulfillment anywhere in history; what has begun spiritually cannot find its fulfillment from any material satisfaction. God created us with these dissatisfactions—not so that we would be ungrateful, but so we would be unsated. The thing that God began by creating this cosmos, and the thing God continues personally in each man and woman, searches for an outlet beyond our current limits. The heavenly liturgy is the last step of a journey the first step of which we have taken. And we want perfection.

The life cycle of a *homo adorans*, then, consists of all the adjustments—some large, dramatic, and grievous, some small, ordinary, and humdrum—that God applies to his human creatures as he transforms them into liturgists. If one does not know the end, one cannot understand steps in the process. As a child does not understand his discipline until he understands the maturity his parents want for him, so we do not have an inkling about the true purpose of our trials and chastisements until we understand the end for which God has designed us. Moral theology cannot understand the disciplines imposed on a liturgical ascetic, whose tribulations as a saint-in-the-making will look perverted when measured against the moral outlook alone. We are referencing Job's friends here. Succeeding as a son is different from succeeding as a servant. The goalposts really have been moved, beyond the simple threshold of the pearly gates all the way up to the portal of the perichoresis of the Trinity. The hypostatic union has changed everything.

Medieval pilgrims made pilgrimages to Jerusalem. Man and woman are pilgrims, and their pilgrimage is to the heavenly Jerusalem, where their perfection will be evident when they join the heavenly host in its liturgy. Mary is already there in her perfection, more honorable than the cherubim and more glorious beyond compare than the seraphim. No lesser place can satisfy even the least Christian. No location on earth or in the world will satisfy the person whose perfection requires travel to a foreign land. Already his present home begins to feel strange, even to the sinner on beginning his therapy. So the life cycle of a liturgist, from his inception in the baptismal font to his mature

status, will consist of the constant ascetical realignment of skewed faculties. Liturgical asceticism is preparation for the great Day of Liturgy,
the banquet liturgy of the Messiah, for Judgment Day. That judgment
will be like a great magnetic force with an upward draw, but only
those who have been transformed inside will rise, because only they
will have become the kind of substance this magnet can attract. Only
those who find God attractive will be attracted by God. It is not a
silly thought. There are many people who do not find God attractive
or pleasing to their mind's eye. The task of a human being as his life
unfolds is to make his soul into the correct substance. A magnet will
attract steel, but not brass; heat will make one kind of substance glow,
but incinerate another kind; the face of God will either attract or repel
us, will be felt as either light or fire, heaven or hell. To be in a place of
constant praise to God will be hellish for the egotistical soul. He will
regret not having practiced liturgy when he could have.

We are pilgrims of conversion. To become light and alive requires
that we purge specks of impurities in the soul's core, because self-
will and aversion to humility will produce a soul incapable of being
brightened. Therefore we ask God to perfect our humanity: finish it,
please, accomplish it, make it substantial enough to join the liturgizing of heaven. We beg for spiritual cardiomegaly: enlarge our heart.
Do not let us stop short of being perfected to take our place in the
parousia liturgy. And we need not wait to behold the perfect human
being. Our perfection is growth toward Christ, growth in Christ,
growth in becoming fully Christoform. Perfected anthropology is
revealed by Christology, because a perfect human is assumed into
Christ's liturgical priesthood. When a human being partakes of God's
energy, he experiences theosis, and a saint can be said to be one who
is able to be moved by God's energy. It is glorious; it is glorification;
it is liturgical fulfillment.

Chapter 13

Adam and Eve Confess

And Adam said:

What have I done? I have forfeited my liturgical priesthood. The hesychasm used to be refreshing after a day's labor and day's distractions, but now the silence is no longer soothing, it is of a different kind. I am desolated. I no longer hear the Word speak, so I have lost words to speak. Without revelation, I cannot pray. Apparently my ear is connected to my tongue, because without the Word in the former, the latter prattles nonsense. I used to be attentive to the Word and therefore knew what words to speak in my dominion over the garden; now I interpose my own opinion. His words used to make me older and stronger, but now I only hear my own opinion, my own judgment, my own teaching, so the words of my worship lack power. To my own self I redirect my esteem, my adoration, my reverence, so the words of my worship lack contact. I am just speaking to myself, about myself, for myself, to myself. My liturgy is just sound in the air, as ephemeral as my own existence on the earth. In stubbornness, my knees have forgotten how to bend.

I consume the sacrifice myself now, but I am strangely less full. I have forgotten how to sing, or at least my songs now seem subdued and without worthwhile subject matter. Amity is gone because the friendship has crumbled. I no longer speak from the heart, preferring now to keep secret what is in it. We are no longer on cordial terms and have lost agreement of the heart. What I want for myself seems no longer to be what he wants for me, and what he wants for me I scorn.

What have I done to the cosmos? I have pitched it into the death I brought into existence. Creatures rebuke me for it; the heavens reprimand me for it; the earth reproves me for the thorns and thistles it now produces. The ground is cursed because of my disobedience, and it constantly reminds me of the fact. With enough toil, I produce something to eat, but it is not satisfactory to me. I am not sure how many more years this food can keep me alive; I will have to build bigger barns. The Spirit that used to animate all things is diminished, and I grow more inanimate by the day. Objects are faded and washed out because they are illumined only by the physical sun overhead and no other light. I see only the outer surfaces of things because matter has become opaque and I cannot see a thing's substance or an animal's name. It is as though I have lost my ontological vision. Time has become monotonous, uninteresting, and tedious, and each day passes uneventfully. My life is all *chronos*, with no *kairos*. I sense motion but no movement; my pathway is all flatland with no ascent; nothing takes me farther up or farther in. It feels as though creation waits with eager longing for the revealing of the sons of God and to be set free from the bondage to decay into which I have sold it. It seems to be groaning with labor pains even now. I wish there could be a do-over—if not by me, then by a Second Adam, a New Adam. But, alas, I suppose all my descendants to be too weak for the task, damaged now by my original sin, and none of them could pick up the work I have dropped and bring it to completion.

And Eve said:

What have I done? I have forfeited my liturgical priesthood. I thought the fruit would enlighten, but my mind has darkened instead. I thought knowledge was in the fruit and that the wise path would be going to it directly, impatiently, autonomously. Obedience and temperance and forbearance and steadfastness and fidelity seemed too slow. Surely something so pleasing to the eye and appetite could not be fatal. Surely God would not let me die. It seemed as though God were withholding from me, and I did not expect him to retaliate if I therefore withheld from him. The prohibition first became a doubt, then a dare. The serpent neglected to mention that God, being infinite, could know evil without being subject to its experience, but I, being finite, could only know evil the way I know all things, that is, by experience. The serpent also neglected to say that this greater knowledge would have one day been given safely, freely, without reserve. Being a delight to the eyes is not sufficient to fix the goodness of a thing; it must retain its place in the hierarchy.

I saw the effect the fruit had in the mind of the man when he could not shamelessly admit what he had done and instead blamed me. I could understand the effect because I also refused to admit fault and blamed the serpent. I feel that we will be dodging responsibility for a long time to come. We will claim the fault lies elsewhere, anywhere, everywhere but in ourselves, making a daily mockery of God and his commandments. I seem to have lost the sagacity I once had, and now I am making bad decisions. I was created to give life, to be the Great Mother, but instead I feel selfish and miserly, holding in rather than giving out, suppressing instead of liberating. I still expect to bring forth children, but childbearing pain will be multiplied. The equal dominion that I had with the man over everything in the garden is forgotten now that he rules over me. There is enmity between the serpent and me, and I suspect the total history of the progeny that come from the man and me will be a chronicle of this conflict. I wish there could be a do-over—if not by me, then by a New Eve, a Second Eve who could blot out my fault. But, alas, I suppose all my descendants to be too weak for the task unless some daughter of mine receives grace from the first moment of her existence. Though the Dragon would stand before this woman when she was about to bear a son, to pursue her and devour him, perhaps in the last day, at the very end, he could be vanquished.

And Adam and Eve concluded:

What has happened? Things have gone wrong *above* us: the Father's voice sounds stern, his face appears grim, and we are in terror of his commands. We dreaded his footsteps when we heard them in the garden; how would we feel about them now, here in Hades? Would they stir hope? Might we this time call out repentantly, expectantly, hopefully? Or is it too late for us now? Things have gone wrong *within* us: our faculties resist our control; passions have become unwieldy; appetite and ire defy intellect; our souls cease to communicate life and health and immortality to our bodies. Things have gone wrong *below* us: harmony with the animals is gone; we are deaf to the music of the heavenly spheres; toil and pain are our allotment.

The three tremors—above, within, and below—are related. Failing our priesthood, we fail our sovereignty. Having stepped out of the hierarchy above, we have plunged ourselves and the world below into anarchy. Having pinched off the channel to heaven, the center no longer holds. We have lost the footing of our liturgical place in the cosmos. We were created to stand under God, beside our neighbor, and over creation, but our inflated hubris has floated upward in an attempt to stand beside God, over our neighbor, and beyond creation. Wisdom from the tree without the Gardener's blessing proved to be a sham. From this paradise, this garden, this Eden, we were to begin our journey toward heaven, but we deserted our training, abandoned our self-control, went limp before the contest for the crown even began. We were to increase from the image of God to the likeness of God, but we lost heart here, east of Eden.

When we ate the fruit from the tree in the middle of the garden, we committed idolatry. When we sought our own definition of good and evil, we committed idolatry. When we disbelieved God's warning that even touching the tree would bring us death, we committed idolatry. Unwilling to wait for wisdom and receive it directly from God, we turned to the fruit of the tree as an ersatz source of knowledge. We set up a counterfeit ontology—one in which lethal fruit did not kill, divine promise did not merit patience, and good and evil could be fabricated. We made laws for ourselves, instead of receiving Torah from the Creator, and this was idolatry.

We have undergone a naking. [Note from the eavesdropper: "nake" is a verb used for peeling; when you remove a nut's shell or an orange's rind, there occurs a *naking*, and you may describe the orange or nut as *naked*.] We were naked of our Robe of Glory. In its place, we now wear a garment of skin, a later nature, which our children will mistake as our original and true human nature. But they should be told, in no uncertain terms, that its mortal character came about after our deed and is not the true human nature. In the garments of skin there is no grace that wells up naturally within, and life only continues as long as death is postponed. Would that God be as clever a redeemer as he is a creator and that one day he will be able to untie the knots by which we have bound ourselves.

"Oh, Eve, dare we hope that the love we once felt from him is tenacious enough to pursue our race? Might our children one day see our fall as a *felix culpa*? But why would any Shepherd leave the ninety-nine faithful ranks of angels to come after one lost human race in jealousy for its liturgy?"

"Oh, Adam, why would he, himself, undertake a salvation so costly? And how would he go about it?"

Chapter 14

Because We Are Sinners

One day Jesus went with an official named Jairus intending to heal his daughter who was at the point of death, and as the two set off a large crowd pressed upon him. There was a woman in the crowd who had been afflicted for twelve years with internal bleeding. She had found no help from other physicians and had spent all she had on their consultations. But she heard about Jesus and believed that if she could but touch his clothes she would be cured. Why she did not confront him face-to-face we are not told. She came up behind him, touched his cloak, and by this contact was healed.

Liturgy is the cloak Jesus leaves behind for us to touch. It is our contact with Jesus now that he has risen and ascended. Liturgy is our taction with the Lamb of God. With our own fingers, we feel a grazing touch of his sacramental cloak, as she felt with hers. She reached out as he was passing by through a large crowd. He now moves across the centuries through the huge crowd of mankind—do we notice? Dare we have enough hope to come up behind him in the crowd and touch the liturgy that trails behind him? This daughter's faith saved her, and she departed cured of her affliction. It can be the same for us. Sin is bleeding to death, and liturgy heals us by stopping what slowly drains us of life. To be in communion with God was life for Adam and Eve; to be alienated from God is death for Adam and Eve's children; to receive God's caresses again is resurrection, and this is made possible by the New Adam, whose cloak the Church, the New Eve, holds out to the world to touch.

Sin is death. Liturgy is life. This is why sin and liturgy cannot coexist in the same person. In order to achieve liturgy, the hemorrhaging inside must be stopped. Therefore, to make liturgists out of us, grace cauterizes. Everything that happens to us spiritually is intended by God to heal the original wound, the original bleeding, the original sin of Adam and Eve, and restore our liturgical stature. The motive for every action God takes with sinners is his merciful intention to heal his sons and daughters who are at the point of death. Every question about the redemptive actions of God, and the faithful response of the wayward person, can be summarized by the answer "because we are sinners".

Why does God love us? Because we are sinners. Why do we seek God? Because we are sinners. Why does mercy give joy? Because we are sinners. Why do we submit to God's discipline? Because we are sinners. Why God's providence? Because we are sinners. Why repentance? Because we are sinners. Why tears? Because we are sinners. Why do we suffer? Because we are sinners. Why do we pray? Because we are sinners. Why faith? Because we are sinners. Why hope? Because we are sinners. Why love? Because we are sinners. Why was the law delivered to Moses? Because we are sinners. Why were prophets sent? Because we are sinners. Why does the *Logos* operate invisibly throughout the world? Because we are sinners. Why the Church militant? Because we are sinners. Why the sacraments, especially Baptism? Because we are sinners. Why the second plank, penance? Because we are sinners. Why all the sacraments, especially the Eucharist? Because we are sinners. Why the hierarchy that sanctifies, instructs, and shepherds? Because we are sinners. Why spiritual directors? Because we are sinners. Why death? Because we are sinners. Why does God accompany us through the valley of the shadow of death? Because we are sinners. Why does God merit our reverence? Because we are sinners. Why pray without ceasing? Because we are sinners. Why must we work out our salvation with fear and trembling? Because we are sinners.

The happiness we feel from one glance by God causes more jubilation than all the pleasures that can be offered by the world because we are sinners. There is more rejoicing among the angels in heaven over one rescued than over the safe ninety-nine because we are sinners. We must be healed by Christ's stripes because we are sinners. Even God's strikes content us because we are sinners. Our voices thrill when we rejoice that Christ has trampled down death because we are sinners. The sound of joy and gladness, the voices of bride and bridegroom, give thanks to the Lord, who is God, whose love endures forever because we are sinners.

Because we are sinners, the Tridentine liturgy begins by connecting the *asperges* with hyssop that cleanses; we confess to Almighty God, Blessed Mary ever Virgin, Blessed John the Baptist, the holy apostles Peter and Paul, all the angels and saints, and our brothers and sisters that we have sinned in thought, word, and deed; we ask God to cleanse the lips of the Gospel reader as once he cleansed the lips of the prophet Isaiah with his burning coal; we ask the spotless Host offered to the living and true God to atone for numberless sins, offenses, and negligences; we receive God's mercy when we offer the Chalice of salvation; we beg that the reception of the Lord's Body not become our judgment and damnation.

Because we are sinners, the Divine Liturgy of Saint John Chrysostom prays for peace from above and salvation of souls; for deliverance from affliction, wrath, danger, and necessity; it asks for salvation through the intercessions of the Theotokos; it begs Holy God, Holy Mighty, Holy Immortal to have mercy.

And because we are sinners, the Mass of the Second Vatican Council counsels that we must acknowledge our sins to prepare ourselves to celebrate the sacred mysteries; confesses that by our grievous fault we have greatly sinned in thoughts, words, deeds, and failures to act; acknowledges that the Lord who heals the contrite of heart and intercedes at the right hand of the Father came to call sinners; gives glory to God in the highest and peace to men of goodwill by praising the Lamb of God for taking away the sins of the world; has the deacon or priest ask Almighty God to cleanse his heart and lips before he proclaims the holy Gospel and kiss the Gospel book so that through its words sins may be wiped away; bids the priest to wash his hands as a sign of being washed from iniquity and cleansed from sin; and thrice begs the Lamb of God, who takes away the sins of the world, to have mercy.

This is not a juridical affair; this is a love affair. Love is operating on the deep level where liturgy encounters sin and applies God's cure. The energies of God's love are redemptive, and the synergies of man's worship must be repentant. Divine, righteous love cleanses human, decayed love when they meet, and God's purging gives urgency to human contrition. The more intense our self-recognition of sin, the more fervent our thanksgiving; the more severe our self-condemnation, the more spirited our Eucharist. We so mourn the loss of liturgy that accompanied the loss of original justice that now, in our state of original sin, whatever hint of the communion that Eden once held for mankind causes jubilation. We experience this liturgical savor of Eden in contrast to our present state of life. We experience it as a sharp contrast with sin, but when love welcomes the sinner, then the pain of that contrast stirs our hope instead of causing despair. Tears that are bitter can turn sweet. Tears that are bitter and despondent can become tears of gratitude and fervor. This spiritual alchemy is amazing to behold in a liturgical life.

Jesus healed. Liturgy heals. Liturgy is like the hemorrhaging woman being healed by the light stroke of Jesus' cloak as he passes by; like the son who lay sick at Capernaum being healed at the moment when Jesus tells his father it shall be done; like the mother-in-law of Simon having her fever rebuked, and many others being healed that evening; like the leper who believed he would be cleansed if Jesus willed it, and Jesus did, and he was; like the servant of the Centurion being healed even after his master confessed unworthiness to have Jesus come under his roof; like the paralyzed man let down through the roof so his healing could reveal his forgiveness; like the man whose shriveled hand was healed on the Sabbath, when it is unlawful to do good; like the only son of a widow rising up again; like the daughter of Jairus waking up from death's repose (to whom Jesus was going when he was interrupted by the bleeding woman); like two blind men whose sight was restored when they called out for mercy; like a possessed mute whose demon will no longer silence him; like a crippled man who could carry his mat though he never did reach the pool as he had waited thirty-eight years to do; like an unknown number at Gennesaret who were healed of various ailments, even some who simply touched his clothing; like the demon-possessed girl whose Canaanite mother won her parlay with Jesus by observing that even dogs get crumbs from the table; like a man who was deaf and almost dumb having his ears opened (*ephphatha*) and tongue loosened; like a possessed blind and mute man who could see and talk again when his demon was expelled; like vision slowly clearing when Jesus spit on the eyes of the blind Bethsaidan; like a man born blind who saw the light of the world after he washed off mud and saliva in the pool of Siloam; like a woman who could straighten up after eighteen years; like the swollen man healed in front of a prominent Pharisee on the Sabbath; like not one, not two, but ten lepers; like

Bartimaeus begging for the mercy of being able to see; like Lazarus coming out, being unwrapped, and let go.

Jesus healed. And he explained why. It is a sign of forgiving sins. But now we know his authority to forgive sins. And with faith-eyes open we can see sins being forgiven in every liturgy. We believe it—no paralytics required. How is Adam ever going to learn to do liturgy again after he has become an amnesiac and cripple? God will have to kneel down again, as he did at Adam's creation from clay. Kneeling beside Adam, God will have to show him how to speak and move his feet, the way a parent teaches a child to talk and walk. This God did by himself becoming an Adam—the New Adam, the Second Adam, the last (eschatological) Adam, the restored Adam, the liturgical Adam. Our God kneels to heal our iniquity in a *kenosis* that is educational, remedial, therapeutic, and resurrectional.

SIN

Chapter 15

Satan's Hatred for Liturgists

Satan hates liturgists. This hatred is the cause of his animosity toward man. He spread his celestial rebellion to the terrestrial sphere in order to put a stop to the faint strains of liturgy he was hearing from below his Luciferian post. Created to be a servant of God, as is every created being, he was placed in his particular position upon the hierarchical ladder to convey the descending agapic glory of God and the ascending Eucharistic doxology of creation. But Satan would not serve. Angels have a double function: first, to glorify God unceasingly and, second, to help people to be saved. (The twin purposes of liturgy are recognizable on the rails of the hierarchical ladder.) Satan forsook both. His idolatry was his refusal to serve the cosmic liturgy, and in his enmity he will not serve our salvation. He broke hierarchy in favor of anarchy. He chafed under the rule of the high priest of heaven, and in pursuit of his autonomy he obscured the ontological currents of agape and Eucharist. Opaquing the veil between heaven and earth, he clouded the love that God was showering upon his creation and diverted to himself the glory creation wanted to give its Creator. He was a blockage in the arterial circulation of the cosmos.

This seriously damaged the potential of the world for cosmic liturgy. The world had been created as theophany (to reveal God), as sacrament (to heal and empower embodied souls), and as symbol (to unite God and man). *Sym* + *baleo* literally means to throw together, and the ancient Greeks used it to name a sign or token that established recognition. A coin that had been broken apart could later be "thrown together"—the two parts could be *symbolized*—as a sign of mutual identification and connection. If the world had maintained its symbolic meaning, then the cosmos could be vocabulary in the liturgical dialogue between God and man. We can express this state of affairs more accurately if we use symbolize as a verb than if we just say that the world is full of symbols. A world created by the *Logos* could "symbolize us with God"—throw us together with God. The *Logos* left traces of himself in creation's *logoi* that could operate as intelligibility, and this reasonable order could aid the communication between Creator and man. The cosmos was strewn with evidences of God's love and mercy designed with the purpose of symbolizing, of throwing us together with God.

This symbolic, liturgical capacity of the cosmos is exactly what Satan sets out to deconstruct. His entire battle plan, which stretches across the entire length of human history from the Garden of Eden in Genesis to the heavenly Jerusalem in Revelation, is to undermine the union (religion) God desired to have with us. Satan substitutes *dia+baleo* for *sym+baleo*: he prefers that we not be thrown together with God, but thrown apart from God, and he manages to utilize the created world toward that end. His work is to estrange, alienate, and distance a creature from his Creator. He is the first victim of his own diabolical power, for he is himself a creature made by God with a place in the liturgical orbit of the heavens, and when he rebelled against God's love, it caused an equally opposite reaction. He careened out of heaven when he repulsed the power of God's love. "How you are fallen from heaven, O Day Star, son of Dawn!" marveled the prophet Isaiah. "You said in your heart, 'I will ascend to heaven; above the stars of God I will set my throne on high; I will sit on the mount of assembly in the far north; I will ascend above the heights of the clouds, I will make myself like the Most High'" (Is 14:12–14).

El Diablo was so successful at his diabolical work that his corruption of mankind's noetic faculty means the innocent material world no longer symbolizes us with God; it diabolizes us from God. The fault does not lie with any material objects; it lies in our faulty treatment of them. The problem is not money, sex, or beer; it is avarice, lust, and gluttony. Good things have a bad effect. This is one of the mysteries of iniquity: by the warp he caused in man, a world that God had pronounced "Very Good!" can now be misconstrued. It is the mystery of the world's worldliness. Good things that could have served as evidence of God now attract us to themselves and distract us from him. A world that could have symbolized us with God instead feeds our appetites of avarice, covetousness, vanity, gluttony, envy, et cetera. Instead of the world witnessing the Creator's love and raising our eyes to heaven, Satan has made us downcast. Sin has made the material world carnal.

Satan had already stopped up his ears against the liturgy of heaven, and with the damage done to the cosmic hierarchy, he thought he was ruling over a silent planet. But then, from the very dust of the ground, the Lord God formed a liturgist and blew into his nostrils the breath of life and settled the man in paradise. It was not good for the liturgist to sing alone, but none of the wild animals or birds of the air were adequate harmonizers; they had their share in the created cosmic liturgy, but they were incapable of joining the man in *logike latreia*. So the Lord God divided the body, rib to rib, flesh to flesh, and made a partner liturgist. This Satan could not abide, so the snake immediately came to disrupt their liturgy. Satan hates man because he is envious of man—and the term is meant in its medieval meaning, not its weaker modern meaning: envy is being saddened by someone's good fortune and gladdened by someone's ill fortune. Satan envies man: he is enraged that God would love the human person, and he will be glad over the alienation he causes. So Satan will tempt them to sin, to miss the mark with their homage, and join him in his idolatry. More than anything, he wants to throw us apart from the altar.

The contest over true and false liturgy can be seen in the Old Testament, too, once we look for it. The premier story there is the Exodus, and it is a story about true worship and Pharaoh's unwillingness to allow it. Pharaoh is Satan's surrogate. What is the reason that Moses gives to Pharaoh for letting his slave force go? "That they may hold a *feast to me* in the wilderness" (Ex 5:1; all emphases added); the Lord God tells Moses to tell Pharaoh to "let my people go, that they may *serve me*" (Ex 7:16, 8:1, 8:20, 9:1, 9:13, 10:3). The Exodus miracle is for the sake of a liturgical feast, and this is well understood by Pharaoh, even though his idolater's heart will not recognize the supreme God. "Who is *the LORD*, that I should heed his voice and let Israel go?" (Ex 5:2). Step by step we see the struggle unfold between worship being allowed or forbidden. At issue throughout the Exodus narrative is a question of service. The text continues to use the verb "to serve" for both the people's bondage in Egypt and their service to the Lord. Pharaoh insists the people exist to serve him, but God insists the people exist to serve him. The point of conflict between Pharaoh and the God of Israel revolves around whose service is the more important. God demands from the Israelites an attachment that is exclusive, and this Satan will not abide. The first tablet of the Ten Commandments received soon after emphasizes exactly this. The Israelites are commanded to remember—commanded!—that Yahweh is the one who brought them out of the house of bondage, so they should have no other gods; not fasten upon anything in heaven above, in the earth beneath, or in the water under the earth; not serve them or bow down to their graven image; not use the name of the Lord in an irreverent manner but hold his name holy; and they should remember the day that God hallowed. These are each liturgical reverences that come from obedience. The Torah is about true worship, true orthodoxy, true fidelity. The way the law and the prophets can be fulfilled, then, is by perfect worship. The intention of the law and the prophets is put into effect when we have no other God and we honor his name in his day. That is why Jesus said that nothing is erased or canceled: he did not come to abolish the law.

The prophets are no less concerned with right worship than is the law. Sometimes a shabby reading of the Old Testament pits prophet against priest, profane against sacred, world against temple, but this is a false reading. The prophet does not mind someone going into the temple; the prophet is only bothered if that person does not take the temple with him when he comes back out again. The problem is not the performance of sacrifice; the problem is the superficiality of the sacrifice. The lamb is offered up, but not the heart; the flesh of the lamb is burnt, but the sin is not burned out of the heart. When Isaiah says that the Lord does not care for a multitude of sacrifices, that the Lord does not find pleasure in the blood of lambs and goats, that incense is an abomination to him, it is because Isaiah has already spent half of that first chapter describing the condition of the people in rebellion against him, not knowing their owner, being ladened with wickedness, trampling his courts, lacking a single sound spot on their body. When Jeremiah says that frankincense does not make a sacrifice pleasing, it is because frankincense will not perfume the stench of murder and adultery. When Ezekiel calls the people harlots for chasing after strange gods, he additionally predicts a renewal of true sacrificial worship in the future when our nuptial union with the true God is consummated. And when Hosea voices God begging for mercy and not sacrifice, knowledge of God rather than burnt offerings, he is regretting that the rituals are hollow.

Satan is a man-hater because he cannot abide liturgy, and his entire diabolical endeavor is to cut off liturgy. This is the command he gives to his fellow fallen angels, the demons, who tempt and torment mankind. The demons make their attack on liturgy at Satan's behest (next chapter). They excite the passions of men so that their souls will not be able to pray as they should.

If one does not adore God, one will claim to be God.

Chapter 16

The Work of the Demons

The less resistance we give to the demons, the less awareness we have of their activity. A fish does not notice the water until he is out of it, and a sinner does not notice the demons until he tries to escape them. This resistance is exactly the training the desert ascetics underwent, and they shared what they learned about the diabolical stratagems so that others could more effectively engage the struggle. Evagrius of Pontus listened to the experiential wisdom of the desert athletes and followed it upstream to sin's origination in eight *logismoi*. Evagrius discusses them especially in the monastic context, but the therapy is relevant to every baptized ascetic, and liturgical dogmatics sees in the "eight evil thoughts" an increasing intensification of the obstacles to liturgy.

First, gluttony. By this Evagrius means more than simple over-eating. He says the demon of gluttony suggests to the monk temporal concerns over illness, scarcity of what one needs in order to live, or isolation that separates one from aid and assistance. Doubts about God's providence makes one hedge one's bets, and the abandon required to experience liturgical love is curbed by a caution arising from self-concern. One cannot set sail into the deep waters of liturgy because one is clinging to the shoreline. It is the equivalent of a liturgical prenuptial agreement with God: before I enter into a spousal relationship with God at the baptismal font, I list the goods I currently have and that I want to be returned in case we divorce. This demon of gluttony makes us apprehensive before the altar, fearful to go into the deep.

Second, lust. Liturgy is done with the body, so the demons attack the purity of the body. Evagrius is thinking of the demon of impurity who tempts the ascetic to give up the virtue of chastity, and this demon equally attacks the monastic vow and the conjugal vow. Chastity is the successful integration of sexuality within a person and is practiced according to one's state of life. The celibate practices chastity in the form of continence, and married people in the form of conjugal chastity. Our liturgical life is an act of the whole person, and that includes our bodily existence. All religions have intuited a connection between sexual purity and religious cult. In the Christian case, Paul speaks adamantly about the body being a temple of the Holy Spirit because we are gifted with the Holy Spirit. "He who is united to the Lord becomes one spirit with him. Shun immorality. Every other sin which a man commits is outside the body; but the immoral man sins against his own body. Do you not know that your body is a temple of the Holy Spirit within you ... ?" (1 Cor 6:17–19). This is the body that God will raise from the dead for everlasting liturgy, so remember that it is not meant for sexual immorality (1 Cor 6:14, 13). The word Evagrius uses to name this second evil thought is *porneia*, which has associations of fornication, i.e., unfaithfulness, and has applicability to idolatry, since the Old Testament represents the relationship between God and his people under the figure of a marriage.

Third, avarice. This is not merely an accumulation of money, it is the love of money as a means to secure ourselves. Evagrius says the demon of avarice parades images of an uncertain future before the mind: old age, inability to perform manual labor, famines, sickness, and poverty. But the bite of each of these for the monk is the shame that comes from accepting the necessities of life from others. We would rather depend on ourselves, and the world, than be dependent on God. But liturgy is not possible without reckless trust. Liturgy must be practiced on the cusp between life and death. God said to the man who built bigger and bigger barns in order to eat, drink, and be merry for many years: "Fool! This night your soul is required of you" (Lk 12:20). Love of money turns our attention outward, away from our soul, which a life of liturgy should be preparing for beatitude. The things we accumulate turn into blockages to doxology. Avarice also exposes, like an x-ray, a lack of humility. To the avaricious man, the whole point is not to have to accept help from others (we shall see what this pride looks like vis-à-vis God in the final *logismos*), and this undercuts the communal *koinonia* in which liturgy takes place. Tertullian says the witness that most powerfully struck the pagans was seeing how Christians loved one another. The life of faith manifested itself as devotion to apostolic teaching, fellowship, the breaking of bread, prayers, and holding all things in common (Acts 2:42–45). All these manifestations are cut from the same liturgical cloth.

Fourth, dejection. Evagrius says this demon stirs the soul to sadness over the deprivation of its desires. Combatting this demon requires taking control of memory, for he will direct the soul to the memory of home, parents, and the former life that was surrendered upon submitting to the monastic rule in a search for God. The ascetic in the city must also take control of memory if he is to undertake a glorification of God upon submitting to the rule of the beatitudes. The blessed liturgists are poor in spirit; they mourn and are meek; they hunger for righteousness and are merciful; they are pure in heart and peacemakers; and their possession of the Kingdom of heaven will make them persecuted because of righteousness. When the soul feels weak, such a life can be depressing. But liturgy cannot be done with melancholy. If the demon of dejection succeeds, liturgy is suppressed before it even arises because adulation is incompatible with gloom, laud with despair, glorification with grief, and exaltation with downheartedness. The sad liturgist cannot praise the goodness of God, because he does not feel God's blessings.

Fifth, anger. You cannot do liturgy in anger. Evagrius says this demon boils up wrath and constantly irritates the soul, and he explicitly mentions that the demon strikes at the time of prayer, when it seizes the mind and flashes the picture of the offensive person before one's eyes. The grudge is nurtured, then fanned into anger; then it neutralizes prayer because prayer cannot be made to God with an indignant heart, which is what Evagrius says anger will become if it persists. Once again, the breaking of bread is connected to fellowship, *koinonia*. Our relationship with our neighbor is a condition for effectual liturgy. It does not matter whether our neighbor has angered us or we have angered him. Jesus goes on to treat anger immediately after the beatitudes and explicitly gives this rule for Eucharist: "if you are offering your gift at the altar, and there remember that your brother has something against you, leave your gift there before the altar and go; first be reconciled to your brother, and then come and offer your gift" (Mt 5:23–24). If you are having a feud with your neighbor, your liturgy is futile. It has no useful result. Horizontal love is a condition for vertical love. "If any one says, 'I love God,' and hates his brother, he is a liar" (1 Jn 4:20), and liars cannot liturgize. Liturgy requires truth-telling.

Sixth, despondency. The word Evagrius uses for this *logismos* is *acedia*, and he calls him the "noonday demon" because this demon presses his attack from the fourth hour until the eighth. Evagrius gives an insightful and recognizable description of a person distracted from prayer by boredom. To such a person, the sun barely moves, the day seems fifty hours long, he calculates by the sun's position how long it is until mealtime, and he makes a restless glance out the window to see if perhaps someone is coming to visit. The result in the desert ascetic is a hatred for the place, the life, the manual labor he has taken on. The result in the city ascetic is sloth, which is how the term *acedia* has been translated in the West. It means "sorrow about spiritual good", regret about having to do one's piety, one's prayers, one's liturgy. This is not sloth as laziness; this is sloth as disinclination to labor—to liturgical labor, to be precise. At the root of *leitourgia* is work (*ergon*), service, an office, ministry, and the demon of despondency makes one slothful about one's liturgical duties. The demon in the desert drove the monk to give up the struggle, to move to another place where things are easier, where he might make a success of himself (after all, the demon suggests, it is not the place that is the basis of pleasing God, since he is to be adored everywhere). The demon in the city drives the baptized to give up the struggle, to skip morning prayer when there is an early business meeting, and to ignore the rest of the Liturgy of the Hours when it interrupts other plans we have for the third, sixth, and ninth hour. Sunday is no longer a day of Sabbath rest; it is either treated as another day for profit, or it becomes a day of sloth, which is counterfeit rest. The despondent, slothful person does not have the energy for liturgy. The term *acedia* comes from a Greek word that refers to a "non-caring state", and it fuels a sense of meaninglessness. The despondent liturgist is sullen.

Seventh, vainglory. We tend to treat vainglory and pride as synonyms, but Evagrius makes a distinction. Pride boasts before God, while vainglory boasts before men. In vainglory, the monk is tempted to make his struggles known publicly and hunt after the praise of men; his imagination envisions crowds of people knocking at his door, seeking audience to hear his wisdom; he even imagines attaining to the priesthood. This demon tempts the baptized liturgist in much the same way. The praise of men is always sweet to the ear, and giving fatuous advice is a pleasant pastime. Being discontent about our place in the liturgical hierarchy leaves us excitable. That is why Jesus commands humility in our prayer. Do not be like the hypocrites who love to pray on the street corner in order to be seen. Do not babble like the pagans. Do not perform righteous deeds with the intention that others will notice. Do not blow a trumpet ahead of your almsgiving (Mt 6). The liturgy is about entering the space of God Almighty; it should not be an occasion of flaunting your spirituality. Given that liturgy pours forth from grace, and grace is a gift, there is nothing to boast about.

Eighth, pride. If vainglory was boasting before men, pride boasts before God. About what? Ourselves, our autonomy, our sovereignty, our power, our accomplishment. Evagrius calls this *logismos* the most damaging of all (indeed, for Augustine it was the mother of all other vices), because it induces the monk to deny that God is his helper. Pride is independence from God based on the idea that we are the author of our own salvation. Evagrius adds that it gives the monk a big head in regard to the brethren, considering them stupid if they do not have the same opinion of him that he has of himself. The demon of pride tempts the monk to consider himself the cause of virtuous action; the demon of pride tempts the worshipper to consider himself the cause of his liturgy. Almost all the Christological heresies have an ecclesiological counterpart; this pride is a sort of Pelagian liturgiology.

These are the strategies by which Satan instructs his demons to disrupt our liturgy.

Chapter 17

Sin as Idolatry

There are many concepts that possess a kinship to sin, for example, immorality, iniquity, injustice, wickedness, vice, evil, wrongdoing. None of these is exactly the same as sin, yet if a sense of sinfulness can be detected in them, it comes from the fact that disobedience to God ramifies in other dimensions of our lives. The trespass of God's spiritual commandments shows up as a trespass of societal principles (illegality), moral norms (immorality), ethical dictates (wrongdoing), rights of the human person (injustice), and so forth. Liturgical hamartiology will move past them and consider sin explicitly as an offense against God. The English word "sin" translates the Greek word *hamartia*, which means missing the mark, a failure to stand in the relationship one ought to have with God. And what relationship is that? Liturgical. Sin is insurrection against God's authority, which makes sin a theological category rather than a simple moral or social or juridical category. Sin is the absence, misdirection, or corruption of worship. In other words, sin is the failure to pay homage to God, paying homage to the wrong subject, or paying homage improperly and insincerely. Liturgical dogmatics will understand sin under the liturgical category of idolatry.

The Fall of Adam and Eve was the forfeiture of their liturgical career, their relinquishment of the cosmic liturgy they were created to serve, their distraction from God and redirection to themselves, their stepping out of hierarchy into anarchy. The natural world was created to glorify God, and all natural creatures do so by natural law. There is only one type of creature that can "dis-glorify" God, and that would be the demonic and human creatures in rebellion. In both the human and satanic spirit, pride was the cause, disobedience was the effect, and sorrowful alienation was the result. All creatures will give glory to God unless they turn aside from their natural course, and this is only possible for rational spirits who can make willful acts. Neither inanimate creatures (moon, stars) nor merely animate creatures (dogs, cats) can sin (even though they can be subjected to futility and suffer bondage to corruption by human sin [Rom 8:20–21]). Sin is an act of the will; sin is a bent will; sin is a problem of spirit and not a problem of body. Sin refuses to give to God the glory that all things were created to give. All things are dependent upon the gratuity of God, and this sin resents. All things are created to return thanksgiving to the Almighty, and this sin suppresses. Motivated by self-love (*philautia*), the sinner begrudges his liturgical responsibility, and this discontent breeds animosity, rancor, resentment toward God. The real wound that original sin inflicts is personal, not statutory. So, naturally, this places the human sinner in a contentious and combative relationship with creation, since the human sinner trips up what creation is trying to do as it glorifies, receives favor from, and gives thanks to the Almighty. No wonder there is a tension between man and matter. Of this the philosophers had a glimpse, though they did not understand the whole story or the reason why.

If *hamartia* means missing a mark, what mark is missed? Faith, hope, and love for God. Our faith misses the mark when we aim it on a false trajectory, toward false gods. Our hope misses the mark when it flies recklessly toward any counterfeit power. Our love misses the mark when it is directed toward an ersatz beloved. Liturgy should express the faithful, hopeful, and charitable response of man and woman to their Uncreated Lover, and sin is when we shoot our arrows at all kinds of other targets. The created cosmos is incapable of idolatry, but man idolizes (makes an idol out of) that very same, innocent cosmos. Again, it is a problem of the will. Liturgical hamartiology is concerned with God's motive of love, our failure to react to love, and the cure of our love.

In the Gloria we sing out a patterned response. First we tell God that we praise him, bless him, adore him, glorify him, and give him thanks for his great glory. This, of course, is what we ought to be declaring to the Lord God, the heavenly King, our God and almighty Father. We owe it to him. Then, when the Gloria turns to the Incarnate One, the Only Begotten Son, the Lord God and Lamb of God, i.e., Son of the Father, it begs him to take away sin, and this is initially puzzling. Sin is a moral evil, but evil is a privation—a privation of the good, said Augustine. Sin and evil do not have a positive existence; they are a negation. Sin is a swing and a miss, and evil is an absence. So how do you "take away" something that is absent? How do you save a sinner from something missing? In the same way you save a hole from being empty: by filling it. The sinner must be filled with liturgy. We are talking here about things wanting: want of conformity, want of love, want of trust. How do you remove a want? By providing what is wanted. How do you remove an absence? By restoring what should be. How do you take away sin? By finally hitting the mark, which happens when Christ unites us into his life that is directed always and only toward the Father. We ask him on earth and in heaven to have mercy on us: not only when he took away the sins of the world on the Cross, but even now, while he is seated at the right hand of the Father. Liturgical wisdom instructs wise men and women about the original *logos* of the world so that they might conform willingly to the *Logos*. They willingly discover the world to be an echo chamber for liturgy and love.

Sin does not conform willingly because *philautia* prefers itself to anything else. *Philautia* prefers ego to ecstasy. It resists any outward turn—toward creation, neighbor, but most of all toward God. When God draws near, the selfish will reacts by protecting itself, and the more love is offered, the more resentful it becomes. The destructive spiral is hard to break. The reason sin's animosity is so deep-seated is that God's love is so prodigious. We know this by experience even on the human-to-human level, where the will centered on itself is irritated at being pried open. On the human-to-divine level, the estranged heart even more stubbornly begrudges God's commands, God's mercy, God's goodness. The love from God causes a persistent irritation in the sinner's heart, and this sinful reaction makes liturgizing painful. The sinner is *not* glad "when they said to me, 'Let us go to the house of the LORD!'" (Ps 122:1). At the Judgment Day, the beatific vision will be experienced as miserific, and the light of glory will burn instead of illuminate. Until that day, when liturgy will be hellish to the damned, liturgy will itch and sting the sinner. He will not find satisfaction in sacrament, contentment in celebration, pleasure in providence, happiness at the altar, or delight in doing God's will (Ps 40:8), because he is spiteful. The sinner's homage misses the mark (his worship sins) because it is directed toward himself instead of to the true God.

Original justice meant standing aright and in awe, attentively, and offering the holy oblation in peace; original sin was the forfeiture of this upright liturgical posture. Mankind is now bent over, crippled with a spiritual kyphosis that Augustine described as *incurvatus in se*. With hands clenched around temporal and fading goods, the children of Adam and Eve no longer open their hands in *orans*. With cataracts of sin upon the eye, they no longer see the glory of God radiating from heaven and reflecting back from the earth. The heavenly world has become so imperceptible that they attend only to mundane goods of comfort and wealth and self-esteem. They no longer see either the angels of the nations or even their own guardian angel and have become deaf to the music of the celestial spheres. Created for ascension, they cling instead to the dust from which they were created. Created for deification, they prefer the plaudits of flatterers. All of this is idolatry in action, daily.

On the one hand, we miss the mark with a cultic religion that lacks righteousness. On the other hand, we miss the mark with a puritanical moralism that lacks liturgical expression. The former is a sham religion that the Holy One easily sees through, the latter is a self-directed religion that will always fall short of sainthood. The former thinks we do not have to obey; the latter thinks we do not have to worship. The former commits the idolatry of believing we could flatter God; the latter commits the idolatry of believing we could master God. Both are forms of sinful liturgy for missing the mark of a true liturgy.

Sin is the absence, misdirection, or corruption of doxology. Any of them will cause the same result—whether our doxology is missing, misapplied, or misused. Liturgy concerns glorifying the true God; God is truly love; love goes forth to meet the beloved. Sin does none of these things.

Chapter 18

Evil

I might be wearing thin the patience of the reader by including a chapter on evil in a book on liturgy. The reader will think, "Surely evil has to do with moral wrongs and ethical injustices, not with the lengths of thurible chains or chasuble hemlines. 'Evil' is too potent a word to employ. The deficiency of liturgy may be regrettable or hapless or disturbing, but can one name it liturgical evil?"

I had better begin by defining my terms—both of them.

The outline of *liturgy* has been under construction throughout this whole work, starting from its opening definition in the introduction. Liturgy and dogmatics have been connected for the purpose of enlarging, deepening, thickening the scope of liturgy until we see its substance underneath its accidents. Liturgy is the efficacious pathway from the alpha of divine grace to the omega of human deification, with all that is involved in the divine undertaking to call mankind into the perichoresis of the Trinity, including the creation of visible and invisible realms, including a response to Satan's anarchy in the invisible realm and man's Fall in the visible realm, including salvation history unfolding from Torah to Paschal Mystery, and now including the presence of that mystery in the Church. The redemptive accomplishments of the historical Christ in his human body apply to the redeeming activity of the sacramental Christ in his Mystical Body. That is why the liturgical activity of the Church has dogmatic content and the dogmas of the Church have liturgical form.

The definition of *evil* can be found at various points along the dogmatic timeline of Christian thought. Its initial marker was laid down by Augustine's arguments against the Manichaeans, where he concluded that evil is not something; it is the absence of something. He offered up the famous analogy of darkness being the absence of light, not vice versa. Light is something, and if we wanted to darken a room we could "remove light" by turning off the lamp, blocking up the window, and taping the crack at the base of the door. But darkness is not something, and we could not "remove dark" in a like manner. The removal of dark only comes by the addition of light. Tradition continued to reflect upon the idea and concluded that an additional point should be added. Evil is the privation of good, but privation alone is not necessarily evil. It is not evil if a human being lacks the power to fly; nor is it evil if a bird lacks the power to speak, because these powers were not promised respectively. Therefore, the definition pressed forward to say evil is the lack of a *good that is due*. It is the absence of a perfection that a being ought to have. Flight is not a perfection due to a human being, and speech is not a perfection due to a bird. Evil is the heat that comes from the friction of "ought" rubbing against "is". What ought to be the case? Ought this situation to be different? Ought this person to be treated differently? Ought there to be something more? The application of divine law, natural law, and a refinement of conscience is necessary for perceiving what is evil.

Good is what something is due; evil is the privation of a good. The good is what everything desires (a Scholastic dictum). With that understanding in hand, we can move forward to consider liturgical evil, and immediately our consideration divides first to consider the case of God, second to consider the case of man. It is good that God is worshipped, and it is good for man to worship God. God desires our worship; man in his true state desires to worship God.

First let us consider the fact that God is due worship; he is owed it as a debt; he is worthy of receiving devotion from invisible rational spirits (angels), from visible irrational creatures (cosmos), and from visible rational spirits (human beings). All creatures should give adoration appropriate to their ontology. It is expected of them because it is owed by them. Liturgy is not so much expected by God as it is expected of us. In each realm, non-divine creatures are under obligation, beholden, and indebted for innumerable favors and gifts, starting with being itself.

God does not command liturgy because he is Narcissus, yearning to stare at his own reflection in the idols we will manufacture. If he is staring in any way at his image in the created pool, it is at the *imago*

Dei he selflessly created as man and woman, wishing their fulfillment and perfection. Narcissus stared at his own image in the pond and fell in love with himself; God stares at his *imago Dei* in man and woman and is impelled outward, to fall in love, to fall lovingly toward them in benevolence. The former stare led to *philautia*; the latter stare led to *kenosis*. God commands liturgy because he is truthful, and he truly merits worship. We are describing an ontological case. From God goes forth light, and beyond himself he has created a universe of non-divine mirrors who spread that light by reflection. Angels, creatures, and human beings are created like the walls of a looking-glass chamber so the wave front of truth, beauty, and goodness from God might go everywhere before it returns to him as reflected glory. But as darkness is the privation of light, so evil is a privation of this glorification, a withholding of worship from God,—the mirror's surface clinging to the light as if the light were its possession. Liturgical evil is withholding worship, an act done first by Satan, then by man and woman. The absence of liturgy is an evil.

This privation of the good seems to occur as a result of redirection on our part. It is as though the energy of worship is so great, so deeply embedded in human nature, that it cannot be stifled. Trying to do so is like trying to stop a fire hydrant by cupping one's hands over its open mouth. Our worship sprays in chaotic directions. If we do not choose our final good, we will choose apparent goods; and if we do not choose God, we will liturgize other gods, usually ourselves first. Of the three realms of angel, creature, human being, two are culpable and one is innocent. The stars and the beasts do not have a corruptible free will, so when God is deprived of their worship, it is not because they have withheld it but because we have debased them. Evil is subtraction, and the sin of worldliness we commit is taking the world minus the Kingdom of God. The cosmos is not evil, but something is missing by our fault. Mankind creates worldliness, and Scripture tells us that the world's reaction is to groan in travail and wait to be set free from its bondage (Rom 8:21). The profane yearns for the sacred because sacred and profane are a duplex. The world was not subjected to futility by its own will (Rom 8:20); the fact that all is vanity is caused by the other two realms of creatures culpably using their spiritual freedom for liturgical evil. Satan and his fallen angels commit it freely and intentionally: they break the hierarchy and will not worship God. And man and woman also commit it freely and intentionally: they deny God the glory and obedience and worship he is due, preferring the taste of the fruit from the tree of idolatry. "You will be like God" (Gen 3:5). Evil is the absence of liturgy just as darkness is the absence of light.

Second, let us consider the consequence of evil upon man, because we have just intersected it. Evil is the absence of a perfection that a being should have. First we have said the state of no-liturgy is evil because God is deprived of a laudation he should have, and now, second, we can further say that the state of no-liturgy is also evil for man because he is deprived of a perfection he should have. Human perfection is deification, union with God, the power to liturgize God. Human perfection is to be seated up on high—higher than our earthly state, higher than our political and philosophical ambitions, higher than any temporal throne historical progress can provide. Human perfection is a person's synergistic ascent to the perichoresis of the Trinity that has been offered to him in divine *kenoses* of creation, revelation, crucifixion, and resurrection. Liturgy is being equipped by the power of the Holy Spirit to enter into the relationship the Son has with the Father, and liturgical evil is the absence of this perfection in a human being. It is ugly. The state of no-liturgy is as disgusting as the deprivation of any other good that ought to be found in a human being: the disabling of liturgy is like the laming of a leg, the loss of *logike latreia* is like dementia in the mind, a blinded *nous* is like an eye put out. It is even more obscene that we do these mutilations voluntarily. We do not "look right"; sin warps our humanity.

Mankind was made in a creature-Creator relationship that would have progressed under the terms of original justice wherein God's grace would energize and sanctify the human liturgist. This was intended to be natural, obligatory, and welcome. Liturgy and liturgist were made for each other. In the law of creation, cosmic liturgy was entitled to a righteous human celebrant, and man was due a particular place in the liturgical hierarchy. Liturgical evil breaks the law of creation, dislocating our soul from this hierarchy and disrupting this hierarchy within our soul. That is why liturgy must now run at two levels: the fulfillment of our true life and the correction of our false life. We now conduct our liturgy under two movements, one that occurs under the law of God and one that occurs under the law of sin. Our sacrifice of praise is natural in the former; in the latter it takes on also the quality of a sacrifice of expiation. This, of course, is not something we can do for ourselves, by ourselves. As the sacrifices of a dead person are powerless to give life, so the sacrifices of a sinner are powerless to give holiness. Therefore the expiratory sacrifice must be done by Christ, once for all, on the Cross.

Evil is not something; it is the lack of something. The way to deal with evil is not to remove something (how does one "remove" a hole?) but to restore something (bring light to the darkness). If liturgical evil is the privation of liturgy, then the way to strike it down is to fill the void, which is precisely what Christ does when he shares his liturgy with us. Liturgical evil is a deficiency and a defect: we suffer both an absence of liturgy in our lives and an inadequacy of liturgy when we attempt it. Since an evil is set right by a restoration, the overcoming of liturgical evil requires the Second Adam to restore what was lost by the first Adam when he abandoned liturgy and went his own way. And God's grace abounds! The Second Adam does not simply rebuild the first Adam's incipient liturgy; the Second Adam gives us *his own* liturgy. In excess of our need, Christ fills the deprived liturgist with his own sacrifice in order to bring our liturgy to perfection. He implants in the members of his body the liturgy he does as the God-man. I put this in the present tense, not past, because the Ascension was the definitive entrance of Christ's humanity into God's heavenly realm, and the priesthood he permanently exercises there overflows to our daily Mass. His own liturgy is the gift he places in the hands of his Bride, the replacement of her damaged liturgies, the restoration of her human perfection, the gift that fills the evil void of liturgy.

The cure is supererogatory, beyond our expectations, and the flood of Christ's liturgy into us results in an overflow of virtue and charity. Liturgy is connected to asceticism, justice, morality, charity. The restoration of liturgy involves a spiritual warfare against evils of many varieties, a list of which is rattled off by the apostle Paul: unrighteousness, evil, covetousness, malice, envy, murder, strife, deceit, maliciousness, gossip, slander, hating God, insolence, haughtiness, boastfulness, inventing evil, disobedience to parents, and being faithless, heartless, ruthless. Such passions and vices resulted when men and women "did not see fit to acknowledge God" (Rom 1:28–31).

A person in such a condition cannot liturgize God because impurity destroys holiness. Only he who does justice can live in the presence of the Lord, and living in the presence of the Lord is a functional definition of liturgy. "O LORD, who shall sojourn in your tent? Who shall dwell on your holy mountain? He who walks blamelessly, and does what is right" (Ps 15:1–2). The Psalmist adds that the liturgist must speak truth and not slander, must neither harm nor cast scorn, must honor those who fear the Lord, lend his money without interest, and refuse a bribe against the innocent. To straighten up our liturgy, we must straighten out our morality. The prophets of Israel do not criticize the temple; they criticize people who misuse the temple. When the prophets chastise a liturgical hypocrite for injustice, it is for the purpose of redressing his sacrifice, setting it right.

Our sacrifices were imperfect because they were missing something, so God set out to remedy human liturgy. First, he gave the Torah and the prophets, which together outlined what man must do in order to give him the kind of worship he is due: give it to no other gods (Deut 5:7), give it with loyalty and knowledge of him (Hos 6:6), give it with obedience (1 Sam 15:22), and give it from a heart of flesh and a new spirit (Ezek 11:19). Then he provided that very heart of flesh and that very new spirit required for perfect liturgy, namely, the Sacred Heart of Jesus and the Paraclete whom we invoke over every liturgical act.

To summarize: (i) evil is a privation of the good; (ii) the privation of the highest good is the highest evil; (iii) the highest good is the worship God receives and the worship a deified mankind offers; (iv) therefore, we had to have a chapter on mankind's greatest evil, which is liturgical evil.

Chapter 19

Liturgical Theodicy

Our principle in liturgical dogmatics has been *lex orandi statuat lex credendi*: the law of prayer is the foundation for the law of belief. Many have written about this (myself also), so it has not been given explicit treatment in this work. But now we come to a topic to which the principle applies vividly. Liturgy is foundational for our belief in theodicy (a vindication of God's goodness and justice in the face of the existence of evil). It is so for two reasons.

First, and of lesser consequence, is the fact that liturgy starts on a different foot than theodicy, a term coined by a philosopher (Leibniz) from a root that contains a judicial flavor. The Greek suffix *-dike* refers to justice, rights, a court case: theodicy intends to justify the ways of God to man. Placing oneself in the position of judge over God's actions can be beneficial to intellectual inquiry, but it is not the position from which to commence liturgy. Ask Job. He resisted disputation and the interrogation of his friends; he ignored the hurricane and the earthquake and, instead, listened to the still, small voice. Instead of putting a question to God in the dock, he let God put a question to him. "Where were you when I laid the foundation of the earth?" (Job 38:4). The man who would challenge God is instead challenged by God to tell him about the earth's measurements (38:5), how the sea is held in place (38:8), what causes the dawn (38:12), what is behind the gates of death (38:17), the dwelling places of light, darkness, and snow and hail (38:19, 22), whence come rain and dew (38:28), about the life of lion, mountain goat, deer, and wild donkey (38:39, 39:1, 5), how the horse leaps and the hawk soars (39:20, 26). We can stop. We have already flunked the exam God proctors. To anyone who proposes to examine God in a courtroom constructed by our intelligence God counters, "He who argues with God, let him answer it." And Job replies, "I lay my hand on my mouth" (40:2–4).

Theodicy is not a riddle; it is a contest. It occurs, not in the intellect, but in a different location, namely, our heart. Our heart is asked whether it has faith and whether evil shakes that faith. There was a time when evil did not exist, and the time will come when it will exist no more, but the question put to us in the meantime is what shall we do? What shall we do in this interval between Eden's innocence and heaven's righteousness? In the between time, we must do our liturgy with evil yapping outside the door noisily and stupidly and not let it gain entrance to our hearts.

We tend to categorize faith as a species of knowledge and, therefore, file it in the cabinet drawer of epistemology. We move down a spectrum of knowing from the brightly lit end of certainty to more and more dimly lit probability, then possibility, then doubt, then unlikelihood, until we reach the darkness of impossibility and exclaim "That is where faith is to be found!" But perhaps we can glimpse a different meaning of the word by placing it in a different language game. Looking in its mirror opposite will help. Faith is *fides*; its opposite is *infidelis*. Sometimes we even file that latter word in the same epistemological cabinet to mean a disbelief in certain pieces of information. But we more often use the word *infidelity* in a different context. When we talk about marital infidelity, we are not talking about a lack of knowledge. Here infidelity means disloyalty, and fidelity means loyalty, the fulfillment of a promise, trustworthiness, fealty, allegiance, obligation, solemn promise, surety, confidence (from *fidere*). Now ask again, does evil shake our faith? Such a question asks if our struggle with evil will lead us to infidelity, to unfaithfulness in our nuptial covenant with God. The question of theodicy is the question of whether we will remain allegiant, devoted, fast, and firm. Evil is not a subject to be debated; it is a power to be combated. And theodicy is not a parlor game that intellectually vindicates God in the quandary of evil; it is an ascetical competence to maintain *fides* in God's goodness even in the face of evil.

And this is the second, more important way that liturgy is a privileged place for a liturgical theodicy. Liturgy *is* an act of faith. Liturgy *is* a doing of *fides*. Liturgy is a performance of nuptial fidelity. The platform upon which liturgy stands was built with planks laid by patriarchs and prophets and apostles. The liturgical platform is erected upon Abraham (faith), Moses (Torah), Job (fidelity), David (praise), Peter (a rock), John (beloved), Paul (justification), Stephen (witness), and stretches between the farthest poles that can be found in the question of theodicy. On the one hand, the basic liturgical posture is adopted from Job: God is God, and we are not, and we come to liturgy, not for the purpose of questioning him, but for the purpose of worshipping him. On the other hand, the liturgy celebrates God's response to the problem of evil, namely, the Cross. First, the transcendent God shuts down the curiosity that characterizes Job's friends, and the rationalizing philosophers are sent away when the deacon calls out "The doors! In wisdom, let us be attentive!" Then the imminent God draws back the curtain on his love and lets us lie close to the breast of Jesus (Jn 13:25), which the soldier will soon pierce that we may drink his blood. The problem of evil is not solved; it is settled. It is settled when we find God simultaneously all-powerful and dearly beloved. The liturgy is built upon this constant antinomy, and liturgical dogmatics dwells in the land of antinomy.

An antinomy is when the infinite truth, with its one form, one content, and one spirit, is known by finite minds in pieces that appear to contradict, though they cannot. The Infinite God can know Truth, but citizens of the finite know Truth as truths. We must not pretend the Truth is fragmented when the actual fragmentation is in our reason that knows it. We are looking at a unified ontological object, but the multiple mirrors in our mental kaleidoscope make the world look fragmented. Therefore, acknowledging antinomy consists of integrating the contradictory aspects we are looking at into the one total and harmonious truth that is the case in fact. When apparent contradictions are seen, antinomy does not say that neither the one nor the other is true; antinomy does not say that one is true and the other is false; antinomy says that both the one and the other are true parts of the full Truth (Florensky).

The book of Job is a concentrated experience of contradiction, which is then resolved, but not by lessening the tension Job feels. Lessening the tension is the solution his friends suggest, and Job is told by the still, small voice to leave the tension in place—as Moses was told from the burning bush: "You cannot know my name. But you can know me. I Aм." God is beyond knowing, and therefore human beings cannot judge God, cannot comprehend God's name, cannot see more than God's backside after his glory has passed by. But though God is beyond knowing, he is not beyond loving, which brings us to liturgy. Admittedly, we are tempted to abandon the antinomy and put more emphasis upon the love than the glory, upon the mercy than the justice, upon the forgiveness than the judgment, but that only means we should tighten up our liturgy.

The more thoroughly formed a liturgist is, the less the problem of evil—as a problem—delays him from confronting evil in battle. Satan would be happy if we wrote a hundred books about theodicy instead of extinguishing one passion or slapping one demon. We might, ourselves, be equally happy because it is easier to write the books. But true theologians of the problem of evil suffer and remain steadfast. They remain faithful. They thwart infidelity. And for theologians to understand truly how even evil could be a tool for perfection when wielded by the hand of God, they would have to undergo this divine operation of perfection, which involves liturgically praising God during innocent suffering, glorifying God while condemned and despised, trusting God while being consumed with sorrow to the point of death (Mk 14:34). In other words, they would have to undergo the divine operation of deification and be made to look like Christ. Job was his type in Scripture. In liturgy, Jesus the antitype is our model for liturgical theodicy.

REDEMPTION

Chapter 20

Grace, Liturgy, and Asceticism

Grace is the favor of God toward man that results in their friendship. Grace is the saving, redeeming, regenerating, justifying, gifting, sanctifying energy of God in man, toward man, for man. Grace is unmerited divine gratuity. So what motivates God to show us his favor/grace? Liturgical dogmatics will not answer "the liturgy"—that would be nervy, cultic pride!—but it will answer *with the witness of* liturgy. Grace produces temples of the Holy Trinity, and participation in the perichoresis of the Trinity is our starting point for understanding liturgical grace.

Our ceremonial activity does not arouse (cause, excite, move) God's grace. What hubris that would be! It would place the Christian God on the level of dumb idols who will do the bidding of those who flatter them with religious ceremonies. Scripture warns about misplaced confidence in idols made out of gold, silver, or bronze who cannot see or hear anyway (Rev 9:20, Is 44:9, Deut 4:28). There is no breath in the stone, even one overlaid with gold (Hab 2:19). God warns the Israelites that he will accept no bull from their house or he-goat from their folds, because every beast of the forest is already his, the cattle on a thousand hills are his, the birds of the air and all that moves in the field are his. "If I were hungry, I would not tell you; for the world and all that is in it is mine" (Ps 50:9–12). (Sounds very similar to his conversation with Job.) Our liturgical exchange is with the living God, who has created us, not with a dead idol that we have created.

Yet if God does not *need* our praise, God nevertheless *enjoys* our praise. This determines the relationship between grace and liturgy. So immediately after the Psalmist's harangue, only two verses later, he adds "Offer to God a sacrifice of thanksgiving, and pay your vows to the Most High; and call upon me in the day of trouble; I will deliver you, and you shall glorify me" (Ps 50:14–15). I have no need of sacrifice . . . sacrifice to me a thank offering. We see here a liturgical witness to the phenomenon of grace: God graces those who call upon him, and by calling upon him, they glorify the one who has delivered them. It is an asymmetric exchange, which is why we are doing our part on our knees and he is doing his part from a throne. We bring our needs to liturgy, but the reason we liturgize is not because we are in need. We are looking for grace in liturgy, but we do not liturgize as mercenaries. There are greater and deeper motives at work, motives that arise from the gratitude grace generates. Liturgy is first and foremost an activity of love, love being the cause of *latria* in man and grace in God. Liturgy is an activity between friends, a divine activity of divine friendship, i.e., grace.

God does not create, guard, and redeem his creatures in order to fulfill himself, since he is already filled full in his perichoresis. He nevertheless kenotically pours out his interior love-life as a liturgical ladder for our synergistic ascent into deification. Charity directs us first toward God in liturgical services and, next, to serving our neighbor because he is an object of God's love. This is grace at work; this is liturgy at work. We call it liturgical grace because it fits with the economic descent and sanctifying ascent of liturgy. Liturgical grace adorns and dignifies the human race, which has been given subsistence in order to glorify the Uncreated One. "He who brings thanksgiving as his sacrifice honors me" (Ps 50:23). God has put an amazing power into human hands: he has given us the power to please him. The theological categories of grace—actual, sanctifying, created, uncreated, prevenient, habitual—are conceptual efforts to explain how we have been brought from the abyss of sin to the altar of sacrifice. Liturgy is theological union with God, and the objective of grace is to bring this liturgical union about.

Given our fallen state, the role of liturgical grace takes a different form from what it would have taken if man had remained faithful in Eden. The image of God that Adam and Eve possessed upon their creation was directed toward greater and greater likeness of God, and the divine friendship between God and man would have grown and grown by the power of grace. Adam and Eve would have been directed farther up and farther in by a sanctifying grace that imparted to the soul participation in a divine spirituality impossible to a rational creature by his own unaided power. In the state of original justice, there would have been perfect subjection of reason to God, of sense appetites to reason, and of body to soul. But this nature was damaged by the satanic seducer when he tempted Adam and Eve with disobedient self-determination, so now grace has an additional task to perform in their offspring. Actual grace must now redeem, save, and liberate the captive liturgist who is incapable of performing salutary acts on his own strength. A person must be set free from his abductor before he can return to the divine friendship that undergirds liturgy.

Liturgy is a matter of blessing. The verb has a double meaning that illuminates how closely grace and liturgy are connected. First, blessing indicates the holiness that originates from God ("So God blessed the seventh day and hallowed it", Gen 2:3), and, second, it indicates honoring and glorifying and thanking God ("Bless the LORD, O my soul; and all that is within me, bless his holy name", Ps 103:1). Benevolent love on the part of God (uncreated grace) leads him to bestow a gift (created grace) ordained to eternal life, which stirs up gratitude in the form of a desire to glorify him. That was the sequence the Psalmist had laid out: (i) call upon God; (ii) he will deliver us; (iii) we shall glorify him. Liturgical grace follows the bidirectional paths of liturgical blessing: catabatic sanctification and anabatic *latria*. God sanctifies man, and man glorifies God—the twin purposes or activities of liturgy, again. A blessing of holiness by the Trinity (from the Father, through the Son, by the Holy Spirit) results in man's Eucharistic blessing of the Trinity (to the Father, through the Son, in the Holy Spirit). Grace and liturgy are yoked. In the *divine economy*, salvation comes about when the Father sends the Son, who sends the Holy Spirit. In the *liturgical economy*, deification goes in just the opposite direction: a man is led by the Spirit to the Son, and through the Son he recognizes the Father.

One might be tempted to make a division of labor between divine and human, assigning actions of grace to God and the activity of glorifying to man, but this is misleading according to the tight synergy of liturgy. We have already seen that blessing has a double form that allows it to be ascribed to either God or man, and here we will find that glory also has a double form because human beings are invited to join a Trinitarian action. The Father glorifies the Son by calling him beloved; the Son glorifies the Father by his work of saving the human race; the Son glorifies the Holy Spirit by manifesting and revealing him to the disciples; the Holy Spirit glorifies both Father and Son when those who receive him become children of God and members of Christ's Body; and what the Son and Holy Spirit do in concert for the Father glorifies them both. This perichoresis of glory can be kenotically extended to invite our liturgical ascent into perichoretic doxology. It is a work of grace because it is the benevolent gesture by God (uncreated grace) that bestows the supernatural ability (created grace) to join these exchanges of glory for the sanctification of our soul (sanctifying grace). Glory, then, might be thought of as a divine light that can be shared with human beings as grace. God is the light whose energies we absorb; glorification is the emission of that light in our various states, from our own *nous*, by our own service, in our own charity, as our own purity. Even our asceticism glorifies God by discharging this light in a glorious death, as the baptized prove in their souls during their daily spiritual death and the martyrs prove in their bodies during their literal death.

Grace supplies deficient powers to a person in consideration of the merits of Christ. Without this grace, no supernatural activity would be possible. Without this grace, no supernatural sacramental liturgy would be possible, and no sanctified lives of liturgy would be possible. In the incongruous world into which sin has plunged us, we must be impelled almost against our wishes toward the very thing that is our good. (Not ultimately against our wishes, though.) The starving must be dragged to the dinner table; those in pain but must be forced into hospital; the dying must be coerced to the altar to receive the food of immortality. God gratuitously incites liturgy, and our very lives, our survival, and our redemption depend upon that fact. Our happiness is in liturgy, and God, wishing beatitude for us, infuses us with power for liturgical activity.

Ascent into the perichoresis of the Trinity means involvement in the passage of glory and love flowing between Father, Son, and Holy Spirit. For man, this is a liturgical elevation, a dance of deification, beatitude foretasted in faith now and envisioned in glory then. It is our supreme happiness, and yet we are like a horse or mule that must be curbed with bit and bridle (Ps 32:9). Grace leads sinners into liturgy, sometimes gently with revelations of truth, beauty, and goodness, sometimes forcefully by the hand of providence imposing afflictions. "For the LORD reproves him whom he loves", says Proverbs (3:12) and "for the moment all discipline seems painful rather than pleasant; later it yields the peaceful fruit of righteousness to those who have been trained by it", says Hebrews (12:11). Grace prepares liturgists in an ascetical process begun now. We are not intended to live from one transient act of divine help to the next (actual graces); God desires something more permanent for the soul. The gift of sanctifying grace infuses a supernatural quality in the soul that makes us pleasing to God—a liturgical condition. On sanctifying grace depend our holiness and adoptive sonship—a liturgical status. Sanctifying grace is substantial communication in the inner life of the Holy Trinity—what liturgy eagerly desires even while joyously anticipating.

Liturgical grace is accompanied by liturgical synergy. We have a role to play, too. God does what man is unable to do, but God does not thereby make us inert. We are expected to be responsive after grace has made us responsible (able to respond). *Kenosis* is the word in our definition of liturgy for God's catabatic generosity; *synergy* is the word in our definition for mankind's anabatic response. Synergy adheres when two forces are equal in necessity, though unequal in strength. In liturgy, God's grace energizes and man's zeal synergizes. Liturgical zeal follows liturgical grace. The sacraments of the Church are graces, gifts of Christ, works of the Holy Spirit, and after we are brought to spiritual resurrection, then our liturgical piety follows: the grace of Baptism infuses a zeal for asceticism; the grace of Confirmation empowers a zeal for witness at whatever the cost; the grace of Ordination bestows a zeal for *diakonia*; the grace of Matrimony prepares the zeal of conjugal chastity; the grace of Reconciliation enables zealous acts of reform of life; and the grace of Anointing the Sick causes zealous unification to the Passion of Christ resulting in strength, peace, and courage to suffer. Grace causes liturgical zeal.

If liturgy is an engine of the *exitus* and *redditus* that circulates from the Trinity to us and back again, then liturgical grace is the carburetor of that engine. If liturgy is where all the explosions take place, then liturgical synergy determines the right mixture of grace and response for liturgical combustion, just as the right mixture of fuel and air must be measured for combustion in other engines. Grace brings pneumatic energies into contact with human energies to create the dynamic pressure of liturgy. Grace provides the human liturgist with the powers (graces) required for liturgy. Asceticism is required for liturgy. It is training in self-denial that unbends the sinner's *incurvatus in se*. Purity is a precondition for any priest to enter the temple of Christ's body, whether ordained or baptized; purification from sin and cleansing from transgression are a condition for the baptized to become a temple of the Holy Spirit; grace trains the liturgist in constant prayer in order to present his body as a living sacrifice; noetic vision is required for the liturgist to see spiritual work under the corporeal activity (i.e., to see the *res sacramentum* under the *sacramentum tantum*); a heart of flesh must replace a heart of stone so the liturgist can walk in God's statutes and keep his commandments before, during, and after liturgy; the liturgist must know truth, love the good, and delight in beauty; a body without a soul is dead, and a liturgist without the Holy Spirit does dead liturgy; grace is required for resuscitation; through his gifts of grace, the Holy Spirit awakens faith that configures us to Christ, the high, heavenly liturgist. There is no end to the list of interactions grace and liturgy have.

Chapter 21

The Liturgical *Soter*

Liturgical soteriology tries to comprehend the activity of the *Soter*. It is related to *soteria*, meaning preservation or salvation, and *soizein*, meaning to save or preserve, and *sos*, meaning safety and health, well-being and welfare. Here is our chain of thought.

Sin is offense against God . . .

In liturgical hamartiology, we approached sin under two categories, idolatry and disease, and liturgical soteriology will unite these two definitions. Sin is offense against God that results in our spiritual ill health. Although sin can be defined in other ways, for example, by its ramifications (disobedience, transgression, wrongdoing, iniquity, immorality, etc.), and sins can be distinguished according to their objects (the virtues they oppose, the commandments they violate, whether they concern God, neighbor, or oneself [*CCC* 1853]), if we follow sin far enough upstream to its source, we find the soul admitting "Against you, you only, have I sinned, and done that which is evil in your sight" (Ps 51:4). Idolatry is the cause of our infirmity. If soteriology is the doctrine of salvation, then the *Soter* must remove this cause of our infirmity. He does so by bringing about liturgical recovery of right relationship with God, which heals our sickness of soul.

We do not offend God except by doing something against our own good . . .

The Scholastic theologians admitted that we do not offend God except by doing something contrary to our own good. The damage we do to ourselves is only a consequence of the more fundamental, root problem of withholding liturgy from God. "I am the LORD your God, who brought you out of the land of Egypt, out of the house of bondage. You shall have no other gods before me.... You shall not bow down to them or serve them; for I the LORD your God am a jealous God" (Deut 5:6–9, Ex 20:5, 34:14). Sin is the breakage of covenant and withholding the worship God deserves, worship for which he is jealous.

To do something against our own good is unhealthy ...

We were created to be at ease with God, but now we are at a dis-ease with God. Our abnormal condition makes us uneasy around him. Health is normal and natural and intended in every being God has designed. Health is suitable to the goodness of being and, thus, a kind of ontological descriptor. We might playfully add it as one more transcendental of being: "thing, one, something, good, true, and healthy". Health can therefore be understood as an objective of natural law. Natural law is the rational creature's participation in the eternal law God has written for it, and natural law operates by an imprint of the Divine Light. Natural law is reason discerning between what is good and evil, hale and infirmed. By law, God has decreed our happiness and health! His eternal law commands it, and natural law discerns it. These commandments are not given by God to limit our freedom any more than the orders given by the doctor are intended to deprive us of freedom. Rather, the commandments are a rejuvenation: they develop and cultivate our health. We are attracted naturally to a healthy state that is wholesome, sound, vital, and salutary. A being is unhealthy when it cannot do what it was made to do because something is missing, not operating correctly, or not directed toward the right end. As a result, the being does not look right, does not move appropriately, does not make progress. The wheel is warped, the knife is dull, and the human is worldly. Unhealth can be defined both ontologically and teleologically.

*We fail to respond to God as God when we do not worship him alone as God (*latria*) ...*

Mankind was made for liturgy. Justice is giving another his due; Adam and Eve were created in original justice; the state of original justice recognized that God is due liturgy. Liturgizing God is a wholesome and salutary activity. Liturgy made Adam and Eve prosperous, upright, lively, and healthy, while refraining from liturgy made them bankrupt, fallen, lifeless, and sickly. Mankind lost peace with God because it idolized itself, hoarded glory, esteemed itself, curved inward (*incurvatus in se*), exchanged natural law for a diabolical one, put itself in a bartering position with God, and replaced God's path to deification with one of its own choosing. The creature has a debt of obligation to the Creator upon whom his existence depends, and what is due God in justice is an enforceable obligation, payable on demand. Contingent human creatures should be led to their proper end, namely, thanksgiving. The realization that we are beings *creatio ex nihilo* should inspire a free response of worship. God is justly owed adoration, homage, reverence, honor, and devotion, and we are not to pay it to anyone else. When Satan tried his trick on the Second Adam, this time in a wilderness instead of a garden, he offered Jesus all the kingdoms of the world and their glory if Jesus would only bow down and worship him. But we hear from the *Soter*'s own lips what should be our apotropaic reply, too: "Be gone, Satan!" "You shall worship the Lord your God, and him only shall you serve" (Lk 4:13, quoting Deut 6:13: "You shall fear the LORD your God; you shall serve him"). Sin is offense against God, we said, and we offend God by withholding *latria* from him or bestowing it on an *eidos* (idolatry). There are plenty of idols vying for our attention, and each one causes us a sickness unto death. The Lord Almighty deserves our service, and, if we do anything less, then we are not in the relationship with him that he desires.

Idolatry arouses the jealousy of God ...

When Scripture portrays God as jealous, it is not painting him as childishly egotistical, because Scripture does not confuse jealousy with envy, as we tend to do. Envy means to be gladdened by someone's misfortune and saddened by someone's good fortune. But Scripture is not proposing that God is envious or resentful or suspicious or bitter toward us. Scripture is rather proposing that God is jealous, meaning zealous, watchful, and desirous for

the exclusive devotion that the covenant requires if it is to operate properly. God continually makes covenant with his people,
and covenant requires the appropriate worshipful response. The
prophets say that when God's jealousy is roused, it is because Israel
has failed in her identity as a worship partner, and in zeal God
pursues them. "They have stirred me to jealousy with what is no
god; they have provoked me with their idols" (Deut 32:21). "For
they provoked him to anger with their high places; they moved
him to jealousy with their graven images" (Ps 78:58). God tells his
people, "Take heed to yourselves, lest you forget the covenant of
the LORD your God.... For the LORD your God is a devouring
fire, a jealous God" (Deut 4:23–24). Holiness animates God with
a jealous desire for the righteousness and purity of Zion, which
determines his eschatological plans. Just how far will he go? "I
am jealous for Zion with great jealousy, and I am jealous for her
with great wrath. Thus says the LORD: I will return to Zion, and
will dwell in the midst of Jerusalem, and Jerusalem shall be called
the faithful city, and the mountain of the LORD of hosts, the holy
mountain" (Zech 8:2–3). God cannot bear the estrangement: if
they will not come to him, he will come down to them. This is
jealous love.

The jealousy of God to receive our liturgy results in his sending a Soter ...

Our sin, to repeat, is offense against God. That means an offense
against love, withholding trust, failure to adore, unwillingness to
serve—in other words, a breach or failure to perform an obligation. Sin is a breach of liturgy. So God has sent a savior, a *soter*,
to repair the breach and heal the trespasser. In addition to liturgy's first purpose, which is the glorification of God, God has
coupled a second purpose to liturgy, which is the sanctification
of man. Now liturgy can be recovered, recuperated, and rehabilitated in the wayward offspring of Adam and Eve. Liturgical
soteriology permits us to think of the atonement in covenantal and
relational terms because it recognizes sin as a tear, a rip in relationship. Because a breach is a violation of law, the juridical language
of atonement is not completely done away with, but since the
covenant is injured by both infringement and rupture, the rescuer

whom God sends must perform two miracles: lawfully repairing the breach and therapeutically healing the trespasser. The *Soter* has been engaged in these two tasks since our parents left the garden. This has been his work both as the unincarnate and incarnate Word. And the rescue operation climaxes in his high priesthood. "You, who were dead in trespasses and the uncircumcision of your flesh, God made alive together with him, having forgiven us all our trespasses, having canceled the bond which stood against us with its legal demands; this he set aside, nailing it to the cross" (Col 2:13–14). Soteriology is the gift of righteous liturgy to man and woman through the order of Melchizedek. "The LORD says to my lord: 'Sit at my right hand, till I make your enemies your footstool.' ... The LORD has sworn and will not change his mind, 'You are a priest for ever according to the order of Melchizedek'" (Ps 110:1, 4). These words were prophetically written first of Christ, and now the mystery of his divine priesthood has descended to human agency. Priests are ordained into the order of Melchizedek.

Liturgy is thus soteriological: deliverance from an enemy and restoration to health ...

We can hardly remain healthy in Satan's clutches. A body cannot be considered healthy in the morgue. Soteriology involves salvage, safety, salving. Are we cured after the rescue, or is the rescue our cure? It does not matter if we cannot calculate the timing of a timeless act that reaches from Mount Calvary back to Mount Moriah and forward to Mount Zion. The Incarnation gives back to mankind the possibility of worshipping the true God, but gives it now with a power greater than mankind possessed in Eden. The cult of the first Adam, even if done in original justice, was a human one; the cult of the Second Adam, opened by grace, is a theandric one. God's jealousy is connected to his holiness: "He is a holy God; he is a jealous God" (Josh 24:19). Therefore, the truest and highest worship must be done in holiness. Therefore, the Savior must make his sibling liturgists holy. This command appears in 1 Chronicles 16:29; see also Ps 29:2 and Ps 96:9: "Ascribe to the LORD the glory due his name; ... Worship the LORD in holy attire." Alas, we have no holiness. Hurrah, the *Soter* shares his with us. "Although he was a Son, he learned obedience through what he suffered; and being made perfect he became the source of eternal salvation [*aionios soteria*] to all who obey him, being designated by God a high priest according to the order of Melchizedek" (Heb 5:8–10).

A liturgist is the healthiest kind of person there is . . .

In order for the *Soter* to put things right with God, he will also have to put things right within us; therefore, the light of liturgy will both glorify God and disinfect sin. (This involves liturgical asceticism, which is therapeutic and not masochistic.) We need purity in order to commit liturgy, so sanctification brings holiness. First, the *Soter* quenches our thirst; then something unusual happens to the healed heart of the liturgist: the Holy Spirit enters the liturgist and becomes established there. On the last day of the Feast of Tabernacles, the great day, Jesus stood up and proclaimed that anyone who thirsts can come to him and drink, and "He who believes in me, as the Scripture has said, 'Out of his heart shall flow rivers of living water' " (Jn 7:38). We came in order to drink, and now living waters flow out of our hearts. We got more than we bargained for. The Holy Spirit entering within is a miraculous result of liturgical soteriology. In order to see God as Light, the soul must be in a certain spiritual condition. "When your eye is sound, your whole body is full of light" (Lk 11:34). Just as the created light gives light to the healthy eyes of the body, so the uncreated light gives light to the pure *nous* and illumined heart. Liturgical soteriology enlightens the eye and enlivens the soul, which is descriptive of the liturgy of prophets, apostles, martyrs, saints, and Our Lady. They have clear eyes, bodies full of light, hearts overflowing with living water. The priesthood of Jesus is a resurrection priesthood, foreshadowed by Melchizedek, and resurrection liturgy is the healthiest kind of liturgy anyone can possibly celebrate.

Chapter 22

The Beginning of Death's Death

Question: What is wrong with death? Answer from Scripture: No liturgy.

- "The dead do not praise the Lord, nor do any that go down into silence" (Ps 115:17).
- "In death there is no remembrance of you; in Sheol who can give you praise?" (Ps 6:5).
- "What profit is there in my death, if I go down to the Pit? Will the dust praise you? Will it tell of your faithfulness?" (Ps 30:9).
- "Is your mercy declared in the grave, or your faithfulness in Abaddon?" (Ps 88:11).
- "If the Lord had not been my help, my soul would soon have dwelt in the land of silence" (Ps 94:17).
- "For Sheol cannot thank you, death cannot praise you" (Is 38:18).

What is wrong with death is that the dead do not praise the Lord; they are silent; they do not remember God; they do not recite details of his faithfulness; they do not declare his steadfast love; they do not make thanksgiving. Death is the land of no-liturgy. Sheol is silence, no-praise. In the darkness of death, no one shines in glory to the honor of God. Sin is death; praise is life; without liturgy, we are literally dead men walking.

We are mistaken in our estimate of the tragedy of death. Death is not tragic because my paltry plans come to naught, because my worldly esteem will be almost immediately forgotten, because I will miss out on pleasures in which I had hoped to indulge, because every scheme I make will be abruptly and mercilessly interrupted, not one excepted, because my temporal designs (which are temporary, after all) have a lasting power equivalent to the lifespan of a gnat. The true tragedy of death is that our opportunity to worship is involuntarily cut off by the grave. Death's calamity is not that my horizontal line of history stops short; it is that my vertical line of liturgy is cut off. And it is even more distressing if I cut it off voluntarily. The risk God took on freedom means that we are capable of changing our address from Eden to the land of no-liturgy.

(i) Adam and Eve relocated from Eden into Hades. "Hades" comes from *a+idein*, which means "invisible" (a privative prefix attached to the idea of sight). In Hades, people are deprived of the vision of God, and, in the Fall, Adam and Eve wanted to make themselves invisible to God.

(ii) Adam and Eve relocated from Eden into hell. "Hell" comes from *helan*, which in Anglo Saxon means "a concealed place", like the bushes in which Adam and Eve hid.

(iii) Adam and Eve relocated from Eden into Sheol. This word is of uncertain origin, but means "a cave, a sunken place" that is dark. When we are embarrassed to the point of mortification, we sometimes say we want to sink into the floor and disappear; Adam and Eve wanted to.

Eden had been evacuated and become a land of no-liturgy; Christ called, "Adam, my brother, Eve, my sister, where are you? Liturgize with me!" but there was only silence in response. So Christ had to look in the last, last place where men and women had sunk (Sheol), hidden (hell), and concealed themselves (Hades). He took out his longest and strongest fishing line, unspooled it completely, sank it with the weight of his Cross, and did some really deep-sea fishing. Through the little puddle of water in the baptismal font, he can reach Hades.

What does liturgical thanatology have to say about this? Liturgy is holy, and liturgy trains us for holy things. This suggests that even death can be overcome if the liturgy trains us for a holy death. A holy death is one pleasing to God, one liturgically offered to God (sacrificially). It is a death that has been practiced since the inauguration of our liturgical lives; I mean Baptism. This changes the experience of death, which was the intent and end of salvation history in the first place. Salvation history is an operation of trawling for liturgists, and the Church is the trawl net. Jesus is a carpenter who instructs fishermen how to fish! Did the Galilee disciples object to him stepping out of his wheelhouse? But he had to do it when he commanded them to start going after different catch.

Here is one example. When he finished teaching a crowd of people from the boat, Jesus told Simon to put out into the deep and let down his nets again, and although the disciple had already wasted the night and come up empty, he obeyed and broke his net with the number of fish (Lk 5:4–6). Here is another example. After his Resurrection, Jesus found his disciples unsuccessful after another long night of fishing and told them to cast the net on the right side of the boat. They brought 153 fish to shore without even tearing the net and had breakfast together with Jesus (Jn 21:4–14). What Jesus explained by miracle, he had once explained by parable. "The kingdom of heaven is like a net which was thrown into the sea and ... when it was full, men drew it ashore and ... sorted the good ... [from] the bad" (Mt 13:47–48). Scripture continues to describe Judgment Day as a sorting process: good fish from bad, good fruit from bad, sheep from goats, wheat from tares, wise virgins from foolish ones, blessed from cursed. After fishing through the night of many generations without success, Jesus counsels his apostles to let down the net one more time, to cast the net also from the Gentile side of the boat, to catch everyone and sort them out later. Death gathers us all, but the judgment that comes after death's end divides.

Scripture used the imagery of Job's Leviathan ("Can you draw out Leviathan with a fishhook?" Job 41:1) and Jonah's whale ("so will the Son of man be three days and three nights in the heart of the earth", Mt 12:40), therefore the Church Fathers spoke of Christ baiting Satan. He mounted his flesh on the fishhook of his divinity as bait for the devil. Like a ravenous fish, Satan gulped down the bait of flesh, thinking the body on the Cross to be just one more specimen of what was his lawful prey. He did not know that the one he had swallowed was innocent and would cause Hades to vomit man up like Jonah's whale had done. Christ's descent into Hades had the effect of a divine syrup of ipecac.

Salvation history is a matter of trawling for liturgists, and even being dead does not disqualify someone from the net's catch. The righteous of the Old Testament are not excluded. Christ will harrow hell in order to raise them up as potential liturgists, too. From Sheol's silence came a liturgical shout of praise; from Hades' invisibility came a liturgical gleam of glorification; from hell's dissimulation came forth a liturgically harrowed *imago Dei*. Jesus continues to lower his line to catch the little fishes Tertullian talked about. They are a baby Ichthys (*Iesous Christos, Theo Yios, Soter*— Jesus Christ, Son of God, Savior) whom Jesus means to catch and raise up from the depths to which human nature has sunk.

Christ wants to resurrect liturgists from the mortality in which they find themselves. This mortality is a condition without form, a void, a darkness over the deep, so Jesus repeats an action from the first creation in this second creation: he sends the Spirit of God to move again over the face of the waters (Gen 1:2); he again uses water to rescue and bring back to life. At Baptism, he sends a personal flood to drown our iniquity and boost us up onto his ark; he gives a little water so we can wash our feet with the three visitors by the oaks of Mamre (then—surprise—he ends up washing our feet himself in the upper room); he parts a Red Sea with his cross-staff for our escape from Satan and his demons and the land of bondage; he commands water to flow from his rock, Peter, and it follows us through the desert of sin, lest we die of thirst; he sets up a laver of bronze for washing so we will not die when we enter the tent of meeting; he halts the Jordan so we may pass into the promised land following twelve men who carry stones for a memorial altar; he fills four jars with water to flood the wood and the holocaust when he calls down a fire the prophets of Baal could not summon; he parts the water that Elijah struck so as to go on dry ground to meet the chariots of Israel; as Elijah touched the Jordan with wood and brought up from the bottom the sunken axe head, Christ touches the baptismal font with his Cross and brings up our human nature from the muck of sin in which it lies; he cures the leprosy of any Naaman who has faith enough to obey a prophet's demands; he leads us beside still waters running through green pastures that will restore our soul as we feast in the presence of the demons; he promises that if we give a cup of water to a little one, then we will not lose our reward; he stirs the water of Bethzatha to heal our paralysis; if there is no water for healing our blindness at Bethsaida, he will use his own spit; he asks the Samaritan woman for a mere cup of water and ends up giving her water of eternal life; he pours forth the sacraments of water and blood from his pierced side on the Cross; he turns water into wine at Cana's wedding, and at our Eucharistic nuptials he transubstantiates wine into an endless reserve of blood.

Christ is still fishing for resurrected liturgists. O happy fault of Adam that earned for us so great, so glorious a Redeemer. O happy tree upon which hung the Savior of the world; come, let us worship. O happy tomb, which is the one cave leading out of Hades when all other graves lead into it. O happy death of the Second Adam that returns life to the first Adam.

Liturgy celebrates the happiness of things we would never think to be happy, even death. What once frightened us as a snarling wolf has been tamed to be a little dog, a little shepherd dog, herding us toward our rendezvous with God. The thief becomes a messenger; the sepulcher becomes a birth canal; our pall becomes a swaddling cloth. Death has not been victorious, which we witness with our faith, notarize with our hope, and prove with our love. We can die a liturgical, holy death. Every time we eat this bread and drink this cup, we proclaim the Lord's death until he comes (1 Cor 11:26). We stand at attention, on liturgical guard duty until the day of the resurrection.

Chapter 23

Providence

Most of the time we carelessly think of providence as luck—namely, good luck, for us. When good fortune comes our way and we are pleased with an auspicious state of affairs, then we toss heaven a sideways glance and call it providence. But, in fact, all God's acts of providence have only one purpose and motive: to make us more Christoform, which can only mean being more firmly nailed to our crosses so the Holy Spirit can advance the labor of sanctification in our souls. How can we become true liturgists without being truly Christoform? And how can we be Christoformed without following our Master in every step he took, to every place he went, including Golgotha? Someone exclaims: "I received the job I've always wanted—it must have been God's providence at work." But very few people exclaim: "I have been wounded for my transgressions, and blows have cleansed away evil and strokes have made clean my innermost parts (Prov 20:30); because he has reproved me I know he loves me as a son in whom he delights (Prov 3:12); and although the moment of discipline seems painful at the time, it yields the peaceable fruit of righteousness to those who have been trained by it (Heb 12:11)—it must have been God's providence at work."

Silouan the Athonite said that temptations allowed by God are like winds that God blows. When a flame is first lit and is very fragile, a very small wind can snuff it out. A match can be extinguished with a small puff when it is first lit, so at the beginning, God's providence acts with restraint. But when the flame has taken hold and sets fire to a larger mass of wood, then a stronger wind does not extinguish the fire; it actually makes the fire burn more hotly. One blows upon a kindling fire to make it blaze, to inflame it further until it can receive another log. And when the fire is strong enough, you can blow on it as hard as you want without threat of extinguishing it. The wind only results in making the fire flare brighter. We are referencing Job, now, not his friends. Job's friends did not understand providence. But Job is an Old Testament type of Christ: the innocent one whose suffering is perfection. Our liturgical model for providence is the man Jesus, of whom Job was the type. If we suffer with thanksgiving, it is liturgical suffering.

What are some essential virtues for committing liturgy, and how do we arrive at them? *Humility* is essential, but humility will feel like humiliation so long as we have an ounce of pride. *Patience* is essential, but patience cannot be had instantaneously; it must be forged by perseverance through trials. *Wisdom* is essential, but that means driving away all despair, forgetfulness, lack of understanding, and negligence, and taking away all unclean, crafty, and blameworthy thoughts from our smitten hearts and darkened minds (Morning Prayer to the Most Holy Mother of God). *Prudence* is essential, but the very word means the ability to discipline oneself, to govern oneself by healthy reason instead of by the unhealthy reason we possess now. *Justice* is essential, seeing from a God's-eye view and not from our narcissism. *Forgiveness* is essential, and we are told by our Lord how to jumpstart that: start forgiving those who trespass against us. *Faith* is essential, but it is more than following the path dimly lit by our own reason; it is, rather, a venturing beyond those limits into the darkness wherein God is our only guide. *Hope* is essential, but in a stronger measure than merely wishing something nice might happen; rather, a leap of hope is demanded of us. *Love* is essential, but not the sort that attends our own self-esteem, that protects our egos against bruising, that watches over our goods; rather, we must be stripped of false love before we can be clothed in true love. Providence must set to work.

We may say that the origin, unfolding, and end of providence is to cultivate people capable of liturgy. Providence trains our voice for the choir of liturgists, drills our marching step for the legion of liturgists, schools our natures for the civitas of liturgists. God is making us into witnesses, martyrs (*martyria*). And to what do we witness? The Cross and Resurrection—not only found outside Jerusalem centuries ago, but also the cross and resurrection working in our souls. Cross and resurrection are the two instruments God uses in his divine surgery on our liturgical hearts. They are the equipment our divine cardiologist will use to bring our dead heart back to beating. No one may excuse himself by saying he cannot be a witness because he was not there with the apostles when the Holy Spirit descended at Pentecost. The miracle to which we are asked to witness is the presence of the Holy Spirit in our own hearts. We witness with lives resurrected from death, delivered from the devil, and liberated from sin.

Tracking providence in our lives does not require us to look outside to some enigmatic flow of history, peeking under fateful events like flipping over tarot cards. We can track providence by introspective attention, a hesychastic EKG, a searching in the soul to discover those touches by God, whether painful or not, that overcome our reluctance to draw nearer to him and so relinquish the hold we have on ourselves in favor of the hold he takes of us. Providence is a kind of farsightedness by God, and we do not understand it because we are too shortsighted. His foresight is a prudent anticipation of what is required for every single individual, at every single moment, to advance farther in conversion. Liturgical providence is God's prudential preparation for a final cosmic liturgy, and that requires preparing every voice for the choir, every word for the poem, every shard of glass for the rose window. A sacristan will prepare all things for a human, earthly liturgy; the divine sacristan overseeing history will prepare all persons for the final, messianic liturgy.

Providence is a name for the life cycle of liturgists. As the caterpillar's life cycle yields up a butterfly, man's life cycle yields up a liturgist. Both go through a complete metamorphosis. Jesus was sent to bring us out of slavery, as Moses was sent to bring the Israelites out of Egypt, and those who accept God's overture to them are brought to life again. Once they were not a people, but now they are the Church, God's people, a chosen race, a royal priesthood, a holy nation, and they move through history proclaiming the excellencies of God who called them out of darkness into light (1 Pet 2:9–10). Providence guides their pathway through the world, through the grave, and they sing their liturgy without abatement.

I do not intend to say that providence is always painful. I only intend to say that even what is painful is part of providence. One does not wait impatiently for the trials to end before noticing the providential hand of God, since the hand of God is always upon us for the purpose of leading us deeper into our personal liturgy. It weighs all things and spares no things. If a key does not yet fit the lock, it must be cut again. Often our lives must be cut again and again until they are in the right shape to fit the stone altar and contribute to the final Eucharist. The potter's hand is not stilled until the vessel is the right shape, the shape he has previsioned to hold the precise amount of glory he desires from this person in the final liturgy. The artist's hand is not stilled until the particular piece of glass has taken on the right hue, more opaque in some people and more brightly transparent in other people, but each contributing to the rose window the artist is constructing. Although the shaping process will distress the selfish heart, the same process will delight the selfless heart, because at some point our experience of providence turns the corner from preparation to anticipation. The making ready becomes itself a foretaste. The Holy Spirit will begin to dwell in the home even before it is fully prepared and furnished, bringing in his train his seven gifts. If a believer finds himself equipped with wisdom, understanding, counsel, fortitude, knowledge, piety, and fear of the Lord, then he can know that providence has been afoot. God is producing a liturgist by preparing a prophet, priest, king, theologian, saint, ascetic, martyr, crucified.

God's purpose in all things is to nudge us closer to his Kingdom. Providence acts on us like a weight, a magnet, a gravity, a spiritual pressure. Its remote term is the messianic banquet, but its proximate term is the place where we can have a foretaste of that banquet. The pathway home goes through the Church, past the font, confessional, altar. By our earthly liturgy, providence gives us a prefigurement and foreshadowing of the heavenly liturgy. The Old Testament types revealed the antitypes of the New Covenant, but these, in turn, point to a final consummation. Our earthly sacraments and liturgies are types of an eschatological antitype, and that is the ultimate aim of providence.

If you wonder what God is up to inside you, look at that final liturgy: he is providentially preparing you to take part in it. And do not think that because you do not believe in God he is not hard at work forming your life for beatitude and preparing you to meet him one day. Providence works on unbelievers, too.

CHRIST AND THE HOLY SPIRIT

Chapter 24

The Liturgy in Christ

These are the densest chapters. Our Lord and our liturgy are united at a depth beyond our comprehension. Without Jesus, we would be talking about human religion instead of liturgy, and the idea of a "liturgical theology" would be in vain. Without liturgical theology, we would be talking about a man residing in historical records instead of in hearts and on altars. Without Christ's perpetual presence in liturgy, we would be talking about the historical Jesus instead of the sacramental Lord of the Church. The salvific work of Jesus was done once, but it is not yet done. Its consequences live on as his life is etched onto ours. When iconographers paint an icon, they prepare a preliminary sketch, and, using graphite paper, they transfer the drawing onto a board with an etching stylus that imprints the lines of the image into the gesso on the board's surface so the lines of the figure will remain visible as the board is painted. The Church has such a graphite paper for transferring the icon of Christ. The pages of Scripture hold the outline of the Church given by Christ to the apostles, which can be transferred onto our lives by the liturgical stylus wielded by the hand of the Church, as guided by the Holy Spirit when he places his hand upon hers to direct her motion. The liturgical life consists of making us an image of the Image of God, a brother of the Son, an image of the prototype. His life is etched upon us by liturgical realities. His five wounds on the Cross are transferred to us; his Resurrection-power already stirs in our souls. What was begun historically continues sacramentally. Christology is the doctrine of what was completed in the vine, and liturgical theology is the doctrine of the vine's vitality extending into ever-new branches.

In this chapter, we will look at how Christ's life is lived in us, liturgically.

- Liturgy is receiving the same proposal from Gabriel as the one he brought to Mary: Jesus will live in the hearts of his faithful people when the Holy Spirit overshadows them and their faith is engendered by the power of the Most High at Baptism. Then our souls, too, will magnify the Lord and rejoice in God our savior.
- Liturgy is the manger feed-trough permanently stocked with the food that endures to eternal life so mankind shall not hunger (Jn 6:27, 35).
- Liturgy is our sacramental purification, as commanded by the law, a heart perfected by a grace that shows salvation to our spiritual eyes and lets us depart this life in peace (Lk 2:22–29).
- Liturgy is receiving permanent covenantal relationship with the Father, figured by circumcision and fulfilled in the true *sphragis* of the final covenant (Rom 2:29).
- Liturgy is the household in Nazareth expanding infinitely so we can join the Holy Family as adopted brothers and sisters. (We are, all of us, glad to be up for adoption.)
- Liturgy is shifting our parentage from any natural lineage to join Jesus as a Son of the Covenant in his Father's house.
- Liturgy is joining Jesus in his Baptism, and Jesus joining in our Baptism. Over every modest baptismal font, wherever it is in the world, the heavens open again, the Holy Spirit descends again, and a voice from heaven says that the life the Only Begotten Son lived through the hypostatic union shall be ours, too, by grace (Mk 1:11).
- Liturgy is accompanying Jesus to his ascetic appointment for combat with Satan, a spiritual warfare commenced by Baptism and conducted before the start of any ministry—his or ours.
- Liturgy follows in the wake of Jesus' ministry. Of course there are saving actions only he can do as the Son of God, but the Christian is a *sequela Christi* inspired by his mercy toward sinners, motivated by his compassion for the poor, moved by his pity toward the sick, compelled by his ministry of teaching.
- Liturgy is guided by twelve apostles. At the beginning, they were sent to proclaim "the kingdom of heaven is at hand"

(Mt 10:7), and at the end they are honored by the holy city Jerusalem for being the "twelve foundations, and on them the twelve names of the twelve apostles of the Lamb" (Rev 21:14). In between that first mission and that final fruition, liturgists are taught, sanctified, and shepherded (prophet, priest, king) by the successors of the apostles.

- Liturgy happens on Mount Tabor, which, with Mount Hermon, had already shouted for joy at God's name (Ps 89:12). It was a rendezvous place for Elijah and Moses. It could have been a place for a new Feast of Tabernacles, if Jesus had not refused Peter's offer of three booths in favor of completing his mission on another mount, Mount Golgotha, and becoming the true Tent for us all. On this mount, the bright cloud came overshadowing again (*episkiazein*), as once it had overshadowed Mary at the Annunciation (same verb), and the voice from heaven spoke again (as at the Jordan) with the instructions required for all liturgy: "Listen to him."

- Liturgy must be constantly reminded about the confusion of Palm Sunday: the city of Man sings Hosanna at the scent of triumphalism, but the city of God remembers that the King arrives on a beast of burden that will take him to the courtyards of the Sanhedrin and Pilate.

- Liturgy requires the cleansing of the temple wherein it is celebrated. A Christian's body is a temple of the Holy Spirit (1 Cor 6:19); the Christian himself is God's temple because God's Spirit dwells in him (1 Cor 3:16); therefore, as Jesus overturned the tables of the robbers to refresh his Father's house of prayer, so our temples must be cleansed from immorality before we can make liturgy with them.

- Liturgy is a life-giving, penetrating radiation released from the explosion of the Paschal Mystery.

- Liturgy is the high priestly prayer of Jesus (Jn 17) being repeated on the ordained priest's lips daily and weekly. Liturgy is an exercise of the priestly office of Jesus Christ (*Sacrosanctum concilium* 7) as he continues his priestly work through the agency of his Church (83). What he prayed, we pray: unity, indwelling, glory, and giving.

- Liturgy is companionship with Jesus. To break bread (*panis*) together (*cum*) is companionship, and this is enjoyed not only by the Twelve in the upper room, but through the ages in every nation, at every time, by every person who draws near to the table.

- Liturgy is facing, each in our own way, persecution by a world that killed the Lord of Life when he arrived.
- Liturgy requires us to study ourselves for signs of Judas, who valued cause and coin over the Kingdom offered by Jesus; for signs of Peter, who feared recognition and being named a follower of the Galilean; for signs of Caiaphas' self-preserving prudence, Pilate's debilitating cowardice, Herod's counterfeit curiosity, the crowd's deriding mockery. To commit liturgy requires us to examine whether we find Jesus a threat to some deeply hidden self-love.
- Liturgy is the beloved one receiving Mary for his mother.
- Liturgy is fruit sprouting from the tree of the Cross.
- Liturgy is standing guard at the tomb, not with soldiers commanded by Pilate and Pharisee to squelch rumors of resurrection, but with the women who were sentinels of the Resurrection to make sure it was proclaimed when it did happen. They were first messengers: they became angels (*angelos*). Liturgy is the gospelizing of Mary Magdalen, who was apostle to the apostles.
- Liturgy is listening to the angels say "He is not here." Wherever you think you have locked him, wherever you think you have buried him, wherever you think you have left him behind, he is not there. He is on the loose.
- Liturgy is sung in the great echo chamber of the empty tomb, sweetening our song by its acoustics.
- Liturgy is the empty tomb turned sideways, filled with water, and used for a baptismal font.
- Liturgy is becoming the feet of Christ, pierced, to trample down death by death. That is why we must learn to die: so we can trample down death wherever we come across it.
- Liturgy is a caravan of believers in the Lord of Life, the New Adam, the chief cornerstone, the head, the holy one, the judge, the King of kings, the Prince of peace, the Son of God, the Son of Man, the Word made flesh, Emmanuel, the Good Shepherd, the Bridegroom, the Bread of life, the Lamb of God, the way and truth and life. No wonder the Catholic caravan is so capacious: he is all things.

- Liturgy is the work of God, an *opus Dei*. And what is the work of God? "Jesus answered them, 'This is the work of God, that you believe in him whom he has sent'" (Jn 6:29). Liturgy is not only actions of the body; it is also belief in the heart that is firm, convicted, unyielding, and steadfast. That is the real reason that Baptism is the gate to the world of liturgy.
- Liturgy is not just a remembrance of a historical event; it is remembrance of the mystery that was transacted by that historical event. But the mysterious element is not limited to this historical point alone; it goes on into personal experience. Liturgy is participation at the personal level in the Passion and Cross of Christ within the sacramental life of the Church.
- Liturgy burns by a spiritual accelerant that puts us in direct contact with the fire of Pentecost. Liturgy blazes when our simmering coal is blown upon by the wind of Pentecost. Liturgy catholicizes when it speaks to devout persons from every nation in their own tongue.
- Liturgy is catabatic: worshipping Jesus' first descent (by the Holy Spirit incarnate of the Virgin Mary) and welcoming Jesus' second descent (to Hades, where mankind lies muted and fettered).
- Liturgy is anabatic: following behind Christ's first ascension (up to Golgotha) and rejoicing at his second Ascension (up to heaven). The *kenosis* of the second Person of the Trinity has invited our synergistic ascent into the perichoresis of the Trinity.
- Liturgy is drawing near to Christ, as did Nicodemus, Zacchaeus, Mary Magdalen, Peter, James, and John. They approached him in Jerusalem or on the shores of Galilee; we approach him after his little and great entrances when we go forward in the Communion line. We walk toward Christ in the Communion line and then turn and return to our place in the nave. But one day we will not. We will not turn, but will continue to go on, farther, upward, directly to him through the altar gate. Our walk in the Communion line during our lifetime helps us to know the path, to make sure of our footing, and to get up some speed for the final jump.

Chapter 25

Christ in the Liturgy

Having looked at Christ's life liturgically in the previous chapter, in the present one we will look at the Mass Christologically.

Jesus' life is theandric. Two natures are united in one Person (*hypostasis*) without confusion, separation, change, or division. This hypostatic union is unique, yet shared: he is the Only Begotten Son, incarnate of the Virgin Mary by the Holy Spirit, but men and women who are led by this same Spirit are also sons of God because they receive the Spirit of adoption, by whom they cry "Abba! Father!" (Rom 8:14–15). Being baptized into Christ creates members of his Body, and the blueprint of Christ's life is imprinted on them. That blueprint will be made more lucid in the spiritual warfare that follows their empowering immersion. The head sanctifies his members; the source creates the effects; the prototype is stamped upon the ectype; Jesus is the image of the Father, and faithful believers become images of him; the God-man determines our spiritual growth in Godmanhood by the work commenced by the Holy Spirit.

That is why we sense an analogy between Christology and ecclesiology. The latter is the former stretched out to its full length. Ecclesiology is Christology being completed by extension beyond the Ascension into our time, the time of the Church *totus Christus*. The Church is the dynamic incorporation of men and women into Christ, which means that Christianity is not a system of ideas; it is sacramental unity. For these reasons, *Lumen gentium* says the mystery of the Church is compared to the mystery of the incarnate Word "by no weak analogy" (*Lumen gentium* 8). In Jesus himself, the divine and human work perichoretically and reciprocally, each oriented toward the other and compenetrating the other even while distinctness is preserved. There is an analogous action in the mystery of the

Church. Here also the divine and human work perichoretically and reciprocally in the liturgy, with God's work compenetrating human activity. The Mass is the simultaneous action of Christ and the People of God, an action whereby God sanctifies the world in Christ and the human race worships the Father through the Son of God in the Holy Spirit (*General Instruction of the Roman Missal* 16). If asked whether liturgy is the work of God or the activity of man, the answer is "Yes." This is true even though priority must be given to the *opus Dei*. When I stumbled on the happy statement that liturgy is "the work of God and the activity of man", it was to assert paradoxically both a cooperation and a primacy. When the East calls it synergy, it is because the agents are equal in necessity but unequal in importance. When the West speaks of first and second causes, it is because it is entirely from God as from its first cause and entirely from us as from its second cause.

This should mean that when liturgical theology looks for a shadow of the Church in the Mass, the body whose shadow it actually sees turns out to be Christ himself. Liturgical theology carefully watches the Church in motion to discern the *lex credendi* from the liturgy's *lex orandi* and discovers it is watching Christ himself stride through the Divine Liturgy. Christ's Liturgy moves human liturgy. Liturgical Christology, then, is dogma about Jesus read off the liturgy. This includes the liturgical year that celebrates his mysteries of redemption in such a way as to make them present; it includes the Divine Office that places his praise of the Father upon our lips; it includes all the sacred actions and activities of the Christian life. But for now, here, we will take the Mass for a detailed example.

The inclination to see Christ in the liturgy has struck many commentators over the centuries, although most of the time their efforts are now ridiculed by modern scholars. They are derided for overlaying the chronology of Jesus' life upon the structural sequence of the Mass, for example, aligning his teaching in Galilee with the Liturgy of the Word, his approach to Jerusalem with the Offertory, and his death and Resurrection with the fraction rite and comingling. I will not join this smug disapproval because I think those commentators did something perfectly natural. They looked at the liturgy and saw Christ; they looked with sacramental eyes and saw the continued activity of Christ; they looked at earth and saw heaven, especially in the one who descended from heaven and walked upon this earth; they realized that the success and completion of an act did not automatically require rendering it in the past tense; they looked at the *liturgia tantum* and saw the *res tantum* under it; they looked at the activity of human liturgy and saw Christ's work. But to avoid being dismissed out of hand here, when we look at the Mass, we will not focus on the historical life of Christ but, rather, on the soteriological activity of Christ.

Here is the Church; here is the steeple; open the doors, and how many reminders of Christ face us straightaway? The crucifix, the altar, the Book of the Gospels, the priest (Christ the head) and deacon (Christ the servant), the assembly (Christ's Body)—they are all easy to see because they are underlined in smoke when they are incensed. Pagan temples were usually quite small, needing a room only large enough to accommodate one priest's approach to altar and idol, but Christ has remodeled the pagan temple for his house of worship, expanding the square footage so that the royal priesthood of the baptized can also come inside. The baptized priesthood does not watch from outside; they sit smack-dab in the middle of the temple. There is still division of sanctuary and nave in order to make ministerial activity visible, but the whole nave is incensed when the priest circumambulates it in the Orthodox liturgy.

The first liturgical act of the morning has already happened: the faithful have gotten out of their beds and come. "Where two or three are gathered in my name, there am I in the midst of them" (Mt 18:20). A people has been created by Christ—his people—and he summons them here. They do not bring themselves; he convokes them. They are gathered here because he desires them to be here. He calls them not only from the Jews but also from the Gentiles, a fact Saint Paul finds clarified by the prophet: "As indeed [God] says in Hosea, 'Those who were not my people I will call "my people"'" (Rom 9:25). Salvation history is a story of collecting. God is a pack-rat; he saves things. He even saves people who do not initially appear very useful. First he salvages eight people and two animals of every kind; then he stops by Ur of Chaldea to collect Abraham; then he forms Jacob's descendants in the mud pit into a nation at his great *Qahal Yahweh* at the foot of Mount Sinai. Plenty more gathering by judges and kings and prophets must go on, until he decides to build a yet bigger barn for his biggest collection yet. The *Qahal Yahweh* will become the *ekklesia Theou* of the latter days. "You are a chosen race, a royal priesthood, a holy nation.... Once you were no people but now you are God's people" (1 Pet 2:9–10), and since they are the Lord's people, they come to the Lord's house, on the Lord's day, to the Lord's table, for the Lord's supper. When the people are gathered, then the priest approaches the altar with the ministers while the Entrance Chant is sung.

Having assembled his royal and baptized priests, Christ will begin his liturgical work through his ministerial priest. The two priesthoods differ from one another in essence, and not only in degree, and their diversity exists at the mode of participation in the priesthood of Christ. Both the teaching Church and the taught Church have their task to do. The latter is the fellowship, and the former is the means to fellowship. The ministers do not serve themselves; they are taken into the order of clerics in order to maintain and promote the baptismal priesthood of the entire People of God leading to full ecclesial realization. Both minister and laity are liturgists; both minister and laity have a liturgy to do; the priest acts *in persona Christi Capitis* in the Body of Christ. Do not say the laity cooperates with the priest in the liturgy; say, rather, the laity and priest co-operate the liturgy.

The Introductory Rites. The Trinity is twice designated. The liturgy is done in the name of Father, Son, and Holy Spirit, and the people are greeted in the grace of Jesus, the love of God, and the communion of the Holy Spirit. The second Person of the Trinity, the Son, the Incarnate One, has a central place in the triangle above, in heaven, and in the triangle below, on earth. What we are about to do is an activity of glorifying God and sanctifying man, and these are the two duties that Christ performed in communion with the Holy Spirit. The people reply to the greeting by honoring the priest's ordination: "And with your spirit." When the priest was ordained, the bishop asked the Lord to "pour out upon this servant of yours the blessing of the Holy Spirit in the grace and power of the priesthood." The bishop made this epiclesis through Christ our Lord. The people make this same response to the deacon, because when he was ordained, the bishop asked the Lord to "send forth upon him the Holy Spirit, that he may be strengthened by the gift of your sevenfold grace to carry out faithfully the work of the ministry." We are not just greeting the minister personally; we are acknowledging the spirit of Christ he received at ordination. It is not the priest's liturgy; it is not our liturgy; it is Christ's liturgy. Christ comes from the Father's throne to this altar in order to accomplish the mystery of our salvation, and the man who stands at that altar does not act on his own authority; he rather acts in the spirit of Christ. This exchange is so important that it is made five times during the Mass: at this greeting, from the ambo, before the Eucharistic Prayer, at the sharing of peace, and at the dismissal.

The Penitential Act. What did Jesus come to do? Bring the Kingdom of God. And what is the first reaction that this should elicit from us? Penitence, sorrow for sin, conversion of life. Those who begged forgiveness could recognize Jesus as the Christ (the penitent thief), and those who did not, could not (the other thief). Therefore, as we come into the presence of Christ in the Mass, we begin with the penitential act of acknowledging our sins because otherwise we would not be prepared to celebrate the sacred mysteries. However, when we make this confession, we are not left on our own. It is true that we are standing face to face with Almighty God, but at that moment we are also shoulder to shoulder with Christ our brother and with all his friends: with Mary ever Virgin, all the angels, all the saints, and the brothers and sisters present, all of whom will pray for us to the Lord our God.

Kyrie and Gloria. We were standing before the Father in the penitential act; now we turn and address Jesus directly in the Kyrie. Why were you sent? To heal the contrite heart. What did you come to do? To call sinners. What are you doing even now at the right hand of the Father? Interceding for us. We are his purpose; his activity is for our sake. In the Gloria, we give Jesus four names (Only Begotten Son, Lord God, Lamb of God, Son of the Father) and again turn to center upon his activity. What does he do? Take away sins, have mercy on us, and receive our prayer. Who else could do it? He alone is the Holy One, the Lord, the Most High. Yet we still beg him to have mercy on us even in his glory sitting at the right hand of the Father. His mercy comes to us from two locations: on the Cross, where he took away the sins of the world, and at the right hand of the Father, where he is seated now.

Liturgy of the Word. Liturgy is proclamation, and proclamation produces the hierarchical structure of the Church. God-ordained hierarchy exists in its prophetic, priestly, and kingly *munera* to make announcement of the good news effectively. The Son is the *Logos*, the Word made flesh; in the Mass, that Son is present as the Word proclaimed and proclaiming. The lector acknowledges this fact when he concludes the reading, not in his own name, not with a footnote reference, not by common cause, but by referring to what has just transpired as "the word of the Lord". The assembly does not thank the reader, is not grateful to the reader for his instruction and kindly wishes, but instead exclaims out loud "Thanks be to God." Something more serious is going on than didactic instruction of the sort one could receive in school. The word of the Lord is being spoken because the Word of the Lord is speaking. That is why, in the absence of a deacon, the priest bows at the altar before going to the ambo and asks almighty God to cleanse his heart and lips in order worthily to proclaim a holy Gospel (holy good news), and at its conclusion either the deacon or priest quietly begs, "Through the words of the Gospel may our sins be wiped away." Serious business. The book is accompanied with candles and incense, as though Jesus himself were returning to Jerusalem, this time with honor. The Liturgy of the Word is not a matter of instruction, education, schooling; it is a matter of wiping away sins, cleansing hearts, our salvation. These latter benefits were accomplished on the Cross, so when the holy Gospel is announced, we trace its sign on forehead, lips, and breast. The holiness of the action of reading requires such a response. The Gospel we are about to hear is from Christ himself and should have an impact on our thoughts, speech, and will. The deacon or priest precedes this triple crossing with a sign of the cross on a book that he will kiss at the end, so when the people mark their lips, it is as if they were kissing the book from afar. The Scriptures are love letters. We are in love with Jesus, who is about to speak to us. Making the triple sign of the cross also indicates that we thoroughly belong to Jesus, who gave us a sign of his sovereignty at Baptism.

The Homily. The homily is part of the liturgical action, not an intermission during it, and therefore is as intimately tied to the activity of Christ as all other parts of the liturgy, even though the role of the human homilist might tempt us to forget it. Perhaps better than saying the Scriptures *are* the word of God, we could say that the Scriptures *contain* the Word of God: they are a manger in which the *Logos* is laid, and the homilist should not do a Bible study, even less should he call attention to what he opines. He should instead get out of the way so the crowd can elbow its way forward to see the Incarnate One, as did the shepherds and wise men when they arrived. The homily is a point when past meets present (how do the commands of God apply to us?) and when heaven meets earth (how does the eternal word apply to our temporal and current circumstance?). This takes time because our minds are usually running too rapidly. Therefore the instructions in the rubrics say to avoid haste, favor meditation, and observe a period of silence after the readings and at the conclusion of the homily. A human voice has been banging on our eardrum; we need the moment of silence for Christ's voice to enter our hearts.

The Creed. It is puzzling to the modern ear to hear the ancient Church refer to the Creed as a symbol—the Symbol of Faith. We think only material objects can be symbols. But symbol (from *sym+ballein*) throws two things together in an act of recognition, like halves of a coin split and now reunited, and when we profess the Creed, our faith is united to the collection of truths God has revealed. Therefore, the rubrics speak of the Creed as a response of the whole gathered people, a joining together with the readings just proclaimed from Scripture and expounded by the homily. That is why we are invited to sing the Creed as a solemn pronouncement of the rule of faith by which we live. The majority of the Nicene Creed concerns Jesus. According to the way lines are broken in the sacramentary, four lines are about the Father, four lines are about the Holy Spirit, and four lines are about the Church, but nineteen lines are about Jesus. As we recite the *mirabilia Dei* whose name is Jesus, it should be as if we can see him before all ages, consubstantial with God, coming down from heaven for us men and our salvation; and after he has been incarnated, we see him dying, rising, ascending, and enthroning at the right hand of the Father. "I believe"—I *must* believe—all these Church doctrines about Jesus if I am going to step over the threshold from the Liturgy of the Word to the Liturgy of the Eucharist. The Creed symbolizes the faith one must have in order to do what the Church has gathered to do, and if someone does not have that faith yet (e.g., a catechumen) or anymore (e.g., someone excommunicated), he is dismissed.

Preparation of the Gifts. What is about to occur could only be accomplished by the God-man, so when the deacon or priest pours water into the wine, he prays "By the mystery of this water and wine may we come to share in the divinity of Christ, who humbled himself to share in our humanity." The Divine Exchange is being confessed. The priest asks that his sacrifice and the laity's may be acceptable to God, and we know that even a humble spirit and contrite heart are not sufficient for making a satisfactory offering. The word comes from *satis* (enough) + *facere* (to make, do, perform), and no sinner can do enough to overcome the alienation from God he has caused. This would be a predicament were we making our own human sacrifice, by our own human power, in our own human religion. But thanks be to God, in the Sacrifice of the Mass about to occur, we find Christ both offered and offerer. He is Victim, and he is Priest. By his assurance we may confidently pray that the Lord will accept both the priest's sacrifice and ours, not by any other assurance.

Eucharistic Prayer. The hierarchy of the Trinity descends upon the altar without disruption of its form: *eucharistia* is given to the most merciful Father, through his Son, by an offering sanctified by the Holy Spirit. The most profound and intimate characteristic of Christianity is being disclosed: we worship the unknown Father through a known Son by means of an active Spirit he gave us. With his natural religion, man has an instinct to worship a deity; in Christianity, God has a human face. The prayer and action are directed to the Father because Jesus always directed himself to his Father, and now we are joining him. He provides us our liturgical orientation. The Father receives thanksgiving, acclamation, epiclesis, a narrative of the institution, anamnesis, oblation, intercessions, and doxology, but all this is done through Christ, with Christ, and in Christ, in the unity of the Holy Spirit. Christ did not punt his thanksgiving to us, ceasing any more to offer it and leaving us on our own. "I will not leave you desolate" (Jn 14:18). We have his commandments to keep, and if we love him, he will manifest himself to us and send the Helper in his name. A great multitude surrounds the Lord Jesus, including Mary, all the apostles and saints, the living and the dead, the whole of visible creation and the invisible angelic creation, and we who have just participated in this prayer have been given a place to stand in it during this fleeting Mass until our permanent place is fixed in our heavenly home.

Responses. In response to a prayer and sacrifice that are both thanksgiving and sanctification, a series of actions occur, all rising from, going to, and concerning Jesus. First, we are moved to pray the prayer he gave us. It is his command, and by divine teaching he formed and prepared us, so we now dare to say "Our Father", i.e., the Father of the Son and Holy Spirit and us. Second, a peace that the world has never known and cannot give (Jn 14:27) is passed around. Jesus left it with his apostles, and since God does not look on our sins but instead trains his eye on the faith of his Son's Church, the same peace will be granted to us. The faithful express a mutual charity they have in Christ before they go forward to eat him, and the Body and Blood of Christ are mingled while they offer the sign of peace. Third, the faithful break into song over the accomplishments of the Lamb of God, thrice repeating the most precious gift he bestows on us: "You take away the sins of the world, You take away the sins of the world, You take away the sins of the world." As a result, we can ask for mercy and peace. Fourth, we may take corporeal communion in the sacrifice just made. Look! the priest says. At what? The Lamb of God. Behold! Whom? The one who takes away the sins of the world. Where? Here, look at the Body of Christ being held slightly raised above the chalice. Do not look into the past, at the sky, upon your spiritual imagination, or even at the Book of the Gospels. Look at the Body and Blood, soul and divinity, the whole Christ truly, really, and substantially contained in unique mode under the Eucharistic species. Though we are not worthy for him to enter under our roof, he is coming home with us to heal our soul. We may now possess in purity of heart what has passed our lips as food and be healed for eternity.

Christ has not been idle during the Mass. Our prayers are made through the One who now lives and reigns with the Father and the Holy Spirit, one God, forever and ever, and the graces we receive are ones he won for us. Our reception of Jesus in Communion has triggered the entire liturgy, as Saint John Chrysostom's liturgy says: "Having partaken of the divine, holy, pure, immortal, heavenly, life-creating, and awesome Mysteries of Christ, let us worthily give thanks to the Lord."

Chapter 26

The Perfect Liturgist

The purpose of liturgy is traditionally defined as twofold: the glorification of God and the sanctification of man. (I will add that the latter is for the sake of the former. When the latter happens, then the former happens.) This is true both for sacraments in particular and liturgy in general. According to the *Catechism of the Catholic Church*, the sacraments express "the action of God who sanctifies men, and the action of men who offer worship to God" (1148), and the purpose of liturgical words and actions are for "the glory of God and the sanctification of the faithful" (1157). If we start from this twofold understanding of liturgy's purpose, then only one man who ever lived can be deemed a perfect liturgist. Had I the combined sanctity of Basil, Augustine, Leo, and John Damascene, I still could not be as perfect a liturgist as this man; had I the combined mysticism of Anthony, Gregory, Bernard, and Hildegard, I still could not be as perfect a liturgist as he; had I the combined sufferings of Stephen, Ignatius, Polycarp, and Agatha, I still could not be as perfect a liturgist as he. This perfect liturgist has passed through the heavens (Heb 4:14), offered a perfect canticle of praise to the Father in heaven, and then associated the entirety of mankind with this work of praise. This perfect liturgist gives a kind of glory to God that is beyond our natural human capacity, and then he further increases that glory by conjoining to himself sanctified brothers and sisters who augment the rising splendor. The titles given to this man outline his authority to liturgize God perfectly.

He is *the New Adam*, doing what the old Adam should have done, failed to do, and is now incapable of doing. The old Adam set himself as a rival to God and understood any glory given to God to be in competition with the glory he intended to reserve for himself.

Therefore, mankind abandoned the art of liturgical sacrifice. Fallen Adam finds worship imposing, exacting, onerous, laborious; he liturgizes grudgingly, reluctantly, and calculatingly, for self-advancement or self-promotion. That is why Baptism precedes the entire liturgical and sacramental life: because the old Adam must die before the liturgy of the new aeon can commence. The perfect liturgist must restore rectified worship to the human race.

He is *Lord of Life* because liturgy and life are concurrent and conjoined. Sin is amnesia; forgetfulness of God is death. The silence of Hades is a mark of damnation; the praise of heaven is a mark of salvation. In order to come to life again, a person must put the name of God upon his lips at all times, in all places, and in all circumstances, as this man did. A sign of biological life is motion; a sign of spiritual life is liturgy. Joining the perichoresis of the Trinity quickens one's substantiality. This man's liturgical union with his heavenly Father vitalized his mercy and ministry, his pity and preaching. This worshipful devotion had such contact with the divine vitality that it made even his death life-giving. He is not Lord of Life because he skipped death; he became Lord of Life when he overcame death.

He is *Lamb of God*, an offering, sacrifice, service, oblation, whose libated blood is our drink and whose nourishing flesh is our fare. The lamb's flesh burnt on the altar of incense ascends as an evening offering to fill the nostrils of God, and the lamb's flesh on the altar-table descends as viaticum to provision our journey to heaven. Because his flesh is the bread he gives to the world, he is also known as the *Bread of Life*. Our ancestors asked, hopefully, "Can God spread a table in the wilderness?" (Ps 78:19). Our wilderness of sin is more barren than the wilderness of Sinai, so on our lips the question carries even more urgency. Can God give bread or provide meat for his people when we are in such a dismal state? The Israelites were strangers in a strange land; we are strangers in a strange world. Can God feed us in our estranged and alienated slavery? The Lamb of God is the divine response to this question: I am the Bread of life; I came down from heaven to feed you; you will live forever; stop grumbling! (Jn 6:35, 41, 51).

He is the *Word made flesh*. He has dual residency. He belongs at the right hand of God Almighty and has chosen to be at our side. He has twin citizenship. It is his birthright to lead the liturgy in heaven, and his legacy is a liturgy led on earth. He does not simply send messages to memories through holy writ; he additionally pitches his tent on our own ground, takes up a place on our landscape, homesteads with us. The *Logos'* corporeality means he can go where we go, accompany us in body as well as in soul, and, although we are not worthy, he can enter under our roof and say the word that will heal our souls. The *Logos is* this word. He says himself. When the uncircumscribable is circumscribed, then the indescribable becomes describable in the words of prophets and apostles, and the Church is given speech for her liturgy. It is liturgy spoken in a divine language because the *Logos* has donated himself as liturgy-speech.

He is *Emmanuel*—literally, God with us. Literally, God incarnate. Literally, a son born of a virgin. God has pitched his tent (*eskenosen*, Jn 1:14) in our neighborhood. The mystery of the Trinity shows itself in every liturgy because God is the one to whom we go, by whom we go, and with whom we go. It is frightening to go into the holy place. Even Moses, God's favored one, was told that man shall not see God and live, and the best he could hope for then was to see God's backside after being told God's face could not be seen. Then—surprise—God became a face. Christianity is the only religion in which God became a face. For us men, and for our salvation, the second Person of the Trinity came down from heaven, and by the Holy Ghost and the Virgin Mary he took on human countenance. From now on, we can see God's human face. From now on, he will accompany us to our liturgical rendezvous with the Father. Without the perfect liturgist as escort, we would be standing on the wrong side of a chasm we dug with our many faults that cripple liturgy: sin, trespass, pride, disobedience, delinquency, unrighteousness, and ungodliness. The obstructions we have posed to liturgical proximity with God are deep and they are wide, but Emmanuel has passed over from the divine side to the human side, and when we are marked by the blood of his Pasch, we can pass over from the human side to the divine side and bring our liturgical praise into the courts of God.

He is *the Holy One* and necessary to us if we are going to conduct a liturgy in the Spirit whom the Father sent in his name. God will never be content with natural worship and natural religion because he wills us to act as children of a divine race who give supernatural worship and practice religion supernaturally. Anyone can worship;

everyone should worship; but not just anyone can commit liturgy. The liturgist must be baptized into the God-man. The liturgist must be holy. "Holy gifts for the holy people of God", says Saint John Chrysostom in his liturgy. Liturgists come through the narrow gate of Baptism to be unified with the Holy One. Liturgists are first made citizens of the chosen people, the royal priesthood, the holy nation, before they can liturgize God (1 Pet 2:9). Baptism grants power to dispossess ourselves (be crucified) and pass over into the hands of God (be resurrected). Such sacrifice depends on holiness; such oblation depends on holiness; and, if we are to make a liturgy out of our lives, such piety depends upon the Holy One. *De-pend* means "to hang from", and we must join Christ hanging from the Cross.

He is the *Son of Man* and *Son of God*. As Messiah, he saves what is lost (Mt 18:12–14), gives his life as a ransom (Mt 20:28), takes his place as Lord of the Sabbath (Mt 12:8), sows good seed (Mt 13:37), is condemned to death (Mt 20:18), rises on the third day (Mt 20:19), and will come with angels in the glory of his Father (Mt 16:27). No wonder the disciples were stymied when he gave them a pop quiz about who people say the Son of Man is. Peter rejects the multiple-choice answers of John the Baptist, Elijah, Jeremiah, or one of the prophets and identifies the Son of Man with the Christ, the Son of the living God (Mt 16:13–16). All known expectations about the Son of Man become connected to the Son of God by a revelation that did not come from flesh and blood but from the Father in heaven. So on Peter the rock he built his Church, and to Peter the rock he gave the keys of the Kingdom of heaven. So began obedience by countless Christians through the centuries to the liturgy he left in the Church's hands.

He is the *Good Shepherd*, whom strangers will not follow but whose voice his own sheep will recognize. He knows them. They know him. The shepherd and the sheep know each other because they spend time with each other. We can *read* the words of the Good Shepherd from the pages of the Bible, but we can *hear* the words of the Good Shepherd in the liturgy. Combined with his voicing of commandments and covenants is the sheep's voicing of jubilation and exultation. He will lay down his life for them, and the more they grow in grace, they will lay down their lives for him, daily. But all this requires attunement of ear so as not to fall for the voice of a stranger. That is why repeated pasturing is necessary every eighth day. That is why it is important to be led by his Cross and crozier to the green pastures beside the quiet waters of Baptism down paths of righteousness that are free from any fear of evil during this earthly shadow of death and be fed in the presence of defeated demons at a table with an overflowing cup promising goodness and mercy. The Good Shepherd desires his flock to dwell forever with him in the liturgical house of the Lord.

These are only a few of the titles of the perfect liturgist who perfectly performs the twin objectives of liturgy to glorify God and sanctify man. As the Son of Man, Jesus gives an adoration, piety, and love to the Father that is beyond our human ability. And as the Son of God, Jesus redeems, consecrates, and sanctifies sinners, which is beyond our human ability. His worship is unique because he is unique. But he is not solitary. His supreme will is that his sacrifice should be perpetuated by the Church in her ministers. When he left, he gave the Church charge of a praise perpetually offered in his name; he gave to his Bride his own power of adoring and praising the Father, and whenever the Church's liturgy rises to God, it is in union with Jesus, supported by Jesus, perfected by Jesus. It is his praise that passes through the lives of the Church, and therefore liturgy is not the performance of a human religion; liturgy is the religion of Christ—the religion he enacted in the flesh before the Father—perpetuated. He bequeathed to his Body and Bride what he accomplished in his sacred humanity and what he continues by his high priestly intercession at the right hand of the Father, what he makes possible by having requested an Advocate for us from the Father. The Church continues the glorifying and sanctifying work of the perfect liturgist.

Chapter 27

Liturgical Spiration

I glance up, look out the window, and say to myself, "It's windy outside." It is a cursory conclusion, but how did I come to it? I am indoors and feel no wind. So I think to myself that, although I do not feel the wind, I can see it. But that is odd. What does wind—alone, by itself—look like? Cup your hands: you are holding air, but what does it look like? Does putting air in motion make it more visible? So I think that although I do not feel or see the wind, I can hear it. But that is odd. What does wind—alone, by itself—sound like? Wind is moving air. Does putting air in motion make it audible? Gradually it comes clear that what I am doing when I conclude from an indoor seat that it is windy outside is detecting the *effects* of the wind. I cannot *see* the wind go by, as I could see a man or a motorcar go by; I cannot *hear* the wind go by, as I could hear a siren or a marching band go by. Rather, I see the effect of the wind on the tree branches, and I hear the result of the wind in the tree leaves.

Now glance up, look around, and say to yourself, "The Holy Spirit is here." Another cursory statement, and how did you come to this conclusion? Jesus puts the metaphor of wind to another use. "The wind blows where it wills, and you hear the sound of it, but you do not know where it comes from or where it goes; so it is with every one who is born of the Spirit" (Jn 3:8). The Holy Spirit does not draw attention to himself, so it is more appropriate to say, as we did about the wind outside, that we sense the Holy Spirit's *effects*. Like the wind, the Holy Spirit eludes direct experience and is known by his energies: wisdom, understanding, counsel, fortitude, knowledge, piety, fear of the Lord, charity, joy, peace, patience, kindness, goodness, generosity, gentleness, faithfulness, modesty, self-control, and chastity are all like so many leaves by which the Spirit gives evidence of himself when he blows through our lives. The effects seem empirical, in a loose sort of way. We detect lives changed and loves exchanged and behaviors altered. At those deeper levels—levels of love and conviction and virtues—we are sensing the effects of the Holy Spirit, and perhaps the more leaves of virtues we sprout, the more evidence of the Spirit we shall have. Bare souls, like bare trees, give little evidence of moving wind.

Consider another example. You are looking at the page of this book, a piece of paper with black ink smudges on it. There is light in the room, or else you could not see the page. Now an experiment: do not look at the page but at the light *between* your eye and the page. Do not look at any object in the room around you, but only at the light in the room. You cannot, because we do not look at light, we look *by means of* light. This was so evident to ancient ophthalmologists that they spoke of an eyebeam coming forth from the eye, crossing the distance of the room, and seizing objects to imprint a mental copy in the mind. We cannot see sunlight; by sunlight we see. This is applicable to the Holy Spirit in that we cannot see him, but there are things we can only see by means of him. "No one can say [or see] 'Jesus is Lord' except by the Holy Spirit" (1 Cor 12:3). "Whatever [the Spirit of truth] hears he will speak, and he will declare to you the things that are to come. He will glorify me, for he will take what is mine and declare it to you" (Jn 16:13–14). Paul gives thanks for the faith of the saints in Ephesus and prays "that the God of our Lord Jesus Christ, the Father of glory, may give you a spirit of wisdom and of revelation in the knowledge of him, having the eyes of your hearts enlightened" (Eph 1:17–18). It is as if the Christians were given spiritual eyebeams.

You are looking at a criminal, on a Cross atop the hill, crucified and scorned, yet you see the Lord Jesus Christ, King of the Universe. He has his own solemnity each year for those who can see him in the right light. You cannot see the light that lets you know him as Lord, but you would not know him as Lord without this light. There was a sequence for Pentecost that begged "Holy Spirit, Lord of Light, from Thy clear celestial height, Thy pure beaming radiance give / ... Light immortal! Light divine! Visit Thou these hearts of Thine, and our inmost being fill."

Christ sends the Spirit, yes, but the Spirit also sends Christ. We are more accustomed to the former because he promised to do so

(Jn 14:16) and then did (Acts 2:1–4), but we should also remember the activity of the Holy Spirit in the life of Jesus, sending him and testifying to him. Confining ourselves to the evangelist Luke alone, we find that the Holy Spirit overshadowed the Virgin Mary and that her child would be called holy, the Son of God (Lk 1:35); he worked Jesus' first recognition by cousin John *in utero* and inspired his mother, Elizabeth, to bless the fruit of Mary's womb (Lk 1:42); he filled John's father, Zechariah, who then prophesied that the horn of salvation had now been raised up (Lk 1:67–69); he came upon Simeon and opened his eyes to see light for the Gentiles and glory to Israel (Lk 2:25–32); he descended upon Jesus in bodily form at the Jordan, commissioning him for public ministry (Lk 3:22); he led Jesus, now full of him, into the wilderness for forty days (Lk 4:1–2); in his power, Jesus returned, causing a report to go out to the countryside (Lk 4:14); he came upon Jesus and anointed him to preach good news and proclaim the year of the Lord (Lk 4:18–19); in him Jesus rejoiced that his Father had revealed hidden things to infants (Lk 10:21); the spiritual cloud overshadowed Jesus again on Tabor, with a voice from heaven reminiscent of the Jordan episode (Lk 9:34–35); Jesus said anyone who blasphemes against him will not be forgiven (Lk 12:10); and Jesus gave promise that the Spirit will teach the apostles what to say (Lk 12:12), which came to pass in the second volume of Luke (Acts 2).

The Spirit's work in the Only Begotten Son of God is different from the Spirit's work on us, nonetheless, he does something for us that is akin to what he did in Jesus. Not the very same, of course. And yet, and yet, "the Spirit himself [bears] witness with our spirit that we are children of God" (Rom 8:16). Men and women are made adopted sons in the Son. "Because you are sons, God has sent the Spirit of his Son into our hearts, crying, 'Abba! Father!'" (Gal 4:6). Therefore, men and women have a share in the filial relationship Jesus has with the Father, and this is the relationship that the Spirit brings to bloom in human beings. And it determines our liturgizing. Thus the Son and Spirit—*logos* and *ruach*—work mutually. Here is an experiment to reveal their synergy. Inhale, hold that breath, and now mouth the Lord's Prayer with lips and tongue but without exhaling: there is no speech. Now take a breath and exhale, open-mouthed, without chopping the flow of air by larynx, lips, and tongue: there is no speech. Word and breath must work together for speech to happen. Similarly, for our liturgical speech, *logos* and *ruach* must work together. We are in Christ, Christ is in us, forming words of worship, but the Spirit must also be breathing out of us if we are to speak those liturgical words. We do not liturgize under our own power, but under the power of the Most High who will overshadow us (which is why Mary is our model for liturgy; see her chapter). Only when the second and third Persons of the Trinity act together in us can we speak liturgically.

The Holy Spirit must *in-spire* us for liturgy: breathe into us. He and we *con-spire* when we jointly confess that Jesus is Lord. Charity is *ex-pired* by the liturgical lungs of the Church because the Holy Spirit breathes life into the behavior of the person as that person leaves the temple's liturgy. The pneumatic respiration we do in the liturgy oxygenates our souls and bodies for piety and politics.

The movement of branches is a sign of the wind blowing, and I propose that the movement of liturgy is a sign of the Holy Spirit spirating. Do you want evidence of the Holy Spirit? Come to the liturgy and see sinners transfigured, elements transubstantiated, time transcended, sacrifices transacted, saints translated, and life transversed. The Holy Spirit's liturgical activity is to bring the People of God across, beyond, to the other side of where they currently stand. He has his own sacramental kenoses. The second Person of the Trinity dwelt in the flesh, and the third Person of the Trinity dwells in the sacraments of the Mystical Body, as the *Catechism* points out. Baptism is a sign of birth into divine life, and by one Spirit we are all baptized (694); Confirmation equips for service through spiritual anointing that configures us to Jesus, whom the Holy Spirit established as Christ, the "Anointed One" (695); in the Eucharist, the Holy Spirit manifests the risen Lord, recalling his word and opening our minds, so as supremely to make present the mystery of Christ (737); Anointing of the Sick gives a particular gift of the Holy Spirit that renews trust and faith in God at a moment of temptation or anguish (1520); the sacrament of Penance experiences the reconciliation the Father accomplished by the death and Resurrection of Christ and accomplishes by sending the Holy Spirit among us for the forgiveness of sins (1449); the Marriage covenant is sealed by the Holy Spirit, who is source of love and renewed fidelity (1624); and in all three degrees of

Orders, the Holy Spirit is outpoured and gifts proper to the ministry bestowed (1573). The epiclesis "is at the heart of each sacramental celebration" (1106).

If an extinguished candlewick sends up a column of smoke and a flaming match is inserted into the smoke, even several inches above the wick, a flame will reappear upon the wick. The eye will not see the fire travel, but the wick will be instantly relit by fire that has traveled the path of the smoke. One thinks of this phenomenon when one sees an altar server kneeling before the altar with incense during the Eucharistic Prayer. A nice column of smoke rises in front of the altar, in front of the priest standing there, and the Church's epicletic prayer rises before God like a column of incense, and in a flash the Holy Spirit comes down: upon the priest, upon the altar, upon the gifts, upon the people. Pentecost all over again. Synergy: the smoke does not cause the fire, but the ascending liturgical prayer is a path by which the Holy Spirit freely comes to us.

Chapter 28

The Holy Spirit's Seven Gifts for Liturgy

The Church wants every Christian to have a personal Pentecost in the form of an illumination of the Holy Spirit that enters heart and *nous*. Augustine said the Holy Spirit is to the Body of Christ what the soul is to a human body. A corpse lacks movement when it is dead, and our souls are cadavers if they do not stir liturgically under the seven gifts of the Holy Spirit. Drawing upon the revelation given to the prophet Isaiah, the Church recognizes seven gifts the Holy Spirit brings with him when he enters: fear of the Lord, piety, knowledge, fortitude, counsel, understanding, and wisdom. The seven gifts belong in their plenitude to Christ because he was endowed with them as true man, but Christ next shares these gifts freely with other members of his Mystical Body by sending the Spirit to infuse every Christian with a permanent endowment that makes the believer grow in holiness and become fit for heaven. I propose that we may consider the gifts of the Holy Spirit as necessary apparatus for liturgy. (The opening definition of each in what follows is a summary taken from Thomas Aquinas.) The seven gifts empower believers to act in a holy, deified way, which is required for making liturgy, so we would like to examine them one by one.

The *Gift of Fear of the Lord* causes a person to avoid sin out of chaste fear. Respect for the sanctity of God moves the creature to give glory to his Creator. True fear of God arises from reverence and love for him. This is very different from a false form of fear that prays with anxiety and tries to placate God out of fear of punishment. Anyone who sings songs of praise in such a frame of mind is a hypocrite, but the fear of the Lord can be perfected by the Holy Spirit in order to advance someone toward perfect liturgy. Servile fear is perfected as filial fear. Pure liturgy only arises from a fear caused by love and

respect for God, as the fear a child has for his parents is more pure than
the fear of a servant because it is moved by gratitude caused by love
and respect. Such reverence is the foundational floor upon which all
liturgy must be built, or else the whole liturgy will be unstable and
unsound. Liturgy is contingent upon conversion, and the fear of God
that leads to conversion is always a simultaneous movement toward
God and withdrawal from evil. Liturgy and morality are mated movements. The soul feels adoration toward God, aversion toward sin, and
charity toward the neighbor. Fear of the Lord instructs us about our
dependence upon God, which awakens awe at his majesty, which in
turn refines and clarifies the glory we render. Fear of the Lord causes
humility and obedience, without which liturgy cannot be celebrated.
In this sense, Jesus himself had the gift of fear of the Lord! He obeyed
his Father's will that led him through the valley of the anguish of the
Passion on the Cross. This gift enhances hope, and our liturgy must
be done in faith, hope, and love.

The *Gift of Piety* is revering God with filial affection. Its very name
indicates that it is relevant to liturgical worship. We have a duty
to God, and to all men on account of their relationship to God.
The only question is whether we can ever show God the kind of
honor and devotion that he deserves? The gift of piety differentiates true liturgy from idolatry. Aristotle said justice is giving another
his due; Thomas applied this definition to explain religion as giving
God what God is due, as God; the gift of liturgical piety perfects our
natural human religion. What we are now able to give God from
our hands is an oblation that his Only Begotten Son placed there.
It is a more perfect piety because it is a supernatural act. We cannot
give true worship to a false god. And since we are prone to falsify
God, our very approach to God must be fixed by the Spirit and not
by ourselves. The Holy Spirit grants us a capacity to pay God the
kind of homage that is appropriate to God (*latria*) because it is a share
in Christ's piety, who, as God-man, honors his Father in the most
fitting way. The gift of piety is a practical participation in the Sonship
of Jesus, which is the pious radiance with which our liturgies should
be filled. We do our liturgy as adopted sons and daughters in Christ.
Then follows a consequence. If we reverence God as loving Father,
we must respect his children, whoever and wherever they are. The
virtue of justice gives God his due religion, and then the virtue of

justice gives the neighbor his due kindness because if anyone says he loves God but hates his brother, he is a liar (1 Jn 4:20). The obligation of piety toward God brings with it an obligation of charity toward anyone whom God loves—which is everyone. This is one love with two objects. Holy piety calls us to justice, and liturgy calls us to solicitude for others. The tradition has always said (most effectively in John Chrysostom) that we must offer our sacrifice both on the altar table and on the altar of the poor.

The Gift of Knowledge is the ability to judge correctly about matters of faith and action. A person judges the truths of faith rightly by this gift, and liturgy must be done "faithfully". An ambiguity is intentional: I mean the liturgy must be done devotedly, reliably, dependably, but first of all I mean the liturgist must be filled with faith. The proclamation of the Gospel caused our conversion, and now the Spirit develops in us a more penetrating assent to the faith that started us off. This means seeing the truths of faith as more than facts or platitudes or proverbs and, rather, seeing the truths of faith as gates to eternal life and Christian perfection. Such knowledge is both practical and theoretical, as is liturgy. This knowledge differentiates between what is and is not consistent with faith, which means it is a requisite for differentiating between what is and is not consistent with liturgy. Spiritual knowledge is illumination more than it is analysis, which means the simple believer equipped with this gift can sometimes know more about liturgy than the scholar. The simple believer can have a supernatural instinct for authentic liturgy since the saints possess sure judgment in matters of faith and practice. This penetrating assent to truth is required if we are going to make true liturgy. What will be proclaimed in Scripture and hymn and icon and symbol and sacrament must be received with spiritual insight. There is one more relevant connection between this gift of knowledge and liturgy. In liturgy we use creation, and this gift of the Spirit allows us to comprehend cosmos correctly. If our finite life is corrupted by sin, we will misperceive finite things as things for our exploitation. We will fail to look through the creation to the Creator and instead lapse into worldliness. But the gift of knowledge protects our liturgy from profanity. The gift of knowledge puts creation on display as theophanic testimony, and we can see matter sacramentally. The gift of knowledge harmonizes with liturgy by placing the cosmic creation against its true, eternal horizon so that we can judge how earthly things are related to eternal life and Christian perfection. This gift produces effects of introspection, detachment from the material things, and repentance for the misuse of things—all necessary gifts for the liturgist.

The *Gift of Fortitude* is a firmness of mind in doing good and avoiding evil. It brings the natural virtue of fortitude to perfection. It fortifies and reinforces our courage with a supernatural strength infused by God. With this gift, a person is able to endure pain and suffering, resist evil, and persevere to everlasting life. On this side of Judgment Day, our liturgy is a song sung in a foreign land (Ps 137:4), far away from our hoped for Zion. Liturgy is not flight from the world—it is the balm of hope we need by the waters of Babylon. Liturgy is a firmness of mind and spirit against the cosmic powers of this present darkness (Eph 6:12). Liturgy is a secret spring of oil that keeps the lamp lit. Liturgy is a secret foretaste of the beatitude that gives us the hope that nerves fortitude. Liturgy is a temporal anticipation of eternity, the eighth day in the midst of the seven, and as such it draws upon the supernatural confidence this gift provides. The gift of fortitude enables the liturgist to hurl songs of joy against affliction, confidence against despair, assurance against doubt, trust against uncertainty, life against death, songs of resurrection against the crosses we now bear. Christ has trampled down death by his death, and the Holy Spirit gives us endurance until Hades cracks for good. At the darkest point, liturgy prays with fortitude: "Eternal rest grant unto them, O Lord, and let perpetual light shine upon them." What we are talking about, of course, is patience. Our impatience is remedied by God, not by our own efforts. (This is fortunate, since we become impatient with our impatience!) Liturgical kneeling is a posture of fortitude. There should to be no cessation of liturgy across our lives. Its constant presence accompanies us up to the point of passage to eternal life, and beyond. The gift of fortitude trains us in sacrifice, increasing its scale and exertion in our lives. Fortitude makes faith venerable, something only accomplished by the twin sisters of patience and obedience.

The *Gift of Counsel* allows a person to be directed by God in matters necessary for his salvation. It is a gift of docility, which is not high on the list of desires by modern people but which delights the liturgist. *Docilitas* is the ability to take advice, sprung not from false modesty but from the desire for real understanding. It requires a silence in the person that is a prerequisite to perceiving reality. This is a silence the liturgy should practice constantly. Docility is ingredient to the cardinal virtue of prudence, but while natural prudence operates under the enlightenment of reason, the gift of counsel brings prudence to perfection by operating under the guidance of the Holy Spirit. Prudence needs perfecting because in modern language it has taken on a quality of reservation, synonymous with judiciousness, caution, wariness. To the contrary, the Holy Spirit will often counsel what looks unwise in the eyes of the world, like recklessness in mercy and impulsiveness in love. This is because our ego usually conditions prudence to ask whether a certain act will lead to our own happiness, while the gift of counsel leads a person to ask whether a certain act will lead to holiness. Will this act lead to heaven? Liturgy contains an itinerary to heaven. Counsel listens to an interior spiritual voice instead of to external advice or heady reason, and to make sure we are not listening to ourselves, our ears must be trained by liturgy. Liturgy's repetitive recitation of God's ways and commandments will teach us whose voice to listen for. Man is in a constant state of searching; the liturgical life is a counseled search for deification.

The *Gift of Understanding* is penetrating insight into the heart of things, and most especially into those higher truths that are necessary for our eternal salvation. It is the ability to "see" God, which we do through all the devices that liturgy uses. We may say it bestows a "liturgical intuition" that moves beyond the surface to the substance. When the gift of understanding discloses the hidden meaning of Sacred Scripture, it allows the typological reading of symbols and figures and events, and when this gift discloses the hidden meaning of liturgy, it allows the mystagogical reading of sacraments and signs and symbols. The liturgy is a privileged place where these two sapiential aptitudes—typology and mystagogy—occur cooperatively and existentially. The gift of understanding shows God at work in our lives in all events, pleasant or painful, by revealing the spiritual ends toward which all events tend. God has only one purpose in mind for us, and it is a liturgical one: so to sanctify us that we can glorify him. He has this purpose because he himself wants to be understood, and only love can understand love. The Holy Spirit gives a supernatural light that pierces the finite boundaries in which we live and shows the true meaning of the path we walk. We are called to eternal beatific communion with God in the liturgy of the heavenly Jerusalem, and the gift of understanding provides us with a right appraisal of that ultimate end so that we may align all our human deeds now in relation to it. In our current pilgrim condition, we are still on the way to purity of heart, which is to will one thing, and by this gift we perceive what that one thing should be. The reason we rejoice in liturgy is because we comprehend our final good.

The *Gift of Wisdom* is judgment about divine things and the ability to judge and direct human affairs according to divine truth. That divine truth is proposed in Scripture and Creed, and in the Orthodox liturgy, it is the deacon's job to poke us in the ribs to listen for it. At the entrance prayer, he says "Wisdom. Arise"; before identifying the epistle reading, he says "Wisdom. Let us be attentive"; to prepare believers for the reading of the Gospel, he says, "Wisdom. Arise. Let us hear the holy Gospel. Peace be with all"; at the Prayer of the Faithful, he again calls for Wisdom; and immediately before the Symbol of Faith, he announces "In wisdom, let us be attentive!" The liturgy is conducted in wisdom, which is only to say that it is conducted in the Holy Spirit, who is the principal liturgist. With this gift, even someone considered theologically uneducated can have great theological insight into the Christian truths celebrated in liturgy. Wisdom is a rudder to liturgy. There are so many other causes and rulers we are tempted to serve, so many idols who make idle promises. Wisdom rescues us from them and inspires connatural contemplation of divine things. It rises from loving union with God by which we may, in turn, see and evaluate all things from his point of view, a God's-eye point of view. To give true worship to the true God requires true wisdom, and this must come from a higher source than our own minds. In turn, wisdom gives us the ability to direct our human affairs according to divine truth. Wisdom is the bridge from cultic, sacramental, public liturgy to mystical, spiritual, personal liturgy. Liturgical asceticism orders our relationship to the created world because wisdom weighs reality properly. Piety makes wisdom manifest because we pray what we believe, reverence, and adore. Charity makes wisdom manifest because we peacefully love our neighbor and have arranged everything in tranquility.

We conclude by observing that all seven of these gifts protect us from idolatry and lead us to true and truthful liturgy.

ECCLESIOLOGY

Chapter 29

The Church's Abcedarium

And the Church said:

A
A for agape, the power of love
I received from the Father by Son and by Dove.
A is for Adam, from whose seed forlorn
will arise all my children after being twice born.
A is for Altar, a lavish-set board:
new manna for man, a true feast on my Lord.
A is for angel, celestial companion
whose liturgy's sung this side of death's canyon.
A is for the ascetics I find
in both desert and city enjoying new mind.
A is for Adam, the first man who fell;
destined for heaven, he risked life in hell.
A for apostate, deserting my Creed,
forsaking all life-giving help that they need.
A is for Advent. Oh, let us begin!
a year full of grace God has hidden herein.

B
B is for Bethlehem, city of bread:
which housed without honor my King and my Head.
B is both Body and Bride: two allowed
to name my full union with Christ my espoused.
B is for Bible, words apostles did write,
with tradition united I can share the full light.
B is for blessing, my duty and joy

to grant grace to mankind and Satan annoy.
B is for vision, beatific someday
when faith will erupt and God's face we'll survey.
B is for Body and Blood and the Bread
which I serve altogether to raise men from the dead.

C

C is *my* letter, the same as for 'cross';
by its power alone I redeem mankind's loss.
C is for Chalice, a cup full of blood:
I serve to my children the Lamb's sanguine flood.
C is Communion I have in two kinds:
with God under bread and with all of mankind.
C is for catechumens I've carried
preparing them for death in the font to be buried.
C is for catholic, which on Peter's barque
unites as my one, holy, apostolic mark.
C is for chrism, an oil that I spread
to strengthen believers now risen from the dead.
C is for Canon, all things holding fast:
the Scripture, a law, or the Creed, or the Mass.

D

D is for Devil, the most ancient foe
who seeks to afflict my sad children with woe.
D is for Death, a beast let off chain
causing sorrow and mourning, my children's worst bane.
D is for Deacon, my cleric who serves
in the pattern of Jesus, who new life preserves.
D is for Dogma, the most certain truth
that overcomes age and gives minds their new youth.

E

E is for Eve, the mother of life
who instead gave her children a share of her strife
E is for Eucharist, heavenly bread
which angels desire but mankind is fed.
E is the End, the great Eschaton

toward which I move history, its full paragon.
E is Exsultet—I can't still my voice:
with glorious lightning my buildings rejoice.

F
F is for Faith, a first-given gift
bestowed by a Spirit both Holy and swift.
F is for Font, a place to expunge
sins original and personal by conversional plunge.
F is for Feast: occasions to celebrate
when I with devotion will creation consecrate.
F, Filioque—my two halves still bicker;
on coming to terms I wish they were quicker.

G
G for *Gaudete*, a song of full praise;
with reverence, rejoicing, bright glory I raise.
G is for Graveside, where we make our homes
so long as we suffer this wound in our bones.
G is for *Gnosis*, a wisdom unknown
unless it should come to mankind from God's throne.
G is for Glory, when at our repose
our reason for being will finally disclose.
G is for Grace, a balm I receive
to bestow to all sinners who come and believe.

H
H is for Hope, a second-given gift
that fills even sinners with heavenward drift.
H is for Hades, once fearful and dread,
now conquered and trampled and peaceful instead.
H is for Hierarchy, the ladder of God
by which I near heaven, forgiven and awed.
H is for Hypostatic, a union unique
to the God-man named Jesus, God's saving technique.
H is for Heresy, too, I'm afraid:
when I am not careful my children have strayed.

I

I for Incarnate, the way it was done
to make out of a sinner new daughter or son.
I for Infallible Church without error
Holy Spirit in guard o'er all I am bearer.
I for Iniquity, wicked, unjust
a condition of man I see with disgust.
I is Idolatry, a lost, darkened state
created by Satan's deceptive fruit bait.
I is for Image of God, never lost
despite sin's corruption and death's high-priced cost.

J

J is for Jesus, my Lord, though concealed,
by whose sufferings and stripes I was forever healed.
J is Jerusalem, God's great templed city
on earth and in heaven, both homelands of pity.

K

K is for *Kapporeth*, the ark's mercy seat
which now enthrones Christ on the altar I meet.
K is *Kenosis*, God's bending of heaven
to give the forlorn a new portion of leaven.
K is for Kerygma, in the Gospel contained;
its preaching my task till the end be maintained.

L

L is for Love, a third-given gift
that sieves out my pride through a spiritual sift.
L is for Liturgy, my holiest act
with which I join heaven by sacrament's pact.
L for *Latria*, the worship reserved
for God only Mighty; none other deserved.
L is for Lamb, sacrificial and pure,
who from upraised Cross brings forth sin's final cure.
L is for Lent, my season of mourning
to prepare for the Paschal day's bright-clad adorning.

M

M is for Mary, the heavenly Queen
in whom my own future-lived bliss can be seen.
M is for Mass, my most glorious function:
miraculous heavenly-earthly conjunction.
M is for Matins: my morning begins
as loud lauding Psalms beg forgiving of sins.
M, Magisterium, my teaching authority,
to sound through the ages my Lord's own sonority.
M is for Martyr, the witnesses strewn
behind my advance to the heavenly noon.
M for Memorial, a great anamnesis
never presented without strong epiclesis.

N

N is for Noah, who took on his ark
those saved from the judgment, like Peter's own barque.
N is Novena, because sometimes I find
I must repeat prayers to express my full mind.
N is *novissimus*, but hard to decide
if it means newest or last about heaven's inside.

O

O is for *Opus Dei*, whose most divine work
is really the labor of my ordained clerk.
O is Oblation, my calling and life;
an action done always, in joy or in strife.
O is for Only Begotten, the Son
who grants us endurance in his race to run.

P

P is for Piety, a trait of my heart:
devotion and reverence and life set apart.
P is for Priesthood, belonging to three:
Christ Jesus the High Priest, his clerics, and me.
P is for Peter, whose confession was made
the keys of the Kingdom, my rock firmly laid.

P is for Pentecost, a tempestuous day
when tongues of the Spirit gave each man his say.
P is for Prayer, my very lifeblood;
my praises uprise and God's graces inflood.
P is for Pope, the vicar of Christ,
who oversees life from Him sacrificed.
P is for Providence, a mystery sublime
that demands I prefer God's will over mine.

Q
Q is for Quiet, hesychastic calm stillness
that lets me find finally a cure for my illness.
Q is for Quelle, the Q source it's called
by scholars who research the Gospel first scrawled.
Q is for Quicken, an act I accomplish
when by font and askesis I am Christ's accomplice.
Q for Qahal, an assembly divine
done at Sinai, Jerusalem, and time beyond time.

R
R is the power of Resurrected new life
shared with me daily, his body, his wife.
R is for *Res*, the sacrament's end
after *tantum* and *et* so my children can mend.
R is for Regeneration Christ gives
to all held in Hades as buried captives.

S
S is for Suffering, one of my states;
Triumphant and Militant are my other two fates.
S is for Sacrament, earth's thinly veiled
contact twixt spirit and matter most frail.
S is for Sinners, of whom I am made,
and yet we are welcomed to heaven, when bade.
S is for Shepherds, with which I am filled:
ordained pastors of Jesus with love he has filled.
S is for Symbol, of which liturgy's made

when my daily oblation on the altar is laid.
S is for Sacrifice, one and the same
whether bloody or bloodless, done in the Lamb's name.

T
T is for Tabor, where first showed the light
to find a safe way through a sinful, dark night.
T is for Tabor, where glory was shown
to apostles for whom it thus far wasn't known.
T for Theotokos, the most holy one
whose felicitous *fiat* salvation has won.
T is for Trinity, perichoresis in motion
that welcomes us in with worship's devotion.
T for a big one: Transubstantiation
of elements prepping our beatification.

U
U is for Union with God the most Holy,
who raises us up by himself become lowly.
U is for Urns, containers of oil
for chrism, ordaining, and healing sin's spoil.

V
V is for Victory, as Christ enjoys now
having finally repaired Eden's life giving bough.
V is for Vigil, because sometimes I pray
from morning till night or from night until day.
V is for Vespers, each daytime to close:
with *Magnificat* of Mary, the Mystical Rose.

W
W for Wisdom! "O let us attend"
my deacon cries out; the reading prehend.
W is Wisdom, Sophia in Greek,
who for the perplexed offers help as they seek.
W is Worship, and may it be done
under ritual and sacrament and new life begun.

X

X is for *chi*, the Greek letter you know
abbreviates Christmas and Christ and *chi rho*.
X also recalls *Ex Opere Operato*:
the action's not mine, it is God's to behold.

Y

Y is for Yahweh, who is the I Am
and like Abram would offer his Son as a Lamb.

Z

Z is for Zechariah, whose *Benedictus* I sing
in praise and thanksgiving each morn to my King.

Chapter 30

The Mystical Liturgical Body

The Dogmatic Constitution on the Church, *Lumen gentium*, can be read as a liturgical dogmatic constitution when it suggests scriptural metaphors for the Church that bear liturgical interpretation. The Lord Jesus set the Church on her course of preaching the good news (5), and now she strides through history as a sheepfold, a vineyard, the house of God, our mother, the spotless spouse, pilgrims in a foreign land, and Christ's Body (6–7). The Church is God's workshop where he fashions saints. The Church is a Bethel (house of God) and a Bethlehem (house of bread). The Church is the restoration by God and the reception by men of the original and eternal destiny of creation itself. All these identities have liturgical characteristics, and we shall look at the metaphors *Lumen gentium* mentions one by one.

1. The Church is a *liturgical sheepfold*. The sheep obey the Good Shepherd and follow him out of the valley of the shadow of death to feed in green pastures, being comforted by his rod and staff, the Cross. In liturgy, the sheep must keep their eyes fixed on the Cross as well as the throne if they are going to keep their steps steady and be saved from meandering through political ideologies, social modalities, philosophical schools. Without the Shepherd, the sheep will divide, then divert, then disjoin. They must obey their Shepherd and do as he says, and what he says to do is to glorify his Father in heaven. The Father knows him, he knows the Father; he knows his sheep, his sheep know him—Jesus is the Mediator between man and God, and he lays down his life to keep his sheep safely in that relationship. The sacrifice of their Shepherd is the same offering the sheep commemorate in the Sacrifice of the Mass. He is always present in his sheepfold, now offering through the ministry of his priests.

The sheep are led to this liturgy by the Shepherd, because it is his liturgy shared with his sheep. Why else do we pray that the priest's sacrifice and ours may be acceptable to God, the almighty Father (the Order of Mass); that the Father would bless these gifts, these offerings, these holy and unblemished sacrifices (Eucharistic Prayer I); that the Bread of life and the Chalice of salvation be offered to God in memorial of the Savior's death and Resurrection (Eucharistic Prayer II); that from the rising of the sun to its setting a pure sacrifice may be made to his name (Eucharistic Prayer III); that the very Sacrifice that God has provided for his Church would truly become a living sacrifice (Eucharistic Prayer IV)? We so pray in order to ask the compassionate Father to grant that, by the power of the Holy Spirit, we may be gathered into one Body as we partake of this one Bread and one Chalice (Eucharistic Prayer for Reconciliation I). We beg the Shepherd to fashion us for himself as an eternal gift. The Father descends to us through Jesus; we ascend through Jesus to the Father. What transpires Christologically is celebrated liturgically. Forgiveness, grace, mercy, clemency, and sanctification descend to the sheep through the Shepherd in Scripture and sacrament, and then arise thanksgiving, acclamation, honor, laud and hymning through the same Shepherd, in the Holy Spirit.

2. The Church is a *liturgical vineyard*. Liturgy is the crop grown in this vineyard. No, better: liturgy is the wine made out of the liturgists who are grown on the vine in this vineyard. The Church does a lot of work forming liturgists: she announces the good tidings of salvation, converts sinners from their ways, preaches faith and penance, prepares her children for the sacraments, teaches them to observe what Christ has commanded, and invites them to works of charity, piety, and the apostolate (*Sacrosanctum concilium* 9). From these liturgists, prepared each according to his deepest need, the wine of liturgy can be pressed. The wine of liturgy is the summit toward which the fruits of these labors are directed. The Church exists because she has been cultivated and tilled by the paternal vinedresser.

We do not create our own field; we do not construct our own vine: we are planted in God's tillage. We liturgize no longer in a desert but from a lush vineyard. Whatever worship someone could accomplish under his own power, whether solo or in community, will never attain the state of liturgy the Church accomplishes under the Holy Spirit's power. Every liturgist is attached to the true vine from whom he receives life. In the same way that no branch can bear fruit except by the power that flows through the vine, so also no liturgy can bear fruit except by branching off of Christ. No sapling in this yard has planted itself. Every branch comes from the graft in Christ's side, opened by the soldier's spear. Liturgy must bear fruit, and every liturgist who does not will be taken away (Jn 15:2). Our aptitude for worship depends upon spiritual pruning; our liturgical life depends upon a liturgical asceticism that issues in the moral life and pursuit of the virtues. Liturgy requires abiding in the vine, for by this God the Father is glorified (Jn 15:8). The plants require spiritual irrigation, so the Holy Spirit descends like a dewfall. In the wilderness, when the dew evaporated, there was bread to eat (Ex 16:14). So also here.

One of Christ's most precious endowments to his Bride is the gift of epiclesis. We come here to make anamnesis and epiclesis over bread and wine. Christ takes over our visible act and gives it a power and worth beyond what it would possess if left in our hands alone. In order to discern this, one must have eyes of faith that see the divine invisible work underneath our human visible activity. A sacrament is when one thing is seen but another thing is understood. The Church is a sacrament because one thing is seen by the world, but faith understands more.

3. The Church is a *liturgical house of God*. The stone rejected by other builders has become the cornerstone of a permanent and unyielding edifice. It is the house of God over which the great Priest rules (Heb 10:21), and within this house green olive trees flourish (Ps 52:8). It is built from twelve stones set up by Joshua (Jesus) in the midst of the Jordan where the feet of the priests bearing the ark of the covenant had stood (Josh 4:9). Scripture says they are there to this day, but we also know that these twelve stones lie at the bottom of every baptismal font because it is the point of passage into the promised land. It is Gilgal, where twelve stones taken out of the Jordan were set up so that when children ask their fathers "What do these stones mean?" they can be told "Israel passed over this Jordan on dry ground" (Josh 4:21–22). When our children ask "What does this Church mean?" they can be told "Christ passed through death, and we have set up this memorial." Jacob put a memorial stone at the foot

of a ladder to heaven, upon which angels descended and ascended (Gen 28:18). A new ladder was footed in Bethlehem, a longer ladder, one that reaches to an even higher heaven.

The stone that the builders rejected has become the cornerstone (Mt 21:42) of a house with doors on all sides for the traffic of liturgists from all nations. The Church is a ballroom in the midst of the city wherein we, today, ourselves, can join in steps choreographed by Christ and danced by martyrs and Mary, apostles and archangels, the elders and the four living creatures, and a great multitude from every nation. The liturgy that goes on in that building is crowded and boisterous, and the floor of the liturgical house would buckle under the weight of so many nations without sufficient foundation. It is founded upon twelve, sturdy apostolic pillars that can bear the weight of any number of occupants. The floor of the Church will not buckle because it has an inerrant, infallible, one, holy, catholic and apostolic foundation poured by the Holy Spirit. "[In Christ Jesus] the whole structure is joined together and grows into a holy temple in the Lord; in whom you also are built into it for a dwelling place of God in the Spirit" (Eph 2:21–22). Into this ballroom are received doubting Thomas and disclaiming Peter, persecuting Paul and tardy Augustine, the inquisitive Zacchaeus and the vigilant Mary Magdalen; all their brothers and sisters continue to be welcomed into it today.

The doors are both entrances and exits. Liturgists can serve the world only if they escape from its fallen condition, but once freed, they can return to the world to free others. This is the liturgical cycle: entering and exiting the Church. Liturgy begins by leaving the world and ends by returning to the world, and in between we are made into new people by spending time upon the altar stone, the rejected cornerstone. Liturgical practice produces an ecclesial identity, which produces an evangelical activity. That is why the place seems to grow: its inside gets bigger than its outside (one definition of "catholic"). The liturgy is never so fully staffed that it will not happily receive another collaborator. The Church swelled as she swallowed Latin and Greek and Syrian and Byzantine and Slavic and European cultures; and now she is already welcoming the stirring southern hemisphere. Her liturgy is catholic in scope and eschatological in scale.

4. The Church is a *liturgical mother*. She is a New Eve, mother and nurturer of the children of God. Her divinized offspring are born

from her liturgical font, commissioned with her liturgical sphragis, fed at her liturgical table, absolved under her liturgical hand, united nuptially in imitation of her own union with Christ, and served by men she orders *in persona Christi Capitis*. The sacraments are liturgical insofar as they put liturgy into motion. Mother Church performs sacraments because she *is* a sacrament: she gives of what she is. The Church is not an institution with sacraments, she is a sacrament with institutions. She is where humanity can be recapitulated and receive a new head; she is where trespassers can be refurbished and made bright and fresh again after the soiling of sin; she is the place where we can pass over from the old aeon into the new.

By the power of God, she gives birth to mystical beings. The Church breeds believers and delivers from her womb Christians whose father is God. This leads me to suggest that every birth of faith is a virgin birth. The birth of faith is not the Church's accomplishment, any more than the birth of Jesus was Joseph's accomplishment. It is the Holy Spirit who conceives faith, and mother Church is the womb where it grows, and the ordained priest stands by like foster-father Joseph, dumbfounded at the miracle, gazing upon the Spirit's handiwork, and not his own. (This is why Joseph has been specially taken as model of the bishop.) The Church is something more than a religious human society because the work our mother does is commissioned and empowered by God. She is herself a witness to the eschaton—a maternal martyr—because she can testify to what happens within her.

The newborns whom she nurses (whether infant or adult) are being formed in soul and service to become latreutic citizens. So as a good mother, she is determined to bring her children to maturity. A mother loves her baby, but she does not hope he will remain infantile all his life. The work she does to nurse and teach and protect her child is to bring him to age. The Church does the work of evangelization, conversion, mystagogy, and catechesis in order to nurse deified liturgists to maturity.

5. The Church is a *liturgical spouse*. She is the mystical Bride of the premier liturgist, Christ, and we may speak of her as either Bride or Body because a bride becomes one body with her groom. That is why Paul used conjugality for a profound lesson of ecclesiology. After citing the Scripture that says a man shall leave his parents, hold

fast to his wife, and become one flesh, Paul says "This is a great mystery, and I mean in reference to Christ and the Church" (Eph 5:32). Christ and his Bride are in union as one body. The Church is the Body of Christ because she is the Bride of Christ. Therefore the energy of Christ activates the Church's mission spiritually (it is activated by the Holy Spirit). As his spouse, she is the mouthpiece of the good news, a bulwark against sin, a glorifier of the Father, bestower of blessings, consecrator of matter, absolver of sin, refresher of souls, a new dawn. She receives from her Bridegroom the three offices of prophet, priest, and king (teacher, sanctifier, and shepherd), making her liturgy inspired, sacerdotal, and sovereign.

As his spouse, she is given a share in the three offices that serve the members of the body: teaching, sanctifying, and shepherding. The Church's *prophetic* liturgy must herald the faith, make faith bear fruit in the lives of the faithful, ward off errors, praise God, instruct, reveal, and enlighten. The Church's *priestly* liturgy must offer up a sacrifice of praise and thanksgiving, propitiation and satisfaction, sanctifying the People of God each day with the effects of the Paschal reconciliation. The Church's *royal* liturgy must strengthen spiritual combat to overcome the kingdom of sin, inspire service in justice and charity, restore creation in its original value, and coordinate individual charisms. The Church is a prophetic teacher of practical morality and mystical wisdom, a sanctifying priest who mediates grace and glory between heaven and earth, and a pastoral sovereign over social and personal contests.

Liturgists are a prophetic, priestly, and royal people. The Church is taken from the side of Jesus as he slept his death on the Cross, as the first Eve was taken from the side of the first Adam during his deep sleep. Upon Jesus' awakening, he began his Resurrection liturgy in union with his Bride and continues to walk with her, within her liturgy, toward the final consummation when he will lift off the veil of sacramentality and show himself in full light. "The holy city, new Jerusalem, [will come] down out of heaven from God, prepared as a bride adorned for her husband", and a loud voice from the throne will say "Behold, the dwelling of God is with men. He will dwell with them, and they shall be his people, and God himself will be with them" as their God (Rev 21:2–3). Perichoresis, co-inherence, conjugality.

6. The Church is a *liturgical pilgrim*. Being on pilgrimage makes a pilgrim; being in liturgy makes a liturgist; the verb makes the noun. The Church is a liturgical pilgrim because she is on a pilgrimage through a foreign land. The Church militant is the one, holy, catholic, and apostolic parade stretching across human centuries. The parade is one because there are not many parades but only one, following one Lord, one faith, one Baptism, and everyone travels in unison; it is holy because it receives marching instructions from the Holy Spirit; it is catholic because there is no people to whom it does not intend to go, and anyone from any nation or culture is welcome to step off the sidewalk into it; and it is apostolic because it is pursuing the first witnesses of Christ by following the directions of their successors.

What is to come has already begun, and what has begun will continue to mature until it is ripe enough to be harvested by God to be joined to the heavenly liturgy. This is the antinomy celebrated on every eighth day. We wait for a Kingdom that has already arrived. We wait for a Messiah whom we already know. We wait for the finality of mysteries we are already celebrating. The Church is the yeast in the dough, raising mankind upward; the roots of the tree, holding mankind fast; water yielded from the stone, slaking mankind's thirst; the key in the lock, given to Peter to forgive sins; the current in the river, moving mankind forward. Whither? Where is this legion, this host, this hierarchical crowd going? We are told in the book of the Revealing: John the eagle-eyed saw mankind parading toward liturgy. He "looked, and behold, [he saw] a great multitude which no man could number, from every nation, from all tribes and peoples and tongues, standing before the throne and before the Lamb, clothed in white robes, with palm branches in their hands, and crying out with a loud voice, 'Salvation belongs to our God who sits upon the throne, and to the Lamb!'" (Rev 7:9–10). This is mankind's end, its place, its position, its term, and the Church on earth exists to prepare us for it. After that, she lays down her tools.

The question for us is whether we will enjoy our destination when we arrive. Will we enjoy giving constant liturgical praise to the Father? Why do we think we shall enjoy it then if we do not enjoy it now? The liturgy we will celebrate then constantly is celebrated now intermittently. The unrepentant sinner will not enjoy it and will continue to hide with Adam and Eve when they hear the sound

of the Lord God walking in the garden in the cool of the day. But
the repentant liturgist will find God's approach blissful because he is
well-practiced at waiting for God to draw near from each Sunday's
altar. Liturgy is the practice station for ecstasy. We practice now what
will we will be doing then. Liturgical faith prepares for vision that
is beatific. The Church grasps paradise in advance, and her liturgy is
heaven tasted on earth. The Church is the inchoate presence of the
final liturgy, the tip of it already beginning. Brothers and sisters of
the Incarnate One join his liturgical activity.

The world had turned its back on the face of God; Christ came to
reboot the liturgy that sin had canceled; and the Church is the world
in its course of transfiguration as it turns its face back to God.

7. The Church is Christ's *liturgical body*. We are told by *Lumen
gentium* that Christ redeemed and remolded mankind in the hypostatic union by overcoming death through his own death and Resurrection, and by communicating his Spirit he mystically constitutes
as his body those brothers of his who are called together from every
nation. In that body, the life of Christ is communicated (7). Liturgy is living this life. First it was lived for us; now it is lived by us,
because it is lived in us. The Church does not merely *use* liturgy, she
is liturgy. "Swim" is a verb, swimmer is the noun; "liturgize" is the
verb, Church is the noun. The Church is first an event, then a thing.
Perhaps this is the most difficult thing for us to realize and the most
important contribution that liturgical ecclesiology can make.

The substance that underlies all the Church's outward manifestations, all her phenomena, all her institutions is the *opus Dei* working
within. The liturgy is an inner gyroscope that maintains the Church's
Christocentric orientation and balance. Without the liturgy spinning
in her belly, the Church would wobble from one cause to another,
from one secular fad to the next passing fancy. Such enthusiasms,
even if benign, still belong to the class of things of which the Church
can never be ultimately made, because flesh and blood will not inherit
the Kingdom of God, nor will the perishable inherit the imperishable (1 Cor 15:50). An imperishable Church must drink from an
eternal liturgy. Christian members do their liturgy as components of
Christ's body. The cells do not live on their own, for themselves, or
by their own power; the cells are elements of the liturgical and Mystical Body. To become a Christian is to be grafted into this Body,

enlivened by the Spirit animating this Body, sent by Christ for the purpose of constituting this Body. The Holy Spirit is the principal liturgist, uniting the real and Mystical Body of the Church with the real and Mystical Body of the Eucharist. We do not have to parcel out the descriptors *mystical* and *real*, as though once the term has been used, it has been spent and cannot be used again. The Church is the Mystical and real Body of Christ, and the Eucharist is the Mystical and real Body of Christ: "real", meaning it can be found in time and history and fact, and "mystical", meaning it is of God and miraculous and supernatural. The Church is a liturgical corporation. She is made up of individual liturgists, but they are united in such a way that she does a corporate liturgy, which is one of the first miracles of Baptism. Her liturgy is done from a collective mind—the mind her children have in Christ Jesus (Phil 2:5).

A Concluding Metaphor

The Scripture metaphors for Church are best, but I will end with one of my own anyway. Mankind stands on a shore, an ocean away from God. The gulf is filled with catastrophes of our own making: pride, rebelliousness, alienation, resentfulness, reluctance, disobedience, transgression. To rectify matters, God parts the sea like a divine Moses so that we can cross over to him on dry land. But we are still petulant. We stiffen our necks and stop up our ears when he calls, so what good will it do for God to shout louder? He roars at the conscience of the pagans, he shouts out the Torah to the Israelites, he hollers by the prophets in Scripture, and there is still no response from our side. Will it then help if he reveals more laws, writes more Scripture, and sends additional prophets? No. So he turns to a new strategy. It is not new to him, only to us. "You were ransomed ... with the precious blood of Christ, like that of a lamb without blemish or spot. He was destined before the foundation of the world but was made manifest at the end of the times for your sake" (1 Pet 1:18–20). God establishes an outpost on our side of the ocean. He must deal with the fact that we become like skittish and nervous birds when he approaches us, so he builds colonies on our shore to give us the comfort of communion. He builds castles out of the wood of his

Cross up and down the coastline so they are easy to find and ready to welcome the curious. They have a nave to rescue us from the judgment flood (à la Noah), and they have a sanctuary window open to the east through which we can see and hear the heavenly Jerusalem (à la Isaiah). The Christian Church is a new creation insofar as she is the presence of heaven on our shoreline, constructed around the aperture of an empty tomb that serves as the echo chamber of the liturgy celebrated therein. These ecclesiastical outposts on our side of the ocean are liturgical portals.

Chapter 31

Sacraments

This chapter may seem to be a cheat. Liturgy and sacrament are so closely interwoven that using one to investigate the other risks being tautological. Nevertheless, we would like "Liturgical Sacramentology" to come at sacraments from a couple of different angles and dilate our understanding.

Ordinary people ordinarily use metaphors when they think about sacraments, and since they are using ordinary speech, I do not mind. When they say "a sacrament contains grace", I am pretty sure they do not mean it in the way a bottle contains wine. They can tell the difference, and I do not feel the need to call in a metaphysician to correct their speech by making it more rarefied and severe. Metaphor is comfortable speech because it is commonplace speech, and any speech about God that is not comfortable because it has become pedantic and esoteric speech is likely to be misleading. (Liturgical speech is very comfortable.) So what sort of metaphors for sacrament might we employ?

First, spatial metaphors. We have already mentioned the most common utterance that says a sacrament contains grace. This does not mean that people think of grace as a reified thing; it means they think of grace as obtainable, charitably offered, enduringly accessible. Grace is contained in this sacrament because it is available in this sacrament. "Contains" is no more troublesome a metaphor than the word "comes", and they equally derive from our spatial orientation. When we say God "comes" with his grace, we do not mean to suggest that God begins to be in a place where he was not before. Neither local motion nor local site is intended. It is silly to pick on certain metaphors and ignore the others when, for example, we say that God was "in Christ" reconciling the world to himself, that the Father "sends" the Son and Holy Spirit, or that they "come" to "give" grace.

We speak in spatial metaphors because we speak as embodied creatures. It is amazing that matter can be used on a soul. Amazing, that is, to the dualist who has erected a strict barrier between the corporeal and incorporeal. He thinks the material sacrament cannot be deployed upon the spiritual soul any more than radiation can be used on the psyche or an ointment can be used on the intellect. But if God is the Creator of both soul and body, and if man is the union of soul and body, then God can be Redeemer of the soul through the body.

We occupy space. Let us get past chafing over that fact and also get past chastising our ordinary speech. We can say that a sacrament is how God "comes down" to us and, indeed, add some other directions, too! A sacrament is how God comes out to us—from the holy gates of the Heavenly Jerusalem. A sacrament is how God comes over to us—from the Emperor's Country beyond the sea. A sacrament is how God comes across to us—overarching from the parousia to our present moment. (We might also add a question of understanding: "How did God come across to you?") A sacrament is how God comes up to us—from the depths of our hearts, since "deep calls to deep" (Ps 42:7) and his "judgments are like the great deep" (Ps 36:6). A sacrament is how God comes through to us—what must God do to get through to us? To what desert must we be taken for our hard heart to be softened, broken, reformed? A sacrament is how God drops in on us—like a friend from next door. A sacrament is how God comes under us—to raise us up to eternal life. We have made the point. A sacrament is how God is around us, by us, with us, et cetera.

Second, symbolic metaphors. Symbol is the coin of the realm in the world of sacrament, so why not make peace with it? The prejudice against calling the sacrament symbolic is because of the untold mischief caused by our reflex action to put "merely" in front of the word "symbol". This temptation gives the impression that a sacrament is like a collage of magazine pictures pasted onto construction paper, instead of reality itself. "It was a symbolic gesture", we say, meaning that instead of giving a true reward, we just make a nod. Symbol has come to mean the absence of a real thing and, worse, sometimes its opposite. But it need not mean this. *Sym+baleo* means to throw together, like the two halves of a broken coin were thrown

back together as a sign of mutual recognition. A sacrament symbolizes, and if it is not functioning thus, then it is useless, like one half
of the broken coin is useless for buying a gumball.

The sacred symbol was something that had been in contact with
the sacred sphere, and in the case of Christian sacraments, words and
elements have been in contact with Christ, who symbol-ized in his
own Person (threw together) the divine and human natures and can
therefore communicate the realm of the sacred to us. Christ is the
primordial sacrament; the Son is symbol of the Father. He who has
seen him has seen the Father, and if someone sees him and does not
see the Father, it is because lack of faith will not let the sacrament
operate symbolically. Sym-bolize is a verb—the action of putting two
halves together, in this case, putting together heaven and earth, God
and man, eternity and time, sacred and profane. But if we have gotten distracted by the noun ("mere symbol") and do not feel the verb
("sym-bolize"), then we stare at the half-coin in our hand instead of
using it to recognize our brother Christ.

Third, sacraments are a yearning. Most mystics say that whatever
touch they receive from God increases their desire; it does not lessen
it. The spiritual nourishment they consume does not satiate their
hunger for God; the spiritual water in their mouth does not slake
their thirst. Why is it not the same with every sacrament? It is the
same with every regular and expected sacrament as it is with every
irregular and unexpected mystical experience. We pursue a God who
runs ahead of us, always slightly out of reach, yet with each sacrament
we tickle the fringe of his garment (his *tzitzit*), and the very chase
fills us with joy. The sacraments do not satiate us, they stimulate us.
These are sacramental sightings of the hidden God. And if he has
disappeared from us at a moment of temptation and trial, the mystics
advise us to sit down where he was last seen and wait. And groan.
And weep. Wait to be strengthened sufficiently by sacramental prayer
so that when God reappears, this time within arm's reach, we may
jump up refreshed and go farther up and farther in after him.

Trainers drag a lure behind them on a rope to teach a falcon to
chase after something; God runs ahead of us with a man-lure bouncing on the end of a sacramental rope trailing behind him. The falconer
swings a lure above his head to call the falcon back to him; God just
may have set the galaxy revolving and the earth rotating for the sole

purpose of luring mankind to himself. Heaven is alluring. Sacraments are sightings of God that draw us forward. It is admittedly odd that some appetites lessen when they are fed, and other appetites increase when they are fed, but that is the way it is, and sacramental grace is of the latter type. Receiving but a drop of water, a drop of wine, a drop of oil, creates more desire because the drop is not enough. It is not meant to satisfy; it is meant to be a pledge. We receive a morsel of bread, but it stirs our hunger for a "feast of fat things ... of fat things full of marrow" (Is 25:6), of which messianic banquet we have a sacramental foretaste.

Fourth, a metaphor of icon. It is popular to explain an icon to Western Christians who have limited experience of them as "a window on heaven", but one day an Orthodox friend said to me "Well, actually, more like a door than a window." I thought this might teach us something about sacraments. Christ does not give us the sacraments instead of himself; rather, he gives himself sacramentally.

The icon does not stand there to be stared at from a distance; it is an encounter with the prototype whose image the icon is. Neither do the sacraments stand there to be stared at from a distance; they are an encounter with the Christ who is the source of the sacraments. The sacraments do not stand between us and Jesus like a wall; they extend from Jesus to us like a bridge. A sacrament solicits a reaction, therefore, the way an icon solicits reaction, too. A liturgical reaction. Neither should be gaped at with idle curiosity and listlessness. A sacrament requires a special kind of looking and beholding; it demands a faithful regard in a gaze that will see behind the veil because the soul is absorbed by the grace it sees. Rather than simply looking to sacraments for illustrative instruction, we should step through the sacraments into new life. As one must learn how to read an icon, so must one also learn how to read a sacrament, lest one fail to discern its depth. The *verbum* is added to the *elementum* to help with exactly that, but it is still a task of faith for us to perform. Jesus said that whoever has seen him has seen the Father, and God's smile is prolonged sacramentally in the Church. Like a fish swimming upstream, we can enter the baptismal flood coming from his side, released by the soldier's spear thrust, and ascend into the bosom of the crucified Christ. We can open our mouth to receive the flow of blood coming from the Sacred Heart of Jesus.

Fifth, a metaphor of light. The whole world was supposed to reveal God, to be transparent to God, to be a repetitive theophany, and we should have looked through every gift to see the Giver behind it. What happened? How did the world become opaque instead of transparent? A window can serve as an illustration. You can see through a window when there is light on both sides, but if it is dark outside and light inside, then the window becomes a mirror, and you see your own reflection instead of the street outside. The cosmos should be a gallery of theophanous windows, but instead it has become a carnival House of Mirrors, distorted in convex or concave reflections, a maze of obstacles. Satan has messed with the lighting of our world by messing with our spiritual eyesight, and ever since our corruption in the Fall, we need a special adjustment of our optical faculties if we are to contemplate God instead of gaze at ourselves.

The proper sacramental lighting of the cosmos needs to be restored by our obedience to the commandments, by the ascetical discipline of our passions, and by the sacramental cures that the Church houses in her medicine chest. Then the True One can reach us through our confrontations with truth; the Beautiful One can display himself through raptures of beauty; and the Good One can work his solicitude for us within acts of goodness. All the things in the world are good images of what we really desire, but we must not let our appetites pause on them. What we desire cannot be filled with anything contained in this world, although everything contained in this world is a sacramental pointer to what we desire. The spread of a sacramental light gives us a completely different world to examine.

Sixth, a maternal metaphor. The Church Fathers saw the water and blood coming from Christ's side on the Cross as representing the symbols of Baptism and Eucharist that create the Church. As God took a rib from Adam's side to fashion a woman, so Christ issued blood and water from his side to fashion the Church. Whether we call the Church the "Body of Christ" or the "Bride of Christ" does not matter, since bride and groom become one body. Adam slept, and the rib was taken from him; Christ slept on the Cross, and the Church was taken from him. Christ is the New Adam, and the Church is the New Eve, mother of salvation, mother of all the truly living. Sacramentality is born from his humanity.

If we looked, we could see this in each of the seven. The font is the uterus of mother Church, from which new Christians are born when her water breaks and by which the person is imprinted with the character that gives rights and obligations. Being in Christ, and having received the Holy Spirit, the chief obligation is personal sanctification through ascetical discipline, and the chief right is the glorification of God through exercising the royal priesthood. But this life must not only be inflowing, it must become outflowing in an apostolate, and therefore Baptism is confirmed with spiritual gifts that make a person Christlike in self-giving charity. This is eternal life, and so it must be nourished on the Eternal One himself at the table of the Eucharist where his Body and Blood, soul and divinity are given for our sustenance. That Christ's sacrifice may continue, the priesthood serves the Church in apostolic succession. That there be a domestic sign of the mystical union Christ has with his Bride, marriage serves the Church as a family unit. When the life of the body is threatened by death, a sacrament is available to salve (heal) the Christian, and when the life of the soul is threatened by sin, a sacrament stands ready to encourage or re-engender charity. We have listed the Sacraments of Initiation, the sacraments at the service of communion, and the sacraments of healing.

Seventh, sacraments are energies. The Eastern Christian tradition carefully preserves the transcendence of God by distinguishing between essence and energy. The essence of God is deepest mystery, unknown and unknowable to any creature, even the highest cherubim and seraphim. And yet, although no created being can know the essence of God, man can know God by his activity, by his movements of creation and redemption, and such are called the energies of God. They are his acts. Then, a human synergy must correspond to the divine energy. The sacraments are unmerited, but they are not automatic. They call for a response to grace by the recipients of grace. The God-man has symbolized (thrown together) the invisible with the visible, the supernatural with the natural, the Uncreated and the created in his sacramental economy. But this economy of unification is supposed to be repeated in each person. The seven sacraments of the Church are not exceptions to our daily life; they permeate our daily life with the Kingdom, the way perfume permeates the water into which it is dropped, the way cells are oxygenated by the air we breathe, the way the dawn colors the landscape. The sacramental effects are not confined inside the Church; these explosions from the altar, rather, spiritualize everything. The sacramental life binds our activity to the Gospel, our love to Christ's charity, our works to the Kingdom's cause, our will to God's mercy, our hearts to his heart, our temporal life to eternal life. We live a symbolic life: thrown together with God. When that happens, there is no moment, no person, no choice, no thing that cannot be blessed and become a reception of grace or an act of worship.

Chapter 32

Home-Sighting

If we have spoken about the inside of the Church, we should speak about her outside, too. The Eucharist is Gibraltar in a tornado. It stands firm. But the little tents we have pitched around its base will be blown away.

The world is a pathway and should not be given any more status than that. When Saint Anthony met the 113-year-old anchorite Paul, who had lived alone in the desert from the age of sixteen, Paul humbly professed he was only a man who would be dust before long. And since he had lived alone without visitors for so many decades, he politely asked Anthony how the human race fared. What government now directs the world? Are new homes being built in ancient cities? Hermit Paul was not asking in the spirit of daily news, because his mind already lived a permanent life. He was asking in the spirit of Ecclesiastes: Can you name anything new that has happened under the sun? (Eccles 1:10). The world he left is ephemeral, but he lives from a place of permanence. Places of permanence are places where the soul grows because one side of the soul is open to heaven. Monasteries and hermit caves are places like that; homes with parents and children are places like that; pilgrimages and spiritual retreats and contemplative classrooms are places like that; but the Church is the primary place of permanence, because she is the agent that feeds all others from the manna she receives daily from heaven on her altar table. Governments and social causes and philosophical schools each take their turn directing the world and then fade away, which is the point Paul was making. After Babylon fell to Persia, and Persia to Greece, and Greece to Rome, does Rome still govern the world? (The correct answer would be "for another three decades", since Anthony and Paul met in 342.) How does the Byzantine Empire fare after 1453? How does the house of Romanoff fare after 1917?

While different governments take their turn directing the world, the Church opens our soul on the side of heaven, and can do so because what is to come is already there. There it is, already. The Church is only a jar of clay, and for now the treasure is held in a weak earthen vessel "to show that the transcendent power belongs to God and not to us" (2 Cor 4:7). The Church is bigger on her inside than she can ever appear to the world on her outside, because the liturgy that goes on inside her is the face-to-face encounter with the one who grasps all creation in his palm. Time spent in what will be our permanent state is of more consequence than all the time we spend on the pathway. In a balance scale, the tray holding the Eucharist would outweigh all the political and social and historical events held in the other tray. The Church is where the new aeon laps upon the temporal shore, where eternity is foretasted, where saints forge their eternal life gradually and steadily, where the liturgy displays for our encouragement the fulfillment of our deepest-seated hope. The Church is not static; by her exercise of liturgy, she is the one entity in the world that is moving, moving forward, moving ahead. She appears rooted and planted because of her stability, but she is actually in motion beneath history moving toward the Kingdom at the pace that tectonic plates move the ocean floor. Knowing that we are all in motion, she offers us a provision, a meal, a viaticum. A viaticum is a supply of provisions for a journey, and while it is understandable how the word came to be applied to the last Eucharist received by a dying person, we live from a steady diet of viatica.

We usually connect the Eucharist with the past—palm branches, Jerusalem, the upper room, Golgotha, the Cross—and rightly enough, since all these are components that staged the Paschal Mystery celebrated by the Eucharist with anamnetic force. But the Eucharist is not about the past. *What* was present on Calvary is present on the altar because *Who* was present on Calvary is still present on the altar. Neither time nor tomb can separate the bloody sacrifice of Calvary from the unbloody Sacrifice of the Mass. The Council of Trent described the reason for the Church in Eucharistic terms and the reason for the Eucharist in ecclesiological terms. When Jesus was about to offer himself on the altar of the Cross, he left his spouse a visible sacrifice because his priesthood was not to be extinguished by his death. The sanguinary sacrifice is re-presentable in the sacramental sacrifice: there and here are the same sacrifice, the same priest, the same victim. Should that sacramental bungee cord ever be broken, or even frayed, the sacrifice of the Church would fall to the ground and crash, and the wreckage remaining would be nothing more than a human ritual. The event remembered would remain divine, but the liturgical memorial is not a divine act unless the anamnesis is placed in our human hands by the Holy Spirit.

Anamnesis means the past made present by its effects, but the Eucharist also makes present the reality at the other end of the spectrum. The Church stretches across a range, but we must be clear about the termini. The two ends of the spectrum of the Church cannot be merely *past and future*, because past and future are two points on the same line. Everyone walking that line is simply hiking a trail along the shadow of death, and if this were the Church's total range of power, then her Eucharist would only be a temporary recess. She would be advising her children to sit down and take a break before resuming their death march, sit down for a moment of silence before resuming their funeral dirge. Instead, in fact, the Church stretches the full length of a spectrum whose first and last points are the first eon and the second. The Church runs the gamut from *history to eschaton*, not past to future, and we come to her to feed on a nourishment that comes from beyond our present timeline. In addition to the Eucharist being connected to the past establishment of the Paschal Mystery, every celebration of the Eucharist is also connected to the final completion of that Paschal Mystery. The Church is where Christ becomes the germ of our future resurrection, and the historical line we walk does not go straight on forever; it has been bent ninety degrees by the Cross so we can begin our ascent. Our vocation in the face of death is to live in hope for the apocalyptic judgment, which we welcome gladly because it restores righteousness to a twisted world. The Church is the place of liturgical untwisting.

The essential function of the Church is to actualize the eschaton in this world, which she does in her Eucharist. We may say the Eucharist "translates" the eschaton. The word "translate" literally and etymologically means picking something up and laying it down in a new location. We know it primarily in its metaphorical adaptation to mean a concept being picked up in one language and laid in another: a "language translation". But it was once used by the Church to speak of picking up bones from a graveyard and laying them in a new home: a "translation of relics". Here we may say that liturgy picks up the new eon and lays it before us: a "Eucharistic translation of the eschaton". The eschaton is laid under our feet by the Church-at-liturgy so that our lives may have a new under-standing, a new sub-stance. The enlightened ones who have passed through the sacrament of illumination, therefore, see the mundane pathway in a new light now. They see the pathways of history, the economies of power, the durability of governments, the demise of rulers, the preciousness of each soul, the immediacy of God—they see how it goes with the world. That is really what the hermit Paul wanted to know.

Do not think, though, that this makes the Church so heavenly minded that she is of no earthly use. We are not treating the lit-urgy as an ecclesiastical depot where Christians await their carriage to heaven. The Church is not concerned with half a human; she is concerned with the whole human, soul and body. If she is concerned with souls—and she is—she is concerned with souls in the state of sin. And sin can be committed in the profane realm as well as in the sacred realm, committed with bodies as well as with souls, committed against bodies as well as against souls. It is true that "against you, you only, have I sinned" (Ps 51:4), but since God does not reside in an exclusively sacred realm, we can also sin against him where he appears in the secular, profane, political realm. Sin is anything contrary to the eternal law, and sin is a failure of genuine love for God and neighbor. We can fail to love God outside as well as inside the Church.

Jesus responded to his litigious bushwhackers by pointing out that they should render to Caesar the things that are Caesar's and to God the things that are God's. In other words, things bearing images belong to the one whose image they bear. Whatever neighbor I meet is God's property; we know this because any and every neighbor bears God's image. When we render to Caesar what has his image, we are being good citizens; when we render to God what has his image, we are being good liturgists. The charity we show to our neighbor is the fulfillment of a liturgical posture toward God. Surrender the coin to Caesar, and surrender your neighbor to God and disentangle him from your own selfish purposes. Our moral duty toward our neighbor is an expression of our liturgical obligation toward God. My neighbor comes with the instruction to handle with care. If someone knocked down an image (statue) of Caesar, he would be guilty of insurrection against Caesar; if someone knocks down an image of God, he would be guilty of insurrection against God. Doing violence against any person is a form of blasphemy.

Therefore, the Church's liturgy does not leave the profane world untouched. Aidan Kavanagh used to define liturgy as doing the world the way the world was meant to be done. When we talk about liturgical ecclesiology, we are not discussing something extraneous, inapplicable, or beside the point. We are actually talking about the very point of the world, namely, its call to holiness. In the liturgy we learn something about the world, and in the world we learn something about liturgy. In the former we learn the telos of the world, and in the latter we discover the scope and details of the Church's evangelization. In each case we are talking about Church, which is kingdom-in-the-world. In the liturgy we learn priestly techniques to offer all things up in oblation; we attend kingly classes about how to rule over all things in God's name; and we develop a priestly talent for interpreting the signs of the times as designs of God. Although we often think of prophets as only one step above a carnival fortune-teller, Scripture presents them as servants of God who are aware of hidden designs. There are laws, directives, and plots hidden by God under the surface, and the liturgical prophet can detect them, like a cat detects tremors before the earthquake strikes. The Old Testament prophet appears to know the future, but what he actually knows is the laws by which God's judgment works, and so he knows what consequences will be brought on by this particular state of affairs. He anticipates the reaction God will have to our action. The liturgical version of Newton's third law states that every action of sin and injustice on our part causes an equal and opposite reaction of wrath and apocalypse on God's part. As my father used to say, wrath is love destroying that which would destroy love.

We could say the liturgist has "sacramental eyes" if we remember the definition of a sacrament as a case where one thing is seen, but another is understood. Our neighbor is seen one way if we use the eyes of envy, avarice, and anger, and in a completely different way if we use sacramental eyes to see him as a child of God. The Church is God's ophthalmologist, dealing with the diagnosis and treatment of disorders of the eye, restoring faith, hope, and love to the eyes of the blind. Our natural sight sees the world in various ways, but baptismal retinal surgery improves our vision. The Church teaches us to see below the surface.

These upper and lower levels—accident and substance—are built into pretty much everything.

- Anthropology: a person is body and soul.
- Sacramentology: *sacramentum tantum* and *res tantum*.
- Christology: Jesus was human and divine.
- Ecclesiology: an institutional dimension and a mystical dimension.
- Liturgiology: ritual and substance.
- Cosmology: creation and the new aeon.

The first term of each pair is empirical, experimental, practical, observable, material, pragmatical, and something you could poke with a stick. The second term of each pair is a mystery present. Liturgical ecclesiology expects us to practice depth-viewing, mystery-viewing when we look at neighbor, history, suffering, death, politics, culture, even coincidence. (Coincidence is what providence is called when God wants to remain anonymous.)

The secular person stays at the level of appearances and on the surface of events. The liturgical prophet, on the other hand, goes deeper to find a more profound meaning. Why do we generally swim on the surface instead of diving to the depths? Because we do not want to risk a new understanding that would upset our privilege, our benefit, our selfishness. Too deep, we think; we might drown, we think; yet that is exactly the depth every baptismal font should measure. Whether a birdbath or a wading pool, the true dimensions of the font must be the same as the dimensions of the Cross: high enough to touch heaven, deep enough that the old Adam cannot escape, and wide enough to embrace every circumstance in charity.

According to a functionalist understanding of the world, things are merely things. According to the sacramental understanding fostered in liturgical ecclesiology, things are more than things. For liturgical eyes, things are media for God, tools for theophany, transparent to

spirit, and wing for the soul. The Church's liturgy trains us to plunge
to the core of matter and feel its sacramental potential; to dive to the
mystery of persons and feel the pleasure they give God; to descend
to the depths where divine law operates and discover that for all who
love God, all things work together for good (Rom 8:28), even suffering and death and denial. No thing in the world is sinful, but any
thing in the world can become an occasion of sin in the scheme of
the devil if we have not put on the whole armor of God (Eph 6:11).
We do not come to liturgy to escape the world, but to suit up for battle. Then the theological virtues of faith, hope, and love infused into
a person in the Church will diffuse from that person into the world.
The outside of liturgy is the world in its course of transfiguration, and
it interests liturgical ecclesiology as much as does the inside of liturgy.

ESCHATOLOGY

Chapter 33

Our Guide Home

We have our most synergistic relationship with the third Person of the Trinity.

That is not true, exactly, since it is an overstatement. The Persons of the Trinity are always united, having equal glory and majesty, none before or after the other, none greater or lesser than the other. The divine substance is not cut up and apportioned among three pieces. The nature, the essence, the energy, and the glory is common to the three. Nevertheless, theological tradition has associated certain attributes of God with certain Persons of the Trinity, the most common example being the association of creating, redeeming, and sanctifying with Father, Son, and Holy Spirit, respectively. The kind of synergy we can have with the Father's creative activity is limited by the fact that a nonexistent being cannot aid in bringing himself into existence; the kind of synergy we can have with the Son's redeeming activity is limited by the fact that a dead person cannot help dig himself up; but we are expected to cooperate in our sanctification, thus I (misleadingly) suggest that we have our most synergistic relationship with the Holy Spirit.

In what kind of activity does the Holy Spirit engage? He gives life, points to Christ, regenerates and renews, assists in prayer, guards and seals, comforts, fills with joy, leads into righteousness, gives fruits and gifts, and enlightens minds, all of which describe the process of sanctification he tenaciously undertakes. And how does the Holy Spirit go about his work? He seems to like to hover over (Gen 1:2), rest upon (Is 11:2), enter within (Ezek 36:26), pour out (Joel 2:28), come upon (1 Sam 16:13), overshadow (Lk 1:35), intercede within (Rom 8:26), inhabit temple-bodies (1 Cor 6:19, 3:16), and dwell within (Jn 14:17). All these verbs seem to indicate that his arrival time and technique are of his own choosing, and often unexpected. He is the supreme stealth agent because the world "neither sees him nor knows him" (Jn 14:17). But the faithful do. And once the Spirit selects his instrument, the instrument can cooperate, like the pen can write once the author picks it up in his hand. We are recipients, but not passive.

Synergy is a cooperation, we know. A co-operation. Two powers are at work, and, though they are unequal in importance, they are equal in necessity. We are led astray by thinking in terms of inverse proportionality, whereby the more effort A exerts, the less effort B needs to exert. Think instead of direct proportionality. Two agents do not each work out of their own power; rather, the first agent employs the power of the second. The Holy Spirit does not move instead of the person; the Holy Spirit moves the person. He energizes, the person synergizes; he animates, the person is made lively; he inspires, the person conspires; he enkindles, the person flares; he illuminates, the person glorifies; he does liturgical work, the person does liturgical activity.

So let us imagine the Holy Spirit hovering over, resting upon, coming upon, and pouring forth onto our liturgical lifetime, flooding the liturgical pathway we gracefully traverse from birth to death. He is our guide to the eschaton. He energizes, animates, inspires, enkindles, illuminates, and works our liturgical activity across it. The length of our liturgical path is only known to us when we have finished walking it. It is like a path of stepping-stones across a river, and we do not know when it will end until we lift our foot and find no stone for our next step. Our sickness unto death is terminal, and our timeline for liturgy has an ending, unlike the eternal timeline we will have in heaven, so we should spend our time here rehearsing for beatitude, fitting our ears and tongue according to their celestial specifications so we can connaturally join the heavenly choir. This is what the Holy Spirit is up to in our lives. He brings every baptized person forward in this adjustment, and a saint is only someone whose customization is completed (and some of them walk among us already). For this purpose, we are given a day for liturgy, a week for liturgy, a year for liturgy, a lifetime for liturgy, and the Church has filled those days and weeks and years with supporting frames for our liturgies.

First, the day. The liturgy of the day is variously known as the Divine Office (*officium divinum*) because it is a divine service or duty for us to conduct, or as the Liturgy of the Hours (*liturgia horarum*) by its hourly arrangement, or as the Breviary (*breviarium*) from its compendium, or as the Work of God (*opus Dei*) because it is. We may imagine the Holy Spirit coming upon that daily liturgy in vertical synergy to synchronize the chimes of our canonical hours with his celestial clock. The hymn of praise that we sing over the course of twenty-four hours is the very hymn of praise that is sung through all the ages in the heavenly places and was brought by the High Priest Jesus into our land of exile. The overshadowing of the Holy Spirit upon our daily office accomplishes a harmonization between earth and heaven, man and angel, time and eternity. Our voiced recitation would sound tinny and cheap without his sonority. "We do not know how to pray as we ought, but the Spirit himself intercedes for us with sighs too deep for words" (Rom 8:26). The Scripture readings, intercessions, psalmody, canticles, and prayers would become pedantic without his inspiration. Liturgy would be done in the spirit of the flesh instead of the spirit of sonship (Gal 4:6–7) without the Spirit of him who raised Jesus from the dead.

How could the Divine Office sanctify the day, and all the human activity in it, without the divine Sanctifier overseeing it? How could the Divine Office take its unity from the heart of Christ if its participants were not anointed by the Holy Spirit and empowered to offer the worship of the New Covenant? "The unity of the Church at prayer is brought about by the Holy Spirit, who is the same in Christ, in the whole Church, and in every baptized person.... There can be [therefore] no Christian prayer without the action of the Holy Spirit who unites the whole Church and leads it through the Son to the Father" (*General Instruction of the Liturgy of the Hours*, 8). From the beginning, Christians have felt an instinct for regular prayer, prayer without ceasing, prayer in the daylit hours and in the nocturnal hours. The Holy Spirit overshadows the days of our life to consecrate our *ora* and our *labora* and gives to us a liturgical responsibility (ability to respond). He overshadows our liturgical day.

Second, the week. A collection of seven of these day units is bundled into a module called the week, and even the pagans sensed that the passage of time was a religious movement, so they tended to name the days of the week after the gods. Israel went farther and integrated liturgical time right into its cosmology, for the creation of the cosmos ended with a good time, a Sabbath. In the beginning of creation, the Spirit of God was moving over the face of the waters (Gen 1:2), and at the end of creation, the final day is blessed, hallowed, set apart as holy, consecrated, sanctified—all these actions sound like liturgical actions, and they are typical of the Spirit. The Sabbath is a day for spiritual life, surrounded on six sides by secular life. The last day of creation affirms the goodness of the Creator, and God's people do not just take a hiatus from labor on this regularly scheduled sabbatical day; they do what God is doing on that day. Keeping the Sabbath is participation in the life of God; that is why the Torah was so strict about it.

Then God added another day because he was triggered to act again. For six days God had labored, on the seventh he had rested, but when mankind fell into sin, he acted again. He interrupted his Sabbath with mercy, as Jesus did (Mt 12:8, Lk 6:5, Lk 6:9, Lk 13:14, Lk 14:3, Jn 5:10, Jn 9:14). Now there is an eighth day, the day of the Resurrection. On the eighth day, the new aeon irrupts: it bursts in, breaks into, forcibly enters the methodical, calendar-tabulated death march in which we find ourselves. It does not upset next week's calendar, bumping the first day of that week to Monday, and the following week to Tuesday, et cetera. The Kingdom of God encountered on the eighth day does not take up space in the kingdom of the world in this way. It is present in the world spiritually. (Rough analogy: the eighth day is not added to time the way another organ is added to the body; it is in time the way the soul is in the body.) The early Church saw Sunday as the day of creation, the day of circumcision, the day of the Resurrection, the day of the Eucharist, and the eschatological day of the age to come—with which of such matters is the Holy Spirit not intimately involved? Sunday takes to itself the title of *dies Domini*, the Lord's day, the day of our master, the day of the Resurrected One "who was descended from David according to the flesh and [was] designated Son of God in power according to the Spirit of holiness by his resurrection from the dead" (Rom 1:3–4). The power of the Holy Spirit makes secular Sunday the ecclesial eighth day. He overshadows our liturgical week.

Third, the year. The days go by, the weeks go by, and now years go by. Earth makes a complete rotation on its axis, and seven of them make up a week; with fifty-two of those, earth makes a complete revolution around the sun. But we are not just spinning and spinning, dizzy with death. The Holy Spirit is suspended above us to interpose a spiritual trajectory upon our gyrations. Now we are going somewhere—toward the eschaton. Now we make progress—toward God. Now we have someplace to be—in beatitude. Cyclical history finds an eternal bedrock, and when the circle touches this bedrock, it becomes a wheel. Then each rotation and each revolution moves us farther along, farther up, and farther in. This is the lesson taught by the Holy Spirit in the Liturgical Year. He sanctifies the ordinary time of a twelve-month calendar with sacred feasts and seasons. He inscribes upon our hearts the mysteries of Christ that redeem us from sin and death. The mysteries are so massive that we cannot take them in by one tasting, so the feast is spread across the twelve-month table. The medieval Church put the zodiac at Christ's service.

Remove the back of your watch, and you will see cogged wheels each moving on its own but interconnecting at certain points. Remove the back of the liturgical year, and you will see more than one organization of time, but all of them interconnect at certain points. The *temporal cycle* is made of seasons that annually commemorate different aspects of our Lord's life. The Holy Spirit is active here. None of these events has expired, none of them is confined to a far-off land or to original witnesses only. The Holy Spirit is the intervening medium through which an encounter with the Incarnate One continues to take place. The *sanctoral cycle* commemorates events in the life of Christ and Our Lady, the lives of saints, and mysteries of our faith. The Holy Spirit is active here, too. We are celebrating holiness as it appears in lives, events, and persons, a holiness that issues from this Spirit.

As we walk toward our death, we are granted only a limited (and unknown) number of liturgical years; threescore and ten, if we are lucky, according to the King James translation of Psalm 90:10. (How many more Easter Vigils will I be allowed? twelve? eighteen?) The Holy Spirit overshadows our liturgical day, week, and year. Along this liturgical pathway are aid stations called the sacraments. The Holy Spirit comes down and rests upon:

- the font and baptized ("Send the Holy Spirit upon the waters of this font. May all who are buried with Christ in the death of Baptism rise also with him to newness of life");
- and the chrismated ("Be sealed with the gift of the Holy Spirit");
- and the heavenly manna ("Make holy, therefore, these gifts, we pray, by sending down your Spirit upon them like the dewfall");
- and sinners (God, the Father of mercies, "has reconciled the world to himself and sent the Holy Spirit among us for the forgiveness of sins");
- and the sick (On the oil: "Send the Holy Spirit, man's Helper and Friend, upon this oil"; on the ill: "Through this holy anointing may the Lord in his love and mercy help you with the grace of the Holy Spirit");
- and clerics (Deacons: "Lord, send forth upon them the Holy Spirit, that they may be strengthened by the gift of your sevenfold grace to carry out faithfully the work of the ministry." Priests: "Hear us, Lord our God, and pour out upon this servant of yours the blessing of the Holy Spirit and the grace and power of the priesthood");
- and the married ("Send down on them the grace of the Holy Spirit, and pour your love into their hearts, that they may remain faithful in the Marriage covenant").

An epiclesis is human petition plus divine concession: (i) we ask, (ii) the Father responds, (iii) the Spirit arrives. His purpose for dwelling graciously within us is to make us a perfect temple of God's glory.

The Holy Spirit's blessings are poured out on many things—the sacramentals, consecrated persons, blessed objects, virgins, religious men and women, church buildings, altars, the domestic church. We have focused here on an overlooked dimension of liturgy, namely, Liturgical Time. Under the Holy Spirit's hand, the liturgy is our pathway to the eschaton.

In our secular sensibility, we think that time pushes us from behind, as if a treadmill were pushing us ineluctably forward. But the Gospel declares that Christ has redeemed time and that the Holy Spirit gives expansion, application, and completion to the Paschal Mystery. When he does, he overshadows time and pulls us forward from *chronos* into *kairos*. Now we punctuate life with discharges of prayer, praise, and thanksgiving, which complement the fullness of divine worship at the Eucharist. The time of the sacred overflows into profane time. Holiness overshadows. An otherwise monotonous (at best) and frightening (at worst) advance of time can be synergized with the renewing work of the Holy Spirit to become an opportunity for attaining holiness. Though the cosmos is temporal/temporary, while we are tilling its fields, we might find an eschatological pearl hidden there by the landowner. When we do, we should sell everything in order to acquire it. We should do so because we have sighted our home.

Chapter 34

The Harrowing of Hell

The field of death can be harrowed to raise a crop of redeemed liturgists.

"No one can enter a strong man's house and plunder his goods, unless he first binds the strong man; then indeed he may plunder his house" (Mk 3:27). Jesus makes this counterargument to those who ludicrously suggest that his power to cast out demons comes from the prince of demons. If Satan's power is defeated, it is not because he is divided; it is because a stronger man has arrived on the scene. This stronger man will set Satan's captives free. We should not think of redemption, salvation, and liberation in abstract terms, but rather emphasize the relational word that normally follows them: "redeemed *from*", "saved *from*", "liberated *from*". From whom? From what? Sin, law, death, wrath, and the devil, answers Paul. A divine plot was hatched by the Trinity to save us from transgression, corruption, and death. Athanasius' answer to Anselm's *cur Deus homo* question runs along three stages: corruption could not be got rid of otherwise than through death; since Christ himself is immortal, he cannot die; therefore, he took to himself from a stainless virgin a body that was capable of death. When he surrendered this body to death, he was able to plunder Hades. Turnabout is fair play. When Satan burgled Eden, he stole the most valuable things in it, namely, potential liturgists. Christ will now turn the Eucharistic tables.

Satan was not tempted by any natural and material good in the garden, but in that garden there were two souls made for liturgical communion with God, and Satan envied them, despised them, hated them. To stop liturgy, Satan burgled Eden and killed the liturgists. Then, in a divine economy of reversal, Christ sacked Hades and stole back the most valuable things in it: all the righteous liturgists who had been stored there, from the righteous Israelites to the just pagans. He blew the gates off Hades' doors and opened heaven's gates for the just who had gone before him. He set about restarting humanity's liturgy. This trampling down of death by his death is written in an icon, too, where we see Christ coming with the dazzling light of the mandorla, the gates of Hades beneath his feet, a skeletal figure (either death or Satan) chained up, bits of hardware floating in the abyss, with a firm grasp on Adam and Eve while the saints of the Old and New Testaments look on. No counterattack will be brooked, either. "You are Peter, and on this rock I will build my Church, and the gates of Hades shall not prevail against it" (Mt 16:18). Hades is now permanently crippled. The only power it has is a power we give it if we now choose alienation, like prisoners remaining in a jail cell with no door.

When Christ was born, a multitude of angels descended to Bethlehem to witness the miracle. When Christ died, a multitude of angels again descended to watch a miracle being made. Becoming a living man was Christ's first kenotic act; becoming a dead man was his second. Christ's human soul, united to his Divine Person, went down into the realm of the dead, while his body with its divinity lay incorruptible in the tomb. The angels cried "Hosanna", as once the citizens of Jerusalem had. Hosanna means "Save, we pray! Give salvation!" and is the most basic liturgical prayer of petition and intercession there is. The Church still prays it constantly as the basic content of her entire liturgy. Hosanna, save, demolish death, restrain Satan, free souls, forgive sins, make reconciliation, and bring to ruin whatever walls isolate someone from God, then or now.

Christ makes one more kenotic act. We have seen him descend from his throne of glory to Bethlehem in order to call contrite hearts to repent, for the Kingdom of God is at hand; we have just seen him descend from the Cross and step across the doorway of Hades to announce that Kingdom to the souls of the just who are dead; but there is one more place, smaller but as baneful, to which he comes. The gates of death that Christ must trample down are found at the threshold of our hearts where they bar us from light and life and liturgy. Christ not only tramples down death by his death, he also tramples down death when he puts us to death, puts our old Adam to death. What Christ did in Hades, and what he will do at the apocalypse, he now does in the sacrament. Baptism is a watery route to the stronger man who can bind our kidnapper. Having been silenced in Sheol, the soul begins to sing. Baptism resuscitates the soul's dormant liturgy.

Sin is forgetfulness of God, and death is the consequence of sin. If we sever a stem from the roots, the flowers will die. If we sever ourselves from God, our liturgy will die. That is how it happened to Adam and Eve. "They heard the sound of the LORD God walking in the garden in the cool of the day, and the man and his wife hid themselves from the presence of the LORD God among the trees of the garden" (Gen 3:8). They transferred their home address from the land of the living to the abode of the dead, the land of no-liturgy. Into Eden they brought invisibility (hades), concealment (hell), and darkness (sheol) because God's footfalls filled them with dread. A dead body cannot feel a pin prick, but a soul is never so dead that it cannot feel the prick of conscience, and the indelible *imago Dei* in the man and woman stirred compunction in them. The question now is whether Adam and Eve will listen with different ears when Christ draws near to them in Hades? It is the same question presented to every sinner at his moment of conversion prior to the sacrament of Baptism and his moment of contrition prior to the sacrament of Penance. Are Adam and Eve and we now as eager to hear the footfalls as once we were terrified by them? When John the Baptist cries, "The Kingdom of heaven is at hand", the question put to us is whether we repent or run. How does the promise of a lifetime of liturgy sound to us? Jesus is on the prowl for a kingdom of priests for God his Father (Rev 1:6) and goes even beyond the ends of the earth to find faithful disciples whom he can make into sacerdotal colleagues.

One meaning of "harrow" is to crack something open, to lacerate and tear open, to vex and to torment, and this certainly describes how the Victor's approach was experienced by Satan and Hades. But another meaning of "harrow" comes from an agricultural sense, and it refers to an implement with iron teeth that is drawn over plowed land to break up clods of earth, remove weeds, stir the soil. Harrow sleds are dragged across the earth to open it, then they cover planted seeds so they can take root and sprout. Dragging the harrow sled across the graves of the cemetery cultivates a new harvest—and one different from what was sown! "What is sown is perishable, what is raised is imperishable. It is sown in dishonor, it is raised in glory. It is sown in weakness, it is raised in power. It is sown a physical body, it is raised a spiritual body. If there is a physical body, there is also a spiritual body. Thus it is written, 'The first man Adam became a living soul'; the last Adam became a life-giving spirit" (1 Cor 15:42–45).

The last Adam became a harrowing, life-giving spirit. When Christ approaches the soul whom he intends to rescue, whether in Hades or at the font, he first lances the sin and then heals the sinner. A patient will fear the divine physician's approach if he is unwilling to have his self-love punctured; but if the sinner has lost patience with the silence of Sheol, if the place of no-liturgy fatigues him, if the Kingdom's approach brings repentance to his throat, then he will welcome the break-up of his unfit home. Harrowing causes distress, but it is all for the sake of resurrection. After this harrowing, the neophyte makes his way straight to the altar for the first of a string of Eucharists over the rest of his life. Baptismal harrowing yields Eucharistic fruit.

Chapter 35

Eschatology

Eschatology concerns the last things, and liturgical eschatology concerns the consequences of those last things as they impact us now. We do not have to wait until later to experience what will last. We think we do because we mistake the eschaton for the letter Z: the final point of the line. Like a creature who can only walk a dotted line in two directions, forward and backward, man is a temporally dimensional creature who can look in only two directions on the dotted line of history, future and past. But in his transcendence, God sees from above, sees the whole line, sees the whole page on which the line is printed. What we describe as yesterday and yore, he sees as *hodie* (today). What we describe as future and forthcoming, he knows as a liturgical *hodie*. We typically sight along the line of history, like a marksman sighting along the barrel of a gun, but God's vision embraces the history, our eye, and the target all at once, and in liturgy God shares his vision with us. The sacrifice of Abraham on Mount Moriah, the sacrifices of the first and second temples on that same mountain, the sacrifice of Jesus on Mount Calvary, the sacrifice of his priest after mounting to the sacramental altar, and the worship that happens in the heavenly Jerusalem (Rev 22:3) have all happened *today*. Liturgy is entering into the *hodie* to receive a new vision that is binocular. The two lenses of binoculars provide depth effect when they are fitted side-by-side; we likewise see with increased depth when we look with a historical lens and an eschatological lens fitted side-by-side. We see history filling up, but we also see what the cup of history is being filled up with, namely, the fullness of time. "When the time had fully come, God sent forth his Son" (Gal 4:4).

Liturgical eschatology poses a fundamental question: Do you really believe in the resurrection? Will it make a difference to you—not later, but between today's sunrise and tonight's sunset?

It would be difficult to walk very far, very easily, or very quickly if one looked no farther than four inches in front of the toe of one's shoe. Far better to raise one's eyes toward the horizon, scanning for obstacles but not fixating upon them. Liturgical eschatology raises our line of sight, extends it, expands it. Without a present liturgical vision of the *telos*, the world looms too large. The world must be placed in context. Our liturgical vision is not a matter of taking our eyes off the world; it is a matter of putting the world in perspective. The immediate is not neglected, but it is placed in proper context so that it does not trip us up. The concerns of the immediate should not overwhelm.

One of the differences between a child and an adult is the ability to judge an event against a larger backdrop. The immature child finds a pain or disappointment so intense because it totally occupies his attention, while a mature adult should know how to weigh the event properly. Someone who attains *natural* maturity will judge this hour within the day, this day within the week, this week within the year, this year within his life; someone who attains *supernatural* maturity will judge things of this world within the context of the next life, which he has already begun living while still in this one. This latter maturity is more difficult to attain than the former. If we relax the eschatological tension line, then our nerves will go limp and a particular trial or sorrow will grieve us because human faith will fail to lift our eyes above it, hope will fail to stand beneath it, and love will fail to surround it. Our virtues must be strengthened by an infused faith, hope, and love effected by the Holy Spirit. Then faith can be convinced that God uses both good and ill to work our deification; hope can be convinced that God's hand is always on the rudder, no matter what happens; love can be convinced to bear all things, believe all things, hope all things, endure all things (1 Cor 13:7). Liturgical eschatology is contingent upon those three theological virtues, and those three together are required for making liturgical worship while walking through the valley of the shadow of death. Liturgical eschatology fears no evil because, even in the presence of our enemies, a table is spread for faith, a head is anointed with hope, and a cup overflows with love.

Going in one direction, we may say that the parousia will be the highest intensification and fulfillment of the liturgy. Going in the other direction, we may say the liturgy is a parousia-like event. "Parousia" means a presence or coming, arriving and entering into a situation, and it was a technical term for the visit of a king. By that definition, liturgy *is* parousia, literally. The King arrives in a true, real, and substantial manner. It is a literal statement that every Eucharist is a parousia: it is the Lord's arrival, the Lord's presence, the visit of our Lord and King. Every Eucharist is a rehearsal for the final parousia that is still to come on our dotted line even though it is already before God's eye as he witnesses our liturgies along that line. This is a unification of the heavenly and earthly liturgies. There are not two liturgies, one in heaven and one on earth; there is one liturgy, in heaven and on earth. In the liturgy, the trumpet of the Word is already summoning us, and yet the seventh angel is still waiting to put his lips to the mouthpiece (Rev 10:7). The King comes—and the result is an increased hope for the King to come! The Gospel announces that Christ has trampled down death—and the result is an increased expectation of death's demise! Every Eucharist radiates the glory of the parousia—and the result is an even more intense yearning for glory to reveal itself! This is the antinomy of liturgical eschatology. If we relax that antinomy between eschaton and history, Church and world, liturgy and the mundane, then we lapse into heresy (a choice, *airesis*) and make a choice either to leave history or to settle into it as our home. Neither is correct.

A person's attitude toward the arrival of the King reveals something about his character, and his character conditions the way he liturgizes. Many commentators on the Psalms have pointed out that the poor are eager for Judgment Day, whereas the rich live in fear of it. The poor have confidence that if the Judge would only arrive to see the injustice with his own eyes, then he would set things right. Their conviction comes from God's own self-revelation that the Judge's arrival will be good news for the poor, freedom for prisoners, recovery of sight for the blind, and freedom for the oppressed (Is 61, the text chosen by Jesus for his first homily, Lk 4). But the rich have a different reaction to Judgment Day. They are less eager for the Judge's arrival because he will show the strength of his arm, scatter the proud in their conceit, cast down the mighty from their throne, and send them away empty (Mary, Magnificat, Lk 1).

Whereas the Church may appear to retreat from the world and engage in self-absorption when she conducts her liturgy, liturgical eschatology reveals that at this precise moment she is, in reality, entering more deeply into the heart of the world than ever before in order to work its liberating transformation. When the world killed Christ, it killed itself. Its deicide was suicide. So when the Church welcomes Christ, it is resuscitating the world. In her liturgy, the Church prepares hearts, not to spurn the King, but to welcome his parousia, not to scorn his love, but to accept the cost of deification. Self-love is being conquered, a step necessary for the eighth day to take root. And when the eighth day takes root in the life of liturgists, they do not remain passive between one celebration and the next one. Their temporal life is not diminished by eschatology. Every moment of their temporal life receives real value from liturgical eschatology. Everything is judged, evaluated, and understood against the light of the eschaton. The service the liturgy gives to the world—the Church's *leitourgia*—is to make this light manifest. The end of man is presented because man in his end state is present: first Jesus, then Mary, then us.

Liturgical eschatology refers every moment of the world's time and every particle of the world's material to the Kingdom of God, because only in that Kingdom do we see the ultimate end and meaning of every moment and matter. Liturgical eschatology sees all things in light of what God cares about, and God does not care about our properties or reputations or flatterers, but about our soul. God called the rich man a fool for building more barns to store his grain because that very night his soul would be demanded of him, and the things he had prepared would belong to someone else. "So is he who lays up treasure for himself, and is not rich toward God" (Lk 12:21). Liturgical eschatology wants to know what matters to God—perhaps the most important dogma of all.

Picture the eschaton this way. If a person had an intense light shining behind him, when that person came into a room, his shadow would enter before his body did. This is the basis for scriptural typology: Christ's shadow (type) entered history before his body did (antitype). The Old Testament foreshadows Jesus because the light of the eschaton shines from behind him and casts the shadow of the Cross down the entire length of the dotted (historical) line on which we walk. Paul says the Israelites were already under the cloud, were baptized into Moses in the cloud and sea, and ate spiritual food and drank spiritual drink, because the spiritual Rock that followed them was Christ (1 Cor 10:1–4). The Israelites were affected by the Cross before it happened. The Paschal Mystery occurred during one particular dot on the line. It thereafter fills every baptismal font and is laid upon every altar table; it theretofore cast its shadow upon every move God made in salvation history: the Cross was the wood of the staff that split the Red Sea in Moses' hand; the water flowing from Christ's side was the floodwater that drowned sin (Noah) and permeated the Jordan with healing power (Naaman); the blood flowing from Christ's side marked the doorposts and lintels of every house in Egypt where slaves ate the Lamb.

It is impossible to keep water from seeping into new spaces through the smallest cracks, and we likewise do not know into what pagan places the saving water from the side of Christ has seeped or how it might have made its way up the hill of the Areopagus (Acts 17:22) where Paul found an altar to a god yet unknown. The Lord of hosts who will prepare a lavish banquet for all the nations (Is 25) is the eschatological Lord of hosts, and all are being gathered to that mountain so he can swallow up the death-veil that is spread over all nations. In the liturgy, we already begin climbing the mountain where that will happen. In the liturgy, we already raise our eyes at the sound of Zion's trumpet shaking the earth. The prophet Joel wants to know who can endure it? He recommends we commence with fasting, weeping, mourning, rending of heart, and offering a true sacrifice (Joel 2)—these are liturgical starts.

The liturgy is something from out of this world in the world. The cultic antinomy of the Church's *leitourgia* is to make the eschaton present to the world, to intersect time with eternity. Liturgy is God's landing pad and man's launching pad. In order to remain true to her mission—her *leitourgia*—the Church must keep this eschatological aroma about her, or else she will become just another temporal agency, a state agent. If the Church loses her saltiness, she will be good for nothing, thrown out, and trampled upon. Liturgical eschatology is essential for ecclesiology. The Church is a sacramental world, and the sacramental world is essentially a link between the world of eternity and the world of today. Her mission, her *leitourgia*, is to be a sacramental wormhole. Her mission, her *leitourgia*, is to display the end, purpose, goal, and ultimate aim of all things. Her mission, her *leitourgia*, is martyrdom (*martyria*: witness). This life is short and is given to us only to gain the other life, the divine life, the eternal life, the godly life, the loving life (agape), the lovely life (beatitude).

We could learn something about eschatology by observing how the eschatological Lord incarnate began his ministry. What was his first message upon entering the public scene? According to Luke, he read from the scroll of Isaiah in the synagogue and said, "Today this Scripture has been fulfilled in your hearing" (Lk 4:21); according to Matthew, he went to Capernaum and began to preach "Repent, for the kingdom of heaven is at hand" (Mt 4:17); according to Mark, he came into Galilee proclaiming "The time is fulfilled, and the kingdom of God is at hand; repent, and believe in the gospel" (Mk 1:15); and according to John, he asks two disciples of John the Baptist "What do you seek?" and in response to their question about where he is staying, he says "Come and see" (Jn 1:38–39). These are all eschatological words: today, repent, believe, kingdom, at hand, come, see. How does the liturgy begin? Also with eschatological words: the Triune name, grace and love and communion, grace and peace, "the Lord be with you", acknowledging sins, preparing to celebrate sacred mysteries, asking prayers of Mary and angels and saints, begging to be brought to everlasting life, *kyrie eleison*, healing contrite hearts, calling sinners, interceding at the right hand of the Father, glory in the highest, peace, the Lamb who takes away sins, the Holy One and Lord Most High—all spoken looking up. Then we look back, in the first reading of the Word, at what Jesus has done to set this eschaton in liturgical motion.

The liturgy is a magnifying glass for seeing eschatologically, and the eschaton is a looking-glass for seeing liturgically. To see eschatologically, we need the magnifying glass of liturgy because liturgy magnifies God—*magnifien*, "to speak or act for the glory or honor of someone". And to see liturgically, we need the looking-glass of eschatology because the eschaton gives us the true picture of things—*mirari*, "to wonder at, to admire" (cf. miracle). Eschatology is liturgical magnification of God, and liturgy is eschatological wonder at God. Neither is telescopic, because the thing we are trying to catch sight of does not lie at a far distance. The Kingdom of God is *at hand*. The Kingdom's grace happens in the liturgical *hodie*. Christ has passed through the gates of heaven, yet the priest holds up the sacrament and says "*Behold* the Lamb of God." The eschatological Christ has been present under sacramental veil ever since he accomplished the Paschal Mystery and was raised up to pass through the heavens now to intercede for us as high priest (Heb 4:14). We have difficulty perceiving his victory because our eyes are myopic. We nearsightedly focus on nothing but the affairs of the world, a world that will cease.

Neither liturgy nor eschaton are irrelevant to life, because life is about letting God love us. We sometimes mistakenly think we go to liturgy so that we can reach God, when, in fact, liturgy exists so that God can reach out to us. He has desired to do so from the foundation of the world and designed liturgy for that purpose. We go to liturgy and pray "thy kingdom of love come, thy love be done." If we already have this life everlasting, what more remains than the enjoyment of that life everlasting? Heaven will be the enjoyment of the perichoretic life of the Trinity that was kenotically extended to flood us *hodie*. Eschatology has to do with final things—that is to say, the condition of things in their final state. When we celebrate the Eucharist and receive the charity of God, we human beings are in our final state, i.e., our eschatological condition.

Chapter 36

Mary (Liturgical Theotokology)

It is well-known that the Second Vatican Council did not issue a separate document on the Blessed Mother but, instead, gave her a chapter at the end of the Dogmatic Constitution on the Church, *Lumen gentium*. "She is hailed as a pre-eminent and singular member of the Church, and as its type and excellent exemplar in faith and charity" (53). The council supposed a connection that we will also suppose here. There is something of a perichoretic relationship between the Church, Mary, and liturgy, each making room for the other, each drawing from the other. The *liturgy* is the Church in motion, the Church caught being most herself; *Mary* is a type of the Church, a personification of the Church; the *Church* is a Marian mystery because this woman is already at the fullness the Church seeks in her liturgical pilgrimage. We should therefore expect to find Marian dimensions in our liturgical life and dimensions of liturgy imprinted on Mary. Mary's life gives us insight into what we do at liturgy, and liturgical dogmatics outlines Mary's identity. Looking upon Mary as a liturgical person reveals not only her identity, but ours, too. Ecclesiology and Theotokology are complementary.

The unique role that Mary played in the history of redemption gives her an unparalleled role in the Church. As Mother of God (*Mater Dei*), Mary is God's way down to us, and as Mother of the Church (*Mater Ecclesiae*), Mary is our way up to God. Her humility annuls any Mariolatry. The Mystical Body depends on the lifeblood of grace, and Mary is the masterpiece of God's grace. Mary is at the juncture of God's descent and man's ascent, and what she was as the historical trysting place for God and man continues in every liturgical tryst. (Tryst: "an agreement between lovers to meet at a certain time and place". A definition of liturgy.) Mary is the model of the spiritual attitude with which the Church celebrates the divine mysteries. Liturgy's catabatic and anabatic character is modeled after Christ's *kenosis* and her *fiat*. Our liturgy should be an expression of the kind of surrender that Mary gave, and though we no longer know Christ according to the flesh, he dwells spiritually in the baptized neophyte. What happened physically in the *Panagia* happens spiritually in a believer. In her *fiat*, she said "let it be done unto me", and in his conversion, the catechumen says "let it be done unto me, too." Christ spiritually enters the baptized. The baptized lives *en Christo*.

Liturgy is a pilgrimage across time and space, and although Mary has completed her journey, she remains a companion with us on ours. Each Christian makes a journey from the city of man to the city of God both within himself (spiritually) and across his lifetime (eschatologically). The city of God consists of all human and celestial beings united in their love for God and united in seeking to glorify him. Each Christian's journey is contingent on God's grace and may go more slowly at one time of his life than another, go at a slower or faster pace than another person's does, but, if predestined, the Christian will depart from love of self to arrive at a greater love of God. This is the pilgrimage of the Church militant to the Church triumphant. At the head of this parade is Jesus, and Mary is first behind him. She is one of us, but farther ahead. She is in the same parade as we are, but nearer the head. The true end of liturgy is to arrive where Mary did. The Church proceeds along the path already trodden by the Virgin Mary (*Redemptoris Mater* 2). She is the image of what we are yet to become.

The pilgrim Church is on her way to meet the Lord who comes, but the Lord has already come to Mary (Feast of the Annunciation) and for Mary (Feast of the Assumption), and yet she still accompanies her children (Feast of the Ascension). She and the angel are alone in icons of the first feast, but Mary is in the midst of the apostles in the icons of the latter two feasts. The icon of the Dormition and the icon of the Ascension reveal liturgical Mariology.

In the icon of the Feast of the Dormition, the apostles have already been sent to the corners of the world to preach the Gospel and establish Eucharistic communities, as if carrying tabernacles of *kerygma* and *koinonia* in their hands, and as Mary completes the course of her earthly life, they are miraculously transported back to Jerusalem to be with the woman who was the tabernacle of the one whom they preach and hand out. She is taken up by the one whom she brought down—it seems only fair—and the icon of Mary's Dormition shows Jesus holding her swaddled soul as the icon of the Nativity shows Mary holding Jesus' swaddled body. She is taken to heaven by the one who came to earth through her. By the voluntary humiliation of the Son, the Mother of God receives glory and is the first among us to participate in the deification of the creature. She is the first, but not the last. Liturgical asceticism is the spiritual warfare required to approach deification. In the Virgin, the Church has already reached the perfection for which the followers of Christ still strive by conquering sin, so she is the sign of the Church's future glory. As a deified human hypostasis, Mary witnesses the possibility of the Church's existence. That is what the apostles are staring at: they see the personal and embodied consequence of the good news they preach.

In the icon of the Feast of the Ascension, Mary again stands in the midst of the apostles. In fact, if one were not familiar with the iconography, this would look like a Marian feast instead of a Christological feast: she and the apostles sometimes take up more than half the board. But that is precisely the point. The Feast of the Ascension is the feast of consummated salvation. There is a vertical track paved between heaven and earth, and by making anabatic Ascension, Christ paves the way for catabatic Pentecost that, when it hits the ground, will spread horizontally to the ends of the earth. The Ascension is not Christ disappearing, it is the activation of the Paschal energy of Christ. So the icon is actually an image of the forty-day-old Church about to be born ten days later. The significance of the icon lies, not in the departure of Christ, but in the significance it has for the Church and the world, which is why the center of gravity of the icon is shared between Christ above and Mary below. The Theotokos is the icon of the Church because there is no other way to write an icon of the Church. She is the Church personified and therefore becomes the axis of the whole composition, placed at the center of the apostolic college immediately below the ruling and ascending Christ. Christ extends a blessing with his right hand, for he has not left his Church orphaned. The angels standing on each side of Mary are guarantors that the ascended Christ will come again in glory. But the Church has work to do in the meantime.

The work the Church is given to do comes out of her character, which is already glimpsed in Mary. She is *doxological* insofar as she offers glory to God with her whole being; she is *Eucharistic* insofar as she embodies Israel's praise and creation's thanksgiving; she is *spiritual* for having enjoyed a personal Annunciation Pentecost in anticipation of the corporate apostolic Pentecost on the disciples; she is *theological* insofar as she enjoys a mystical union with God; she is *ascetical* insofar as her will was conformed to Christ's; she is *intercessory* insofar as she continues in heaven to exercise her maternal role on our behalf; she is an *eschatological* person for being the last of the former age and the first of the final age. These are facets of the liturgical person as much as they are facets of Mary's identity. Liturgical dogmatics looks at Mariology to discover the character traits of liturgists. Mary personally responded, glorified, adored, espoused, and conceived God; the Church liturgically becomes what she is when she responds, glorifies, adores, enters the nuptial mystery, and bears the Eucharistic presence of God.

In *Marialis cultis*, Pope Paul VI identified four liturgical virtues that Mary exemplifies. He said she is (a) the attentive Virgin, (b) the Virgin in prayer, (c) the Virgin Mother, and (d) the Virgin presenting offerings. We could take these four as models of the spiritual attitude with which the Church celebrates the divine mysteries in liturgy.

The Church must be *attentive* to many things in the liturgy, but most of all to the Word of God. The same receptiveness to the Word must be found at every liturgy as was found in Mary, and that receptiveness is called by the same name: faith. Mary listened to God—and she did so long before Gabriel came on the scene. She was a hesychast in Jerusalem before becoming the Theotokos in Nazareth. The Protoevangelium of James says she had been raised in the temple of Jerusalem since age three, in the holy of holies, and the preachers on the Feast of the Presentation of Mary to the temple think this only natural: where better for God's tent to be pitched? The only place Mary, herself a temple for God, could possibly live would be in the temple of Jerusalem. She was a daughter of the sanctuary because she would become the sanctuary for the Only Begotten Son. Because the holiest would dwell in her, therefore she would dwell in the holy of holies. Her soul was nurtured on the word of God in ways that prepared her for giving her *fiat*. She arrived at this state by drawing from the whole history of her people Israel and having her response cultivated by the Holy Spirit. It is the same for us. Mary is a model for how the Church should be attentive to the self-giving of God and responsive in the self-giving of faith. This is a condition for celebrating liturgy.

The Church must remain in *prayer*. After the announcement was made by Gabriel, Mary went to visit Elizabeth, who was prompted by John's uterine kick to call her cousin blessed among women, in addition to calling the fruit of her womb blessed. Mary's response was the Magnificat, which Paul VI calls Mary's prayer par excellence. She poured out a song of the messianic times that mingled the joy of the ancient and new Israel. Our liturgical life is a life of prayer that humbly acknowledges the grace of God reaching out to us from the rejoicing of Abraham, the law of Moses, the hope of the prophets, the faith of Israel, and the love of Jesus. Our liturgical life expresses glorification of God and gratitude for the sanctification of mankind. Our liturgical life draws strength from the daily prayer of the Divine Office, from personal and spiritual prayer, and from repeated prayers in the Mass (Collect, Prayer the Faithful, Eucharistic Prayer, the Lord's Prayer, the Prayer after Communion). The Church is invited in every moment of prayer to assume the posture of Mary, woman of prayer. It would not be difficult to picture her prayer life as encompassing the six forms of prayer named by the *Catechism*: blessing, adoration, petition, intercession, thanksgiving, praise. As the only icon of the Church there is, we see Mary in the *orans* position.

The Church is the *Virgin Mother* of her children. Some will fail to understand how virginity and maternity can be united, thinking that if one is a virgin one cannot be a mother, and if one is a mother one cannot be a virgin, but actually this title combines purity with fruitfulness. The latter is made possible by the former. Her miraculous motherhood comes from her virginal purity. Mary's pure, undivided, virginal heart lets her respond to the overshadowing action of God, and that makes the birth of the Savior possible. She set no hindrance to grace's work, there was no opaqueness in her to obscure the divine light. Virginity is precisely this transparency to God, and virginity opens her to motherhood. This Marian mystery is a prototype for the Mystical Body to celebrate the divine mysteries worthily. The motherhood of the Church that gives birth to her many children similarly depends upon a virginal purity. It is why the Church must be in a state of perpetual reformation: *ecclesia semper reformanda*. Obedience to the commandments precedes and prepares the Church's celebration of liturgical nuptial mysteries. Liturgical asceticism is requisite

for the Eucharistic feast and for the maternal identity of the Church
to take full force. The first identity of the Church is not bureaucratic;
it is maternal. Mary carried the Life of the world in her womb, and
the Church carries regenerative life in her font of Baptism (which
Augustine called the uterus of mother Church), and in neither case
is the appearance of divine life our own accomplishment. The Word
can be born sacramentally in the stable of our heart only by the Holy
Spirit's prevenient action.

The Church lives by *presenting offerings*. Mary presented Jesus to
God at both the beginning and the end of her Son's mission: in the
temple, when the Presentation of Jesus fulfilled the commandment in
Exodus 13:12 for a family to offer their firstborn son to God, and on
Calvary, where Mary united herself with a maternal heart to his sacrifice, consenting to his immolation. The sword that Simeon foretold
would pierce her soul cleaved the natural union of mother and son
and let her offer her son to the Father. The liturgy lives by the same
action. The liturgy only lives through oblation. Mary's life shows a
mingling of oblations: first she offered herself, at the Annunciation,
then she offered her Son, standing beneath his Cross. We likewise
offer Jesus in the Sacrifice of the Mass, and when we do so, we must
be offering ourselves with him. The excellence of the Sacrifice of
the Mass comes from the fact that it is in substance the same sacrifice
as that of the Cross. Jesus continues really to offer himself, the same
victim present on Calvary's altar before Mary's eyes and present on
the liturgical altar before our eyes. The Church's liturgy must always,
always stand under the Cross, united to his sacrifice. If the Church
wanders from this location, she will have lost her reason for being.

Eve came from the first Adam as he slept. The Second Adam came
from the New Eve, and upon his later sleep of death on the Cross
came the Church, true mother of the living. Mary, a deified human
hypostasis, is the mother of a restored liturgical humanity. In herself,
she links holiness and humility, sanctity and submission, reverence
and resignation. Her soul, she says, magnifies the Lord and rejoices
in her Savior, and she is the one through whom God will give help
to Israel, his servant, scattering the proud in their conceit and casting
down the mighty, so he can exalt the lowly and fill the hungry with
good things. She glorifies God even as she serves the sanctification of
man: she is a woman of liturgy.

CONCLUSION

We have not been addressing dogmas about the liturgy, we have been trying to find a way to think about dogmas liturgically and rest them upon the Church's *lex orandi*.

Dogmas are not only to be believed, they are to be obeyed. This latter dimension is opened up by treating dogmas liturgically.

God must be the source of dogma, but that does not make a problem for resting dogma on liturgy, since I understand liturgy to be primarily the work of God and only secondarily the activity of man. If liturgy were only the creative activity of men, then dogma could not rest upon it because dogma would be a result of our creativity. No, dogma must be a consequence of divine revelation. But what is the purpose of revelation?

In one sense, it has no "purpose", since it is an act of the absolutely free and sovereign will of God. But even free acts done by man are directed toward an end and have a "purpose" in that sense, so with all due apophatic humility, let us consider God's purpose in revelation. It is not to fill library shelves. It is not for footnotes. God's purpose in revelation is to receive creatures into his glory. He shows himself for us to see and, therefore, worship. Perfected and beatified creatures are presented with God, through his energies, and they acquire revelation by receiving, knowing, and doing. The knowing (i.e., dogma) lies in between an act by God and a response by man. This definition of revelation already shows its connection to our definition of liturgy. God's purpose in revelation is to extend kenotically the perichoresis of the Trinity to allow creatures to participate synergistically in his glory and ascend to their final beatitude, which consists of recognizing, knowing, and worshipping God eternally. If dogma is a consequence of revelation, then liturgical dogmatics is revelation received, known, and done. A dogma is to be obeyed.

God is *received* in liturgy. We did not say that knowledge about God is received in liturgy, though that is also true. The idea of liturgical dogmatics involves more than the modest claim that liturgy is one source of information about God. Rather, the idea asserts that God himself, the mystery, the source of life, the Creator and Redeemer, gives himself in liturgies that make present redemptive and revelatory acts. The historical acts of redemption occurred once upon a time and then passed on. They remain in memory (spirituality), in inspired memory (Scripture), and in consequence (under the new state of affairs brought into history), but is it possible for us to receive the actor himself? Only if the *Logos* continues to give himself so that we do not have to listen to echoes of the past but can listen to his living voice. Liturgy is connected to the *mirabilia Dei* but does not present them as memorabilia. Liturgy presents them as ongoing works of God in the mysteries that it tenderly holds forth.

God is *known* in liturgy. The verb in that sentence has been stretched beyond normal application, but we are accustomed to its elasticity. It is different to know of John than to know about John or to know John. We come to liturgy, not in order to learn of God (evangelization) or find out about God (catechesis), but to know God. He who knows us has promised to meet us there so that we might know him by experience. We acknowledge that dogmatics is organized intellectually as a systematic body of tenets and principles, and we do not mean to disparage that, since the intellect is the highest gift to man. But one can also systematically organize truth by a grammar of life, which can grasp things that cannot be made intellectually comprehensible because they involve the whole person—including the intellect, but more than intellect alone. There is an additional way of receiving, knowing, and doing that involves asceticism, virtues, piety, and liturgy, all required to make union with mystery, not just have knowledge about mystery. Upon union, dogma has done its job.

And there is a *doing* in liturgy. We receive and know by doing. This holds a key to a more profound knowledge because it arises from love. In 1 Corinthians, Paul says love never ends; in Revelation, John says liturgy will never end. Prophecies will pass away, tongues will cease, and knowledge will pass away (even dogmatic knowledge) because they are partial; and when the perfect comes, the partial will pass away. "For now we see in a mirror dimly, but then face to face. Now I know in part; then I shall understand fully, even as I have been fully understood" (1 Cor 13:12). One does not *not* love God outside the liturgy, just as one does not *not* love one's wife or children when absent from them, but the love for either God, spouse, or children is different when it is in person. When it is a deed. There was a debate between ascetical theologians about what was ultimate and what was penultimate: does agape lead to gnosis, or does gnosis lead to agape? They solved the question by realizing that God *is* love; therefore, one cannot know him without loving him, cannot love him without knowing him. To know him, one must do him: one must liturgize God. Gnosis is a divine vision, and love remains a permanent part of our knowledge of God. Liturgical dogmatics is a divine vision of love, and we therefore know it to be true (*dokein*).

Liturgical dogmatics stands upon the tripod of faith, hope, and love. Hope champions faith, and faith is ordained to charity, which is a bond of perfection. Our perfection is deification, which is union with God, and so the faithful dogmas exist primarily for motivating us hopefully toward this loving union. (I do not mean "optimistically", I mean being motivated by the theological gift of hope.) The dogmas are less for intellectual satisfaction, despite the pleasure theological study gives a few, and more for protecting faith, hope, and love so that they can do their job once infused in us. Liturgical dogmas protect the life of the Church, which means we can see dogmas in service to health. In addition to being didactic, they are therapeutic. Dogmas are definitive, not so much because they describe God (God cannot be de-scribed, outlined, explained), but more because they mark the boundaries between life and death. At some moment or another, whether along the way or on the deathbed, a person will face dogmatic questions like "Was my life meaningful? Will I be forgiven? What is my destiny?" Dogmatic questions like that propel us into the sacred. Liturgy addresses dogmatic questions like that. If your liturgy does not present questions of such consequence, then you are doing it wrong.

In order to be taught dogma, we need a pedagogue. Unfortunately, that word has drifted from its original meaning and come to be understood as a lecturer, an instructor, a docent. But if we follow the word's etymology, we find that the pedagogue was the slave who escorted children to school, from *paidos* (child) and *agein* (to lead). Liturgical dogmaticians should be slaves, pedagogues, bondservants to Christ, who himself freely took the form of a slave for us (Phil 2:7). He leads us to the Father by training the virtuous life, gracing the soul, deifying a person. The Divine Pedagogue is practical, not theoretical, and so in a flash the divide between dogma and morality is overcome (norms of thought versus norms of action).

Basil the Great differentiated two types of Christian teachings according to who knows them and according to the form in which they are found. By the former characteristic, he distinguished teachings that are publicly proclaimed from teachings reserved to members of the household of faith; and by the latter characteristic, he distinguished teachings received from written sources from teachings given secretly through the apostolic tradition. As important as *public and written* teachings are, Basil says that, without the *secret and unwritten* teachings, the Gospel would be fatally mutilated. The examples he gives of the latter are signing ourselves with the cross, facing east for prayer, words of the Eucharistic Prayer, blessings of baptismal water and chrismation oil, and Sunday as the eighth day. What is interesting to us here are the names he gives to the two types of teachings. He calls the public, written teachings *kerygma*, and the unwritten, hidden teachings *dogma*. The kerygma is the Christian Gospel in its public form: evangelism is kerygmatic; apostolic witness is kerygmatic; good news conveyed to the unbaptized is kerygmatic. Dogma is the Christian Gospel veiled from the uninitiated: how to pray is dogmatic; the eighth day is dogmatic; knowledge of the Trinity is dogmatic. For Basil, the *dogmata* were the total complex of unwritten habits, the whole structure of liturgical and sacramental life. And what he really meant by "knowing them in secret" was that we could only know them by way of "the mysteries", the secrets, the sacraments. We would have to do the Christian rites. We would receive and know *by doing*. Liturgical dogmatics.

Liturgical dogma therefore involves beauty and behavior in addition to precepts and principles. Under the patronage of liturgy, dogmas have an aesthetic dimension. Dogmas are believed, but they are also obeyed and wondered. They are concerned with what is true—true about God, oneself, and the world—and we can have a glimpse of such truth through beauty. Beauty is a knowledge of the deep reality of things as God understands them. Beauty reveals ontological reality— but only to the healthy eye! Therefore, to be a dogmatician one must be an ascetic. Liturgical dogmaticians must be hesychasts, because dogmas are for contemplation. The prophet Isaiah told us that the one who comes to reveal God will have no majestic bearing to catch our eye, no beauty to draw us to him. He will be spurned and avoided by men and held in no esteem, yet the eyes of faith will see beauty in him and seek him dogmatically when he presents himself to their liturgical gaze.

Only like can know like. We can know God only if we see God in glory, and we can see God in glory only if we are ourselves glorified. That is, knowing God is contingent upon liturgy. We acquire liturgical dogmatics by receiving, knowing, and doing liturgy.

SUBJECT INDEX

abcedarium, the Church's, 185–92
Abraham, 23, 125, 160, 192, 230, 241
Adam: age of, 48; in Church's
    abcedarium, 185; confession of,
    91–92, 93–94; in Eve's confession,
    92–93; Eve's creation FROM,
    242; and healing of sin, 99;
    worship abandonment, 167–68
Adam and Eve: creation purposes, 55,
    83–84, 85, 113, 130–31, 136–37;
    departure from Eden, 142; and
    fear of God, 25, 85, 228; God's
    frequent presence, 64; liturgical
    alienation, 113, 116; perfection
    yearning, 88; Satan's burglary, 226
adoration, for approaching God, 21,
    22. See also worship
Advent, in Church's abcedarium, 185
altar, in Church's abcedarium, 185,
    188
altar and angels, 66–68, 73
am-ing, 54
anabatic movement, in liturgy, 72–73
angels: and Christ's Resurrection,
    156, 170, 227; in Church's
    abcedarium, 185, 186;
    commonalities with man, 66–73;
    glorification function, 21, 55, 103,
    119; Jacob's experience, 57, 195–
    96; and Mary, 154, 238, 239, 240,
    241; during Mass celebration, 162,
    165; and material world, 65–66,
    84; and rescue of sinners, 94, 96,
    103; sin's consequence, 116
anger, 24, 110–11
Annunciation, 155, 238, 240, 242
Anointing of the Sick, 133, 175,
    223–24

Anselm, 226
apostles, 154–55, 238–39
approaching God, conditions for,
    19–24
Aristotle, 47, 55, 178
Ascension, 72, 157, 238, 239–40
asceticism, 23–24, 85, 89–90, 133, 134
assembling God's Church, 34–35, 36,
    158, 160, 228
Athanasius, 226
attentiveness, Mary's example, 240–41
Augustine, 42, 57, 112, 115, 116,
    117–18, 177, 196
avarice, 24, 104–5, 109–10
awe pathway, knowing God, 21,
    25–28

Baptism: as aid station, 223–24; for
    assembling God's Church, 35,
    158; in Church's abcedarium,
    187; and death, 61, 62, 142–43,
    168; grace's force, 133; and Holy
    Spirit, 38, 175; and just worship,
    56; as liturgical gateway, 32, 157,
    170, 228; in liturgical perspective
    of Jesus's life, 154, 156; and
    Mary's surrender, 238; and perfect
    liturgist titles, 168, 170, 171; as
    rescue from darkness, 144; and
    sacramental metaphors, 207–8; and
    sin, 96
Basil the Great, 246
beauty and truth, 81
beholding, as revelation invitation, 68
Being/be-ing, 53–54, 133
being-on-the-way, man as, 85
Bethlehem, in Church's abcedarium,
    185

Bible, in Church's abcedarium, 185.
　　See also Scripture
blessing, 131–32, 185–86
body identity, Church's, 200–201
body-soul unity, man's, 84–85
bones comparison, 46–47
Bread of Life, title significance, 168.
　　See also Jesus Christ
bridge function, liturgy, 21–22,
　　25–26, 36–37
Buber, Martin, 20

Caiaphas, 156
candle/smoke imagery, 176
catabatic movement, in liturgy,
　　72–73
century format, advantages, 40
charity and creation, 53
chastity, 24, 108–9, 133
Chesterton, G. K., 82
Christ. See Jesus Christ
Chrysostom, Saint John, 9, 68, 70, 77,
　　97, 166, 179
Church: abcedarium of, 185–92; for
　　actualizing the eschaton, 212–13;
　　body identity, 200–201; as gathered
　　people, 88, 160–61; house of God
　　identity, 195–96; inside reminders
　　of Christ, 160; as liturgy in
　　motion, 159, 211, 237; Mary's role,
　　237–42; mother identity, 196–97;
　　pilgrim identity, 199–200; as
　　place of permanence, 210–12; and
　　sacramental metaphors, 206, 207–8;
　　sacramental mission, 234–35;
　　as sacramental unity, 158–59;
　　sheepfold identity, 193–94; shore
　　metaphor, 201–2; spouse identity,
　　197–98; vineyard identity, 194–95
cloak metaphor, for liturgy, 95, 98
coastline metaphor, for Church,
　　201–2
collector, God as, 160–61
communion: in Church's abcedarium,
　　186; mental to actual, 49. See also
　　Eucharist; fellowship

confession, 91–94, 97–98
Confirmation, 62, 133, 175
contradictions and truth, 125–26
Cornelius of Caesarea, 67
cosmos: in Adam's confession,
　　91–92; as definition of world, 74;
　　evil's consequences, 118–20; and
　　liturgical year, 223; as liturgy,
　　54–55, 57–58, 76; and Sabbath,
　　222; Satan's actions, 103–4; time
　　element, 59–60, 81–82. See also
　　creation; world
Council of Trent, 211–12
counsel, as Holy Spirit gift, 180–81
covetousness, 105
creation: continuous nature, 59,
　　77; evil's consequence, 120–21;
　　from God's love, 53–54; God's
　　questions to Job, 123; man's role,
　　83–85; as ordering of chaos, 74,
　　76; and Sabbath, 222; Satan's
　　envy of, 105; sin's consequence,
　　113–14; and Trinity perichoresis,
　　30; as unity symbol, 103–4. See
　　also cosmos
Creed, Christ's liturgical work, 164
Cross: and Church identities, 193; in
　　Church's abcedarium, 186, 188;
　　foreshadowing of, 233–34; hodie
　　perspective, 230; in liturgical
　　perspective of Jesus's life, 155, 156,
　　157; in Mass celebration, 162, 163;
　　and perfect liturgist titles, 170,
　　171; and sacramental metaphors,
　　206, 207. See also Jesus Christ

darkness, 117–18, 119, 121, 148, 180
David, 66, 125
day period, for liturgy, 220–21
deacons/priests, 33, 55, 67–68, 73,
　　161–62, 182, 186, 189, 224
death, 61–62, 95, 141–43, 145, 156,
　　168, 186, 187, 226–28
dejection, demon of, 110
demons, 107–12, 226
despondency/despair, 110, 147, 180

dia+baleo, 104–5
Didache, 35
Diekmann, Godfrey, 48
Diogenes, 82
Dionysius, 55
disease model, sin, 135–37, 139
divine economy, salvation, 131
Divine Office, 60, 159, 220–21
docility, as Holy Spirit gift, 180–81
dogma, overview: in Church's abcedarium, 186; history of investigation approaches, 13–15; task of, 9–11, 243–47; teaching of, 245–46
doubt, demon of, 108, 180
dry bones comparison, Scripture as history, 46
dulia, 22

Easter Vigil prayer, 87, 89
ecclesiology, as extended Christology, 158–59
eight evil thoughts, 108–12
eighth day, 48, 60, 63, 222, 232
Elijah, 144, 155
Elizabeth, 174, 241
Emmanuel, title significance, 169. *See also* Jesus Christ
energies metaphor, for sacraments, 208–9
envy, 105, 137
Ephrem of Syria, 43, 54
eschatology, liturgical, 230–36
eschaton, in Church's abcedarium, 186
essence *vs.* energy of God, 31, 41, 208
eternal life, 62–63. *See also* Baptism; death; time
Eucharist: and angels, 68; and Church identities, 194; in Church's abcedarium, 186; and Holy Spirit, 38–39, 175; as Initiation, 62; in liturgical perspective of Jesus's life, 157; as parousia rehearsal, 232; and sacramental metaphors, 207–8; and

sin, 96, 97; and time, 211–12; as translation of eschaton, 212–13; without anger, 110–11; Zizioulas's existential argument, 13–14
Eucharistic Mary, 240
Eucharistic Prayer, 22–23, 165, 176
Evagrius of Pontus, 88, 108–12
Eve, 54, 83, 92–94, 186, 242. *See also* Adam and Eve
evil, 115, 117–22, 124, 125, 126
existential arguments, Zizioulas's, 13–14
Ezekiel, 106–7

faith: and Church identities, 197, 198; in Church's abcedarium, 186, 187; and the Creed, 164; and dogma, 245; and evil, 124, 126; as fidelity, 124–25; and fortitude, 180; and healing of sin, 95–96, 99; for liturgy, 147; and love, 72; Mary's example, 240–41; and spiritual knowledge, 179–80; and spiritual world, 77; and time perspectives, 231
falcon imagery, 205–6
fallen angels, 107, 119–20. *See also* Satan
fallen world, defining, 75–76. *See also* Adam and Eve; sin
fear: Adam and Eve's, 25, 85, 93, 228; in Church's abcedarium, 187; and idolatry, 22, 25; liturgy's function, 25–26; and love of God, 27–28; and sin, 114, 199–200
fear of Lord, as Holy Spirit gift, 177–78
fearful worship, for knowing God, 21
Feast of Tabernacles, 155
Feast of the Annunciation, 238
Feast of the Ascension, 238, 239–40
Feast of the Assumption, 238
Feast of the Dormition, 238–39
Feasts, in Church's abcedarium, 187
fellowship, 39, 109–11, 161, 178–79, 238

fidelity, 124–25
fire imagery, 146–47, 176
fishing imagery, 142–44, 145
Florensky, Pavel, 15, 16, 46
footnotes, minimization purpose,
 11–13
forgiveness, 99, 147, 162, 175
fortitude, as Holy Spirit gift, 180
frankincense as sacrifice, 106

Gabriel, 154, 240, 241
gathering God's Church, 34–35, 36,
 158, 160, 228
Gaudete, in Church's abcedarium,
 187
Gloria, Christ's liturgical work, 162
glorifying God: and Church
 identities, 193–95; with existence
 of cosmos, 54–55, 57–58, 113; as
 highest human activity, 81–82;
 with just worship, 55–57; as
 liturgy's purpose, 9, 131; as
 man's purpose, 88; role of angels,
 103; sin's consequence, 113–16;
 with thanksgiving, 129–30; time
 element, 59–64; and Trinity
 perichoresis, 30, 131–32. *See also*
 worship
gluttony, demon of, 104–5, 108
gnosis, 187, 245
Gnostics, 47, 61
God, in liturgy's purposes, 9–11.
 See also specific topics, e.g., Adam
 and Eve; grace; love *entries*;
 unknowable God; worship
good, evil's privation of, 118
Good Shepherd, title significance,
 170–71. *See also* Jesus Christ
good things, Satan's corruption of,
 104–5
Gospels, deacon's responsibility,
 67–68
grace, 32, 95–96, 112, 129–34, 154,
 187, 203, 237
Gregory the Great, 42

Hades/hell, 71–72, 142, 143–44, 156,
 187, 190, 226–27
harrowing, meanings of, 228–29
hatred, Satan's, 103–7
healing miracles, 95, 98–99
healthy state, from due worship,
 135–37, 139–40
hell/Hades, 71–72, 142, 143–44, 156,
 187, 190, 226–27
heresy, in Church's abcedarium, 187
Herod, 156
history: Scripture as, 43, 45–46, 153;
 time-oriented, 59, 230
hodie perspective of time, 230–31,
 235–36
holiness hypothesis, 47
holy death. *See* Baptism
Holy One, title significance, 169–70.
 See also Jesus Christ
Holy Spirit: activities of, 34, 59,
 175–76, 219–20; and angels, 7,
 73; and chastity, 109; and Church
 identities, 194, 195, 196, 197, 201;
 in Church's abcedarium, 187,
 188, 190; and Confirmation, 62;
 in Eucharistic Prayer, 22–23; gifts
 for liturgy, 177–82; and grace,
 134; as guide in liturgy, 220–25;
 and illumination, 30, 140, 173–74,
 177, 181–82; and just worship,
 56; for knowing God, 23; in life
 of Jesus, 173–74; and liturgical
 conversations, 48; in liturgical
 perspective of Jesus's life, 154, 155,
 157; for liturgical speech, 174–75;
 as liturgy author, 49; and liturgy's
 purposes, 9–11, 37–39; in Mass
 celebration, 161–62, 164, 165; and
 misfortune, 146; as prayer pathway,
 32; as Scripture author, 49; for
 seeing revelation, 44; signs of, 172–
 73, 175–76; in Trinity energies, 29,
 70; in Trinity's blessing cycle, 131;
 Trinity's glorification cycle, 132;
 witnessing the, 148

homage, for approaching God, 22
homily, Christ's liturgical work, 163–64
hope, 77, 147, 187, 231, 245
Hosea, 107, 160
house of God identity, Church's, 195–96
human dignity, 81–82
humility, 20, 22, 112, 147, 178
hypostatic union, in Church's abcedarium, 187. *See also* Jesus Christ

I AM image, 53–54
icon metaphor, for sacraments, 206
idolatry: in Church's abcedarium, 188; in confession of Adam and Eve, 94; Ezekiel's criticism, 106–7; and fear, 22, 25; misplaced confidence in, 129; piety compared, 178; Satan's, 103, 105; sin as, 113–16, 135–36, 137–38
imago Dei, 81–86, 118–19, 188
Incarnate, in Church's abcedarium, 188. *See also* Jesus Christ
infidelity, 124, 126
Introductory Rites, Christ's liturgical work, 161–62
Irenaeus, 34, 47
Isaiah, 55, 177
is-ing, 54
I-Thou relationship, 20–21

Jacob, 23, 57, 195–96
Jairus, 95
James, 157, 240
jealousy, God's, 136, 137–38, 139–40
Jeremiah, 106
Jerusalem: on earth, 138, 155, 157, 159, 188, 227, 238–39, 240; heavenly, 77, 89, 104, 181, 188, 198, 202, 204, 230
Jesus Christ: and angels, 66–67, 70–72; anger teaching, 110–11; and Church identities, 193–95,

197–98, 200–201; in Church's abcedarium, 185, 187, 188, 189, 190, 191; defeat of death, 227–28; defeat of Satan, 226–27; and Divine Office, 221; and eschatological ministry, 235–36; as fisherman, 142–44, 145; foreshadowing of, 70, 233–34; gathering task, 34, 36, 160, 228; and gifts of Holy Spirit, 177, 178; healing miracles, 95, 98–99; and Holy Spirit's work, 173–75; and just worship, 56; for knowing God, 23; and liturgical conversations, 48; liturgical perspective of His life, 153–57, 158–59; and liturgy for fallen world, 78; in liturgy's purposes, 9–11, 35–38, 39; and man's pilgrimage, 238; in Mass celebration, 158–66, 211–12; as mediator, 36–37, 44, 69, 193; and Nicodemus, 38; as perfect liturgist, 167–71; prayer command, 112; as prayer pathway, 32; and problem of evil, 125; as rescuer of sinners, 138–40, 148, 226–28; response to Satan's temptation, 137; as restoration, 121; and sacramental metaphors, 205, 206, 207–8; for seeing revelation, 44; and sin, 114–15; as teacher, 245–46; and time, 63–64; in Trinity energies, 29; in Trinity's blessing cycle, 131; in Trinity's glorification cycle, 131–32; and Trinity's mystery, 31; and the two Testaments, 42. *See also* Mary
Job, 23, 123–24, 125–26, 147
John, 125, 157, 174, 241, 244
John the Baptist, 228
Jonah, 143
Jordan River, 144, 195
Joseph, 197
Joshua, 195

joy and praise, 27
Judas, 156
Judgment Day, 90, 115, 143, 232
just worship, 55–56, 178–79
justice, 147, 177–78

kapporeth mercy seat, 21, 23, 42, 188
Kavanagh, Aidan, 214
kenosis, 71, 72, 99, 119, 133, 157, 188,
    238
kerygma, 188, 238, 246
knowing God, 19–24, 125–26,
    243–45
knowledge, as Holy Spirit gift,
    179–80
knowledge, in Eve's confession, 92
koinonia, 39, 109–11, 161, 178–79,
    238
Kyrie, Christ's liturgical work, 162

Lamb of God, title significance, 168.
    See also Jesus Christ
latria, 10, 22, 56, 130, 131, 136, 137,
    178, 188. *See also* worship
Lazarus, 45–46
leitourgia, 10, 22, 234–35
Lent, in Church's abcedarium, 188
lex credendi, 13, 43, 47, 123, 159
lex orandi, 13, 43, 47, 123, 159, 243
lifetime period, for liturgy, 223–24
light: and darkness, 118–20, 121,
    148; eschatological perspective of,
    233–34; glory as, 132; as means
    for seeing, 173; as sacramental
    metaphor, 207
liturgical dogmatics, overview:
    history of phrase usage, 13–15;
    importance summarized, 117,
    243–47; investigation approach,
    9–12, 15–16, 40. *See also specific
    topics, e.g.*, Baptism; Mary;
    unknowable God
liturgy, defined/purposes, 9, 25–26,
    34, 47, 117, 167, 188. *See also
    specific topics, e.g.*, Church;
    Eucharist; Holy Spirit; prayer

Liturgy of the Hours, 60, 111, 221
living experience *vs.* formula, 13–14,
    15
Lord of Life, title significance, 168.
    See also Jesus Christ
love: for approaching God, 22; in
    Church's abcedarium, 185, 188;
    and faith, 72; and fear of God,
    25–27, 177–78; and grace, 131; for
    knowing God, 245; for liturgy, 49,
    147; liturgy's function, 25–26, 130,
    245; and sin, 114; and spiritual
    world, 77; and time perspectives,
    231; in Trinity energies, 29, 33
love, God's: as liturgical ladder, 130;
    and misfortune, 146; Satan's
    clouding of, 103–5; and sinners,
    96, 97–98, 115–16
Lumen gentium, 10, 158, 193, 200, 237
lust, 24, 104, 108–9

MacDonald, George, 12
man: as being-on-the-way, 85–86;
    definitions of, 81–83; as highest
    creation, 83–85; pilgrimage
    towards perfection, 87–90. *See also
    specific topics, e.g.*, Adam; faith; sin
Marialis cultis, 240
marriage, 109, 133, 175, 224
Martha, 46
Mary: and angels, 66–67, 68;
    character facets, 240–41; in
    Church's abcedarium, 189, 191;
    and Holy Spirit, 174; in liturgical
    perspective of Jesus's life, 154,
    155, 156, 157; liturgical virtues of,
    241–42; and liturgy's beginning,
    37; nobility of, 81; as perfection,
    89; as spiritual model, 237–42
Mary Magdalen, 156, 157, 196
Mass: as activity of God and man,
    159; Christ's liturgical work,
    161–66; in Church's abcedarium,
    189
maternal metaphor, for sacraments,
    207–8

meekness, for approaching God, 22, 24
melancholy, demon of, 111
Melchizedek, 139, 140
miracles, 45–46, 95, 98–99, 143,
    144–45
money, love of, 109–10
Moses: and bread from heaven, 69;
    cherubim instruction, 66; and
    the Cross, 234; and God's I AM
    message, 53, 83; God's purpose
    for, 148; and Mount Tabor, 155;
    and Pharaoh, 105; and prayer,
    64, 241; and revelation, 41–42;
    seeing/not seeing God, 38, 125,
    169; as Torah foundation, 125
mother identity, Church's, 196–97
motherhood, Mary's example, 240–41
Mount Hermon, 155
Mount Tabor, 155, 191

Naaman, 234
naking, in confession of Adam and
    Eve, 94
Narcissus, 118–19
natural law, 113, 118, 136, 137
natural religion, 26–27, 165, 169
natural revelation, 41–42
Nebuchadnezzar, 54
New Adam, title significance, 167–68.
    See also Jesus Christ
New Testament, function of, 41–42
Nicodemus, 38, 157
Noah, 67, 189, 234
novena, in Church's abcedarium, 189

objective world, defining, 74. See also
    world
oblation, 77, 116, 165, 168, 170, 178,
    189, 190, 214, 242
Old Testament: five ages in, 48;
    foreshadowing in, 70, 149, 233–
    34; function of, 41–42, 109, 122;
    and Holy Spirit, 38; narrative of
    worship conflict, 105–6; prophet's
    knowledge, 214; righteous from,
    143–44, 147

Opus Dei, 157, 159, 189, 200, 221
Ordination, grace's force, 133

Palm Sunday, 155
parousia, 10, 63, 90, 204, 231–33
Paschal Mystery. See Jesus Christ
patience, 147
Paul, 64, 70, 109, 125, 160, 196,
    197–98, 226, 233–34, 244
Paul VI, 240
Penance, 175, 228
penitential act, Christ's liturgical
    work, 162
Pentecost, 148, 157, 176, 190, 239,
    240
perfect liturgist, titles of, 167–71
perfection: and evil, 118, 120; as
    process, 87–88, 180, 181
perichoresis, meanings of, 9, 10
Peter, 125, 144, 155, 156, 157, 170,
    189, 196, 227
Pharaoh, 105–6
philautia, 115, 119
piety, 178–79, 189
Pilate, 155, 156
pilgrim identity, Church's, 199–200
pilgrims, 87–90, 182, 238
Plato, 82, 83
porneia, 109
praise, 26–27, 129–30, 141, 187, 190
prayer: and angels, 66, 67, 68; anger's
    obstacle, 110; and Church
    identities, 194; in Church's
    abcedarium, 189, 190, 191; at
    Easter Vigil, 87, 89; and Holy
    Spirit, 176, 221; with humility,
    112; in liturgical perspective of
    Jesus's life, 155; Mary's example,
    240, 241; in Mass celebration,
    165–66; Nebuchadnezzar's furnace,
    54; and Satan's demons, 110, 111;
    and Scripture, 48; and sin, 96; and
    spiritual world, 77; and time, 60
predestination mystery, 34–35
Preparation of the Gifts, Christ's
    liturgical work, 165

presentation of offerings, Mary's
　　example, 242
pride, 93–94, 109–10, 111, 112, 113,
　　147, 188
priestly liturgy, Church's, 198
priests/deacons, 33, 55, 67–68, 73,
　　161–62, 182, 186, 189, 224
prophetic liturgy, Church's, 198
providence, 146–49, 190
prudence, 147, 181
purity, 134

Ratzinger, Joseph, 13–14
reason, gift of, 81, 84, 85
Reconciliation, grace's force, 133
religious cults, Christ's ending of,
　　37
Responses in Mass, Christ's liturgical
　　work, 166
Resurrection of Christ, 23, 29, 71, 72,
　　153, 156, 159, 175, 190, 194, 198,
　　200, 222
revelation: conditions for receiving,
　　19–24, 44; God's purpose, 40, 44,
　　243–45; and Trinity's mystery, 31;
　　truths about, 40–49
reverence, for approaching God, 22
righteousness, for approaching God,
　　22
Romanides, John, 15
royal liturgy, Church's, 198
Rublev, 29

Sabbath, 222
sacrament, in Church's abcedarium,
　　191
sacramental eyes, 214–15
sacramental world, Church as,
　　234–35
sacraments: as aid stations, 223–24;
　　and Church's mother identity,
　　197; as glorification-sanctification
　　expression, 168; as graces, 133;
　　metaphors for, 203–9; and sin,
　　96

Sacraments of Initiation, 62
sacrifice: in Adam's confession, 91;
　　and angels, 66–67; for approaching
　　God, 22; before Christ, 37; in
　　Church's abcedarium, 188, 190;
　　God's no need for, 129–30; hodie
　　perspective of, 230; and just
　　worship, 56–57; Mary's example,
　　242; and perfect liturgist titles,
　　168; and right worship, 106–7
Sales, Francis de, 16
sanctifying role, Church's, 47, 198
Satan: Christ's baiting of, 143; in
　　Church's abcedarium, 186,
　　188; defeat of, 226–27; demon
　　strategies, 108–12; and evil,
　　119–20; hatred of man, 103–7,
　　226; and Jesus in wilderness, 137;
　　and liturgical perspective of Jesus's
　　life, 154; and loss of spiritual
　　eyesight, 207
Scripture: as communion with God,
　　49; dry bones comparison, 46;
　　function of the two Testaments,
　　41–42; as guidebook, 40–41, 44;
　　as history, 43, 45–46; for liturgy,
　　40–49; in Mass celebration,
　　163–64; organization purposes, 47;
　　outside liturgy, 44–45; and prayer,
　　48; as revelation, 43–44; spiritual
　　meanings, 43–44
Second Vatican Council, 14, 67, 97,
　　237
serpent, in Eve's confession, 92–93.
　　See also Satan
sexual immorality, 24, 104, 108–9
sheepfold identity, Church's, 193–94,
　　198
Sheol, 141, 142, 144
shepherding role, Church's, 193–94,
　　198
shore metaphor, for Church, 201–2
Silouan the Athonite, 146
Simeon, 174, 242
Simon, 143

sin: as Church concern, 213; in Church's abcedarium, 187, 188, 191; in confession of Adam and Eve, 91–94; as death, 228; disease model, 135–37, 139; and fear of God, 25, 26–27; as forgetfulness, 228; and God's actions, 96–98; and healing miracles, 99; and Holy Spirit, 175; as idolatry, 113–16; and liturgy, 95–97, 99; in Mass celebration, 162, 165–66; as offense, 135–36, 138–39; and perfect liturgist titles, 168, 169; from Satan's actions, 105; Satan's demons, 108–12; Trinity's plan, 226–27. See also evil

slaves as teachers, 245–46
smoke/candle imagery, 176
Son of God, title significance, 170. See also Jesus Christ
Son of Man, title significance, 170. See also Jesus Christ
spatial metaphors, for sacraments, 203–4
spouse identity, Church's, 197–98
Stephen, 125
stone imagery, house of God identity, 195–96
subjective world, defining, 75. See also world
suffering and misfortune, 146–49, 180, 188, 191
sym+baleo, 103–5, 204–5
sym+ballein, 164
symbol, in Church's abcedarium, 190
symbolic metaphors, for sacraments, 204–5

teaching role, Church's, 47, 198
temple, body as, 32, 109, 134, 155, 224
Ten Commandments, 106
Tertullian, 110
theodicy, 123–26. See also evil
Thomas Aquinas, 177, 178

Thomas the apostle, 196
time: in Adam's confession, 92; and the Eucharist, 211–12; and liturgy expression, 220–25; visions of, 59–64, 230–36; and world's impermanence, 74, 81, 210–11
today perspective, of time, 230–31, 235–36
Trinity: blessing cycle, 131; in Church's abcedarium, 191; energies of, 29, 33; glorification cycle, 30, 131–32; knowledge of, 29, 30–31, 70–71; as liturgical society, 32; as liturgical unity, 29–31; in liturgy's purposes, 9–11; as mystery, 29, 31, 169; plan for sin, 226–27; revelation's purpose, 243; unity of, 219. See also Holy Spirit; Jesus Christ

understanding, as Holy Spirit gift, 181–82
unknowable God, 19–24, 31, 41, 125–26, 208
Uzziah, King, 55

vainglory, demon of, 111–12
vanity, 55, 105, 119
veneration, for approaching God, 22
Vespers, in Church's abcedarium, 191
vineyard identity, Church's, 194–95
Virgin Mother model, Mary's example, 241–42. See also Mary

water imagery, 144–45, 156, 207, 234. See also Baptism
week period, for liturgy, 221–22
wind imagery, 38, 146–47, 172, 175
window imagery, 207
wisdom, 147, 182, 187, 191
Word, reading of, 162–63
Word, written vs. incarnate Word, 41–42
Word made flesh, title significance, 168–69. See also Jesus Christ

world: judgment perspectives, 231;
liturgical assumptions, 76–78; and
liturgical eschatology, 231–34;
meanings of, 74–76; as pathway,
61, 68, 210, 224–25; and time
perspectives, 59–64, 210–11, 231.
See also cosmos

worship: in Adam's confession, 91;
for approaching God, 22; in
Church's abcedarium, 188, 191;
death's tragedy, 141–42; evil's
privation of, 118–21; and gifts
of Holy Spirit, 118–21, 136–38,
139–40, 178–82; God's due,
118–21, 136–38, 139–40, 178;
as liturgy's purpose, 125; Old
Testament narrative, 105–6. *See
also* glorifying God; *latria*

written word. *See* Scripture

year period, for liturgy, 223
yearning metaphor for sacraments,
205–6

Zacchaeus, 157, 196
Zechariah, 174, 192
Zizioulas, Metropolitan, 13

SCRIPTURE INDEX

Genesis

1:2 . . . . 144, 219
2:3 131
3 75
3:5 120
3:8 228
8:20-21 67
28:18 196

Exodus

3:2 65
5:1 105
5:2 105
7:16 105
8:1 105
8:20 105
9:1 105
9:13 105
10:3 105
13:12 242
14:19 65
14:31 27
16:14 195
20:5 136
25:20 21
33:20 38
34:14 136

Deuteronomy

4:23-24 138
4:28 129
5:6-9 136
5:7 122
6:2 27
6:13 137
10:12 27
10:20 27
30:11-14 43
32:21 138

Joshua

4:9 195
4:20 195
24:14 27
24:19 139

1 Samuel

4:4 21
15:22 122
16:13 219

Tobit

14:2 27

Job

38:4 123
38:5 123
38:8 123
38:12 123
38:17 123
38:19 123
38:22 123
38:28 123
38:39 123
39:1 123
39:5 123
39:20 123
39:26 123
40:2-4 124
41:1 143

Psalms

6:5 141
15:1-2 122
22:23 27
24:7 72
29:2 139
30:9 141
32:9 132
33:8 27
33:18 27

Psalms (*continued*)

36:6 204
37:2 81
40:8 115
42:7 204
50:9-12 129
50:14-15 130
50:23 130
51:4 . . . . 135, 213
52:8 195
78:19 168
78:25 69
78:35 37
78:58 138
88:11 141
89:12 155
90:10 223
91:11 65
94:17 141
96:9 139
96:11 60
103:1 131
110:1 139
110:4 139
115:11 27
115:17 141
118:4 27
122:1 115
137:4 180
141:2 66

Proverbs

3:7 27
3:11 133
3:12 146
20:30 146

Ecclesiastes

1:10 210

Isaiah

6:2 21
6:3 21
6:6 21
11:2 219
14:12-14 104
25 234
25:6 206

38:18 141
40:6-8 81
44:9 129
51:12 81
61 232
63:1 72

Ezekiel

11:19 122
36:26 219
37:1-5 46

Daniel

3 54

Hosea

6:6 122

Joel

2 234
2:28 219

Habakkuk

2:19 129

Zechariah

8:2-3 138

Matthew

1:24 65
2:13 65
4:17 235
5:23-24 111
6 112
10:7 155
12:8 . . . . 170, 222
12:40 143
13:37 170
13:41-42 65
13:47-50 143
16:13-16 170
16:18 227
16:27 170
18:10 . . . . 65, 69
18:12-14 170
18:20 160
20:18 170
20:19 170
20:28 170
21:42 196
24:31 65

Mark

1:11 154
1:15 235
3:27 226
14:34 126

Luke

1 232
1:26-27 65
1:35 . . . . 174, 219
1:42 174
1:67-69 174
2:22-29 154
2:25-32 174
3:22 174
4 232
4:1-2 174
4:8 137
4:14 174
4:18-19 174
4:21 235
5:4-6 143
6:5 222
6:9 222
9:34-35 174
10:21 174
11:34 140
12:10 174
12:12 174
12:20 109
12:21 233
12:28 81
13:14 222
14:3 222
15:10 65

John

1:14 169
1:38 235
3:8 172
3:16 75
5:4 65
5:10 222
6:27 154
6:29 157
6:32-35 69
6:35 . . . . 154, 168

6:41 168
6:46 69
6:51 168
7:38 140
9:14 222
12:25 76
12:31 76
13:25 125
14:9 69
14:16 174
14:17 . . . . 219, 220
14:18 165
14:27 166
15:2 195
15:8 195
15:19 76
16:13-14 173
17 155
17:1 30
17:5 30
17:16 76
17:22 30
17:24 30
20:12 67
21:4-14 143

Acts

2 174
2:1-4 174
2:42-45 110
5:19 66
8:26 66
10:1-4 67
12:7 66
12:23 66
17:22 234
27:23 66

Romans

1:3-4 222
1:28-31 121
2:29 154
8:11 36
8:14-15 158
8:16 174
8:20 119
8:20-21 114

Romans (*continued*)

8:21 119
8:26 . . . . 219, 221
8:28 216
8:29 36
8:30 34
9:25 160

1 Corinthians

3:16 . . . . 155, 219
6:13 109
6:14 109
6:17-19 109
6:19 . . . . 155, 219
10:1-4 234
11:26 145
12:3 173
13:7 231
13:12 245
15:42-45 229
15:50 200

2 Corinthians

3:12 38
3:16-17 38
3:18 38
4:7 211
5:21 78

Galatians

3:26 36
4:4 230
4:6 174
4:6-7 221

Ephesians

1:4-5 70
1:10 70
1:13-14 70
1:17-18 173
1:21 65
2:21-22 196
5:1-2 67
5:32 198
6:11 216

Philippians

2:5 201
2:7 246

Colossians

1:16 65
2:13-14 139

1 Timothy

3:16 71

Hebrews

1:14 . . . . 21, 71
4:14 236
5:8-10 140
9:5 21
10:4 37
10:21 195
12:11 . . . . 133, 146
12:22 78
13:2 21

James

1:10 81

1 Peter

1:10-11 70
1:12 70
1:18-20 201
1:24 81
2:9 170
2:9-10 . . . . 148, 161

1 John

4:20 . . . . 111, 179

Revelation

1:6 228
4:8 21
7:9-10 199
8:3-4 66
8:4 67
9:20 129
10:7 232
21:2-3 198
21:14 155
22:3 230